Pedagogy and Practice in Heritage Studies

CULTURAL HERITAGE STUDIES

UNIVERSITY PRESS OF FLORIDA

Florida A&M University, Tallahassee

Florida Atlantic University, Boca Raton

Florida Gulf Coast University, Ft. Myers

Florida International University, Miami

Florida State University, Tallahassee

New College of Florida, Sarasota

University of Central Florida, Orlando

University of Florida, Gainesville

University of North Florida, Jacksonville

University of South Florida, Tampa

University of West Florida, Pensacola

PEDAGOGY AND PRACTICE

IN

HERITAGE STUDIES

Edited by Susan J. Bender and Phyllis Mauch Messenger

FOREWORD BY PAUL A. SHACKEL

UNIVERSITY PRESS OF FLORIDA

Gainesville / Tallahassee / Tampa / Boca Raton

Pensacola / Orlando / Miami / Jacksonville / Ft. Myers / Sarasota

Cover: Students record observations during Boston University Archaeology Department's field school at Menorca, Spain, during which participants address heritage issues while learning archaeological techniques. Photo courtesy of Ricardo Elia.

This book may be available in an electronic edition.

24 23 22 21 20 19   6 5 4 3 2 1

Library of Congress Cataloging-in-Publication Data
Names: Bender, Susan J., editor. | Messenger, Phyllis Mauch, 1950– editor. |
   Shackel, Paul A., author of foreword.
Title: Pedagogy and practice in heritage studies / edited by Susan J. Bender
   and Phyllis Mauch Messenger ; foreword by Paul A. Shackel.
Other titles: Cultural heritage studies.
Description: Gainesville : University Press of Florida, 2019. | Series:
   Cultural heritage studies | Includes bibliographical references and index.
Identifiers: LCCN 2018018475 | ISBN 9780813056142 (cloth : alk. paper)
Subjects: LCSH: Cultural property—Study and teaching. | National
   characteristics—Study and teaching. | History—Study and teaching. |
   Historic preservation—Study and teaching. | Cultural property—Protection.
Classification: LCC CC135 .P423 2019 | DDC 907.1—dc23
LC record available at https://lccn.loc.gov/2018018475

The University Press of Florida is the scholarly publishing agency for the State University System of Florida, comprising Florida A&M University, Florida Atlantic University, Florida Gulf Coast University, Florida International University, Florida State University, New College of Florida, University of Central Florida, University of Florida, University of North Florida, University of South Florida, and University of West Florida.

University Press of Florida
2046 NE Waldo Road
Suite 2100
Gainesville, FL 32609
http://upress.ufl.edu

Contents

Figures

Tables

Foreword

Keeping Archaeology Socially and Politically Viable
in the Twenty-First Century

The editors, Susan J. Bender and Phyllis Mauch Messenger, bring together a wide range of talented authors in their edited volume *Pedagogy and Practice in Heritage Studies*. The participants provide a range of theoretical and case studies related to pedagogies of heritage and describe the role that archeologists can play in this growing and exciting field of inquiry. The authors are tasked with addressing the question, "How do we make archeology relevant in the twenty-first century?" Throughout this volume the authors provide convincing evidence demonstrating that the pursuit of heritage studies is one avenue to keeping the discipline of archaeology politically and socially viable in this new century. It is a way of understanding communities and accepting differences and recognizing multivocality.

Many of the authors operate in a college or university setting and they show their obligation to engage communities and help recognize, address, and solve societal problems. They grapple with important issues related to how to teach heritage and confront issues like learning theory, assessment considerations, and curriculum design, as well as addressing how heritage fits into the context of conventional archaeological curricula.

Educators have the task of developing an engaged scholarship that has a meaningful critical pedagogy. Critical reflection is an opportunity to place the learning experience into a larger context and show the complexity and varied histories that exist. The student should be able to enter into a critical dialogue rather than accept current social and political situations unquestioningly. Educators should be capable of questioning deep-seated assumptions and myths and raising students' consciousness about the inequalities that exist across society. Heritage studies become socially important to our universities and communities when there is space for this critical reflection, which many will argue is a key to learning. A curriculum in heritage studies can be transformative for students, as it can make the connections between past inequities and existing social problems. A program in heritage studies can strengthen a student's sense of social responsibility and heighten the student's understanding of human differences and commonality.

The authors in this volume will agree that no story is complete if it is told from just one perspective. It is our responsibility as educators to adhere to the "pedagogy of discomfort" (borrowing from Kryder-Reid, this volume), which focuses on "how emotions define how and what one chooses to see, and conversely, not to see." We need to commit to participate in meaningful ways in raising consciousness, working through the issues required for public judgment, and collaboratively crafting resolutions to critical issues. Heritage workers can help to create a past that recognizes and explicitly learns from hidden injustices and difficult histories.

Bender and Messenger have brought together well-established scholars who are urging us to think about how we can operationalize our discipline in new and different ways. Heritage studies with a critical perspective make us think about archaeology in much broader terms. Heritage studies can bring critical thinking skills to the forefront and allow us to expand our subject matter, and allow us to confront our attitudes, stereotypes, and beliefs. Critically examining the past, which is part of the pedagogy of heritage studies, allows us to think about how the past is created, and helps us to move toward a more just future.

Paul A. Shackel
Series Editor

Preface

This volume, *Pedagogy and Practice in Heritage Studies*, and its companion volume, *History and Approaches to Heritage Studies* (edited by Messenger and Bender), had their genesis in two symposia presented at Society for American Archaeology (SAA) annual meetings. At the 77th annual meeting in Memphis, Phyllis Messenger and Susan Bender chaired an electronic symposium, "Lessons from the Trenches: The Pedagogy of Archaeology and Heritage." University Press of Florida editor Meredith Babb expressed interest in a volume on the topic, as did Paul A. Shackel, editor of their Cultural Heritage Series. The following year in Honolulu, Messenger chaired a second symposium, "Lessons from the Trenches II: New Pedagogies of Archaeology and Heritage." In both of these sessions, archaeologists talked about grappling with integrating their work, especially their teaching, into the broader heritage field. Elizabeth Chilton and Larry Zimmerman, who were discussants in the Honolulu session, offered thought-provoking analyses of where we were in the archaeology and heritage enterprise. Participants came away from that session recognizing that we were not alone in trying to rethink and reframe our teaching and learning in archaeology to move beyond seeing ourselves as the authorities in discussions about the past, including stewardship, interpretation, agenda setting, and teaching and learning. Professors Chilton and Zimmerman graciously agreed to write chapters for the project, using their discussions as points of departure.

In the several years that these two volumes have been taking shape, some authors left the project for a variety of reasons. Other authors were invited to contribute a chapter, and still others heard about the project and asked to submit a piece. Paul Shackel's invited chapter on the arc from CRM to heritage became a touchstone for many of the authors as the project developed, and the resulting volumes have profited from each of their contributions. As editors, we have certainly benefited from their perspectives and their contributions to the dialogue, which has become more robust as the project has developed. All the while, the literature on heritage studies and the pedagogy of heritage has continued to proliferate and provide more connections to the pieces being developed for these volumes. We are grateful to the contributing authors, especially as they continued to revisit their chapters in light of new contributions to this rapidly developing literature.

Even as we pursue more robust understandings of the various connections between archaeology and heritage study, we wish to acknowledge the foundation for this work in the early efforts of the Society for American Archaeology's Public Education Committee, so deftly championed by Edward Friedman and George Smith. Many of the authors in this volume, including its editors, initially met in this context; we were encouraged by Friedman and Smith to develop and expand disciplinary practices that were inclusive of a wider range of audiences and professional statuses than had typically been recognized up to that point. We are grateful for their leadership.

We wish to thank the Institute for Advanced Study and the IAS Heritage Collaborative at the University of Minnesota for providing funding and other support that has enabled the editors to convene for several intensive writing and editing weekends. We also thank the Department of Anthropology at Skidmore College for opening up lab space for one of the weekend work sessions. And we thank our anthropologist spouses for feeding us so well during the writing retreats. A special thanks goes to Lewis C. "Skip" Messenger Jr. for preparing the index for this volume.

Introduction

Pedagogy and Practice in Heritage Studies

SUSAN J. BENDER AND PHYLLIS MAUCH MESSENGER

How does teaching heritage fit into the context of conventional archaeology curricula? This is the central question with which the authors included in this volume are grappling. In exploring how to teach archaeology effectively, our authors interrogate with their students the link between contemporary understandings of the past and the present. Through this connection, they open the door to the study of heritage, where heritage is broadly construed as the process through which the past assumes diverse meanings in the present (compare Messenger and Bender 2019; see discussion below). Thus in this collection of rich, detailed case studies, we see common themes (or principles) and ideas emerge that can form the foundation for heritage study in North American archaeology. While lessons from our European colleagues (for example, Harrison 2013; Sørensen and Carman 2009; see also Chilton 2019; Cobb and Croucher 2019), who have a longer history with such considerations, can certainly guide our considerations, it is altogether fitting that American archaeologists craft answers out of the historical trajectory of their own professional tradition (including public archaeology; see Ashmore et al. 2010; Bender and Smith 2000; Lynott and Wylie 2000; Pyburn and Smith 2015). The work in this volume represents a project being constructed from the ground up, in which the everyday work of educators is helping us to characterize the theoretical and practical contours of heritage study (see also Zimmerman 2019).

In this enterprise, the contributors to this and a companion volume, *History and Approaches to Heritage Studies* (Messenger and Bender 2019), are in the midst of crafting a "grounded theory" of heritage study as described by Strauss and Corbin (1998), characterized as a process that begins with an area of study and results in theory emerging from the data. They argue that grounded theories are more likely to resemble reality "because they are drawn from data, are likely to offer insight, enhance understanding, and provide a meaningful guide to action" (1998: 12). Indeed their observation defines precisely what we intend with these volumes. In other words, we hope not to offer a definitive statement on the scope and content of heritage study in archaeology, but rather to offer some insight into how educators are approaching this subject area in their classrooms, to enhance understanding of the range of subjects and activities that constitute heritage study, and to suggest productive avenues for developing our pedagogy into the future. To these ends, we have included in this volume case studies that help us think about pedagogical strategies across an arc of practice: they deal with everything from overarching learning theory and assessment considerations (Moe, White, and McGill), through ideas about curriculum and course design (Elia et al., Hayashida, Henderson and Laracuente, Kryder-Reid, Lerner and Efffland, Pluckhahn, Scham), to specific assignments (Bender, Messenger) that are aimed at stimulating students' historical imagination as well as critical reflection about heritage.

Our authors approach teaching heritage from a multifaceted understanding of what that project entails. A number start with definitions of the heritage domain (for example, Hayashida, Kryder-Reid, McGill, Scham) that draw from scholars from both the European and U.S. traditions (Chilton 2019; Harrison 2013; Little and Shackel 2014; Logan 2012; Shackel 2019; Soderland 2009). Chilton, for example, argues that heritage "includes both tangible and intangible remains of the past and contemporary activities associated with those remains" (2019: 25). Other authors in these volumes infer heritage as an extension of the public archaeology project that "now considers a more diverse public, employs more democratic models of engagement, and reaches out through a wider variety of media and methods" (Pluckhahn: 74; see also Henderson and Laracuente, this volume; Clark 2019; King 2019). Still others consider heritage as "a way of thinking about the material remains of the past" (Elia et al., this volume), where the latter assumes meaning(s) through connection to contemporary cultural contexts. While not all might agree with Harrison's assertion that heritage is a "repackaging of the past for some purpose in the present" (cited in Zimmerman 2019), all would agree that heritage is constructed and malleable, that it is a portal for endowing the past with meaning, and that it points toward a more just future. As a group, the chapters in this volume argue that undergraduates come to our class-rooms largely unaware of their relationship to heritage as "central to iden-tity, to self-esteem and to daily life" (Zimmerman 2019: 216), and that our primary pedagogical project is to make students aware of their own heri-tage, even as they are in dialogue with the heritage of other peoples, past and present.

This theme—of connecting the past to the present and to the future—is initially identified by Moe and dominates the rest of this volume. Indeed, the words "connection" and "link" are probably the most repeated terms in the collection. Several authors argue that encouraging students to de-velop empathy for past and present actors is an effective pedagogical strat-egy for forging meaningful connections (Bender, Kryder-Reid, McGill, Messenger, Scham, White). Others would add that the process of building these connections can lead to critical reflection on contemporary cultural norms and invite students to engage with social and climate justice issues (Hayashida, Kryder-Reid, Lerner and Effland, McGill, Scham). Although not explicitly stated in all chapters in this volume, we suspect that all our authors would agree that an essential component of the heritage pedagogy project includes a commitment to the proposition that "learning about cultures, past and present, is essential for living in a pluralistic society and world" (Moe: 10).

Another type of connection that surfaces repeatedly in this volume entails actively connecting students to diverse stakeholders who are not usually part of the undergraduate classroom dynamic. A number of our contributors seek out opportunities to connect their students to local community groups, teachers in elementary school classrooms, and heri-tage managers, among others (Elia et al., Kryder-Reid, Henderson and Laracuente, Pluckhahn; see also Clark 2019; King 2019). In doing so, stu-dents experience directly the broader, varied meanings that stories about the past can assume and again are encouraged to assess critically who says what about the past and why, and what voices are dominant in this dis-course. In this context, archaeology becomes a powerful tool for learning about the past through the systematic study of material remains, while it is embedded in a wider nexus of knowledge claims (compare Zimmerman

2019). The critical pedagogy that emerges from forging connections of all types promotes self-reflection, supports inclusive representation, and leads to community engagement.

Just as heritage study seeks to make students aware of diverse interests in the past, its pedagogy seeks to enable students to access knowledge about the past in multiple ways. Moe creates a framework for thinking about how students learn and argues persuasively for the importance of assessment in an iterative learning process that encompasses diverse modes of learning (see also McGill, Henderson and Laracuente). Building on this understanding, other chapters outline multiple strategies for encouraging students to learn about contemporary meanings of the past: case studies (McGill), role playing (McGill), ethnographic study (Kryder-Reid, Pluckhahn), applied anthropological techniques (Scham), construction of visual and verbal narratives (Bender, Messenger, White), exchange of student ideas and experiences (Hayashida), and a variety of "hands-on" experiences with educators and heritage managers—including internships (Elia et al., Henderson and Laracuente, Pluckhahn). The overarching theme in these various strategies is that heritage is taught most effectively through a pedagogy that demands student engagement, where critical understandings emerge as students apply concepts learned in one context to resolve problems in another, and their ability to do so attests to the learning that has taken place.

The engaged pedagogies represented in this volume break with traditional approaches to teaching about the human past in two fundamental ways. Conceptually, several contributors argue that approaching the past through the investigation of meaningful themes and questions provides a more effective framework for grasping the meanings of the past than the customary time/space systematics of culture history (Hayashida, Lerner and Effland, Scham). With regard to skills, other contributors (particularly those charged with teaching skills for the practice of public archaeology) make a strong case for expanding student learning beyond the traditional archaeological skill set to include aptitudes in writing or speaking for the public, developing interpretive signage, working collaboratively with community partners, or conducting fieldwork aimed at results other than professional publication (Elia et al., Henderson and Laracuente, Kryder-Reid, Pluckhahn). Of course, teaching conceptual knowledge cannot be neatly divided from teaching skills (see also Cobb and Croucher 2019).

The skills we want our students to practice proficiently flow directly from how we want them to conceptualize the past. Elia and his coauthors make this case when they observe that heritage management is as much a way of thinking about the past as it is a set of skills, and they measure the success of their field school on the evidence of their students "thinking that heritage values, preservation, and stewardship are just as integral to the practice of archaeology as using a trowel or tape measure" (108).

No monolithic answer to this volume's central question—"where should the teaching of heritage reside in conventional archaeology curricula?"—emerges in this volume, and that is to be expected since we are, as Zimmerman (2019) would argue, still early in the process of understanding and building on the linkages among archaeology, heritage, and pedagogical theory. In a number of case studies, heritage understandings emerge out of assignments that in fact weren't even initially designed to that end (for example, Bender, Hayashida, Messenger). The fact that they do suggests that there are many openings in current archaeology pedagogies to help students assess the many meanings of the past in the present, and to encourage them to reflect critically on the fluid nature of heritage claims. In contrast to these examples, several of our case studies illustrate how courses and field experiences can be explicitly designed around key aspects of heritage study, such as ethics education (McGill) or critical heritage studies (Kryder-Reid, McGill, Scham; see also Shackel 2019; Zimmerman 2019). Still other cases demonstrate how teaching archaeological practice can require that students come to understand archaeology as a profession that is embedded in a broader network of practitioners and publics, many with their own views of how the material remains of the past should be managed and interpreted. But what all these case studies share is a perspective wherein teaching about heritage is subsumed or framed by the archaeology curriculum. Hence we see from them how heritage might be fit into this extant structure. And, it is this "fitting in" that leads some authors to consider the knotty issue of the trade-off between teaching archaeology and heritage. For example, Elia and colleagues note the tension in their field school between teaching excavation skills (and getting work done) with finding time for teaching heritage management. Similarly, Pluckhahn explores the tension between teaching archaeological practice as cultural resource management and the rapidly expanding field of public archaeology.

If archaeologists are to teach effectively about heritage, such considerations point to the next step in the project. We are tasked with rethinking our curricula so that students regularly engage increasingly sophisticated concepts of critical heritage study as they progress through our programs. In this way, many of the understandings that emerge in these two volumes might become standard aspects of archaeology curricula rather than sporadic encounters in individual courses. At introductory levels, students might encounter and apply understandings of the relationship between the past and the present and begin to investigate the multiple meanings with which the past can be endowed. In upper level courses, more critical study might be standard, resulting in students seeing the connections between the past and contemporary social and environmental justice issues. In courses that emphasize professional practice, students would encounter the range of interests and issues that heritage professionals might encounter in their work and, when tied to ethical considerations, the implications and consequences of their actions. The engaged pedagogies illustrated in this volume and demanded by this perspective would become standard classroom practice. Such revision would push the ethics-based curriculum envisioned in Bender and Smith (2000) to a new level of conceptual underpinning and move archaeology into dialogue with a broader field of heritage studies and its scholars and practitioners. By encouraging our students to understand how the past is used in the present to construct normative worldviews and visions of our future, we can endow our discipline with a voice that has the potential to have an impact on critical decisions in the communities we inhabit. In the vocabulary of the 1960s, embracing heritage study in our curricula can make archaeology "relevant" in the twenty-first century.

References Cited

Ashmore, Wendy, Dorothy T. Lippert, and Barbara J. Mills (editors)
2010   *Voices in American Archaeology.* Society for American Archaeology Press, Washington, D.C.
Bender, Susan J., and George S. Smith
2000   *Teaching Archaeology in the Twenty-First Century.* Society for American Archaeology Press, Washington, D.C.
Chilton, Elizabeth
2019   The Heritage of Heritage: Defining the Role of the Past in Contemporary Societies. In *History and Approaches to Heritage Studies*, edited by Phyllis Mauch Messenger and Susan J. Bender, pp. 24–31. University Press of Florida, Gainesville.

Clark, Bonnie J.

2019   Making Heritage Happen: The University of Denver Amache Field School. In *History and Approaches to Heritage Studies*, edited by Phyllis Mauch Messenger and Susan J. Bender, pp. 168–180. University Press of Florida, Gainesville.

Cobb, Hannah, and Karina Croucher

2019   Rising, Falling, Assembling: Pedagogy in British Archaeology. In *History and Approaches to Heritage Studies*, edited by Phyllis Mauch Messenger and Susan J. Bender, pp. 181–195. University Press of Florida, Gainesville.

Harrison, Rodney

2013   *Heritage: Critical Approaches.* Routledge, New York.

King, Eleanor M.

2019   African Americans, American Indians, and Heritage. In *History and Approaches to Heritage Studies*, edited by Phyllis Mauch Messenger and Susan J. Bender, pp. 69–86. University Press of Florida, Gainesville.

Little, Barbara J., and Paul A. Shackel

2014   *Archaeology, Heritage, and Civic Engagement: Working toward the Public Good.* Left Coast Press, Walnut Creek, California.

Logan, William

2012   Cultural Diversity, Cultural Heritage and Human Rights: Towards Heritage Management as Human Rights-based Cultural Practice. *International Journal of Heritage Studies* 18(3): 231–244.

Lynott, Mark J., and Alison Wylie (editors)

2000   *Ethics in American Archaeology.* 2nd rev. ed. Society for American Archaeology, Washington, D.C.

Messenger, Phyllis Mauch, and Susan J. Bender

2019   Introduction, In *History and Approaches to Heritage Studies*, edited by Phyllis Mauch Messenger and Susan J. Bender, pp. 1–8. University Press of Florida, Gainesville.

Pyburn, K. Anne, and George S. Smith

2015   "The MATRIX Project (Making Archaeology Teaching Relevant in the XXIst Century): An Approach to the Efficient Sharing of Professional Knowledge and Skills with a Large Audience." In *Sharing Archaeology: Academe, Practice, and the Public*, edited by Peter G. Stone and Zhao Hui, pp. 132–140. Routledge Press, New York.

Shackel, Paul A.

2019   Civic Engagement, Representation, and Social Justice: Moving from CRM to Heritage Studies. In *History and Approaches to Heritage Studies*, edited by Phyllis Mauch Messenger and Susan J. Bender, pp. 9–23. University Press of Florida, Gainesville.

Soderland, Hilary A.

2009   Values and the Evolving Concept of Heritage: The First Century of Archaeology and Law in the United States (1906-2006). In *Heritage Values in Contemporary Society*, edited by George S. Smith, Phyllis Mauch Messenger, and Hilary A. Soderland, pp. 129–144. Left Coast Press, Walnut Creek, California.

Sørensen, Marie Louise Stig, and John Carman (editors)

2009   *Heritage Studies: Methods and Approaches.* Routledge, New York.

Strauss, Anselm L., and Juliet M. Corbin

1998   *Basics of Qualitative Research: Techniques and Procedures for Developing Grounded Theory.* Sage, Thousand Oaks, California.

Zimmerman, Larry J.

2019   Help Needed! Reflections on a Critical Pedagogy of Heritage. In *History and Approaches to Heritage Studies*, edited by Phyllis Mauch Messenger and Susan J. Bender, pp. 215–236. University Press of Florida, Gainesville.

Archaeology in School

Student Learning Outcomes

JEANNE M. MOE

What happens when we teach students about archaeology in K-12 classrooms in the United States? What do they actually learn? What do they understand about archaeology? What do they understand about broader heritage issues such as historic preservation, race, power, and ownership of the past? What knowledge of archaeology and heritage (their own and that of others) will they take with them to their undergraduate and graduate studies? How will it help them engage in heritage-related public discourse as adults?

While archaeology education in precollegiate contexts has been growing over the last thirty years (Smardz-Frost 2004; Smardz and Smith 2000), there has been very little research on what students actually learn about archaeology and what they understand. Archaeology educators are working to rectify the situation and a few research papers have been published in the last decade (Brody et al. 2014; Henderson and Levstik 2016; Levstik et al. 2005; Moe 2016). Additionally, recent dissertations (for example, Davis 1997 [see also Davis 2005]; Moe 2011) and master's theses (for example, Simon 2013) have added to our meager research base.

Using this small research base, this chapter examines our knowledge of what students actually learn, what they understand, and what they remember about archaeology as a result of classroom instruction. The chapter relies primarily on data drawn from formative assessment conducted during the development of Project Archaeology curricula.

History of Project Archaeology

The Archaeological Resources Protection Act (ARPA 1979) and its amendments (1988) require federal land managers in the United States to educate the public about the significance of archaeology sites on public lands and the importance of protecting them (16USC470ii). In 1990, to fulfill the new educational goals of ARPA, the Bureau of Land Management (BLM) partnered with the Forest Service, the National Park Service, and the State of Utah to create an educational program for Utah educators and their students; this program became Project Archaeology. By 1995, Project Archaeology had spread beyond Utah to Alaska, Oregon, New Mexico, Arizona, and Pennsylvania and had laid the infrastructure to become a national education program. In 2001, the national office was transferred to Montana State University under an assistance agreement with BLM and operates as a joint program. The program now serves thirty-eight states and a national and international audience through online courses. To date, Project Archaeology has served more than 17,000 educators who, in turn, reach an estimated 340,000 students each year.

The goal of Project Archaeology is to protect our shared archaeological legacy while providing educators with the tools and professional development they need to fulfill their own requirements. All Project Archaeology curricular materials and professional development for educators are based on four "Enduring Understandings" (what we want students to understand and remember long into the future):

1. Understanding the past is essential for understanding the present and shaping the future.
2. Learning about cultures, past and present, is essential for living in a pluralistic society and world.
3. Archaeology is a systematic way to know about the past.
4. Stewardship of archaeological sites is everyone's responsibility.

Project Archaeology is rooted in archaeological research and encompasses a broad interdisciplinary view of archaeology that includes oral histories from members of descendant communities, geography and environmental sciences, an emphasis on cultures and cultural understanding, architecture, and citizenship both national and global. Following King (2019) and Shackel (2019), Project Archaeology and many archaeology education efforts in the United States are interdisciplinary programs designed to help teachers and students build understanding of their own culture and history and that of others. As such, archaeology education can be seen as one aspect of the broad umbrella of heritage and heritage studies.

Conceptual Understanding of Science through Archaeological Inquiry

Archaeology educators have long understood that classroom teachers do not have the time or motivation to teach archaeology for the sake of teaching archaeology (Smith et al. 1996; White this volume). Instead, most archaeology educators have designed educational materials that allow teachers to use archaeology as a vehicle for teaching critical thinking, scientific and historical inquiry, and civic responsibility. Because archaeology is an engaging topic, it can be a useful tool for teachers to interest students in science and history and to help them grasp fundamental concepts of inquiry and interpretation as required in national educational standards since the late 1990s (Kendall and Marzano 2000; NGA Center/CCSSO 2010). Although archaeology is clearly a useful pedagogical tool, it is difficult to compete for teachers' time in the classroom (Moe in press; White this volume).

First published in 2009, *Project Archaeology: Investigating Shelter* (Letts and Moe 2012) meets the goals of Project Archaeology and the requirements of ARPA and other federal mandates. It is a supplemental curriculum guide for social studies, science, and English language arts. The curriculum guides teachers and their students through a structured archaeological investigation of a real human habitation using authentic data. Students learn to ask research questions, answer them with the data available, draw conclusions about past human lifeways at this site, and support their interpretations with archaeological and historical evidence. Teachers attend professional development workshops to learn how to use the curriculum guide in their classrooms and to learn more about archaeology and descendant communities. Regional and historical shelter investigations each include members of a descendant community to guide students through the inquiry process.

From 2009 to 2011, I studied the efficacy of *Investigating Shelter* to help students understand the concepts of scientific inquiry: specifically, observation, inference, evidence, context, and classification (Moe 2011; results previously published in Moe 2016). This study focused primarily on science inquiry concepts, how students understand these concepts, how they acquire their understanding or misunderstandings, how they apply these concepts, and how they transfer the concepts to other subjects and to everyday life through the study of archaeological inquiry. The study was rooted in the principles of constructivist teaching and learning and in Novak's (1977) theory of education, of which cognition is an important element.

Cognition, Constructivism, and Understanding by Design

Cognition is "the mental action or process of acquiring knowledge and understanding" (Jewell and Abate 2001: 332). It is the internal act of knowing and is, therefore, not directly observable. The relationship between the knowing mind, external reality, and the exact nature of cognition has been debated from many perspectives (epistemological, linguistic, psychological, and so on) since antiquity. Cognitive psychologists, especially Jerome Bruner and David Ausubel (Good and Brofy 1986), applied a cognitive approach to understanding human learning in formal (school) education. Unlike the behaviorists who are interested primarily in the results of learning, the cognitivists are concerned with how learning occurs and what type of knowledge is stored. Under the cognitive approach, learning is centered on the learner rather than on the content to be learned.

Ausubel's notion of meaningful learning occurs when "the entire content of what is to be learned is presented to the learner in final form" in a way that he or she can make sense of it (Good and Brofy 1986: 216–221). Ausubel famously said, "[T]he most important factor influencing the meaningful learning of any new idea is the state of the individual's existing cognitive structure at the time of learning" (Ausubel and Robinson 1969: 143). The goal of instruction is to allow learners to integrate new knowledge with existing knowledge structures for longer retention and the ability to apply it and transfer it to other contexts.

For Ausubel, all knowledge is organized in hierarchical cognitive structures unique to each individual. Within these cognitive structures, minor elements of new knowledge are linked or subsumed under larger, more inclusive concepts (Novak 1977). The most important piece of instruction is to provide cognitive bridges to make it possible for learners to assimilate new knowledge into existing knowledge structures and to remember it long after instruction. This type of learning usually requires advance organizers such as graphs, concept maps, or photographs of the phenomenon to be studied. Learners create new knowledge for themselves within their existing hierarchical structures of knowledge and add to these structures throughout their lives.

Joseph Novak (1977) used Ausubel's assimilation theory to develop a comprehensive learning theory and a theory of education. The main concepts of the theory as used by Novak (1977) are: subsumption, progressive differentiation, integrative reconciliation, and superordinate learning. Only the first three concepts are relevant to this study.

In the course of meaningful learning, new information is linked with existing concepts in existing cognitive structures through an interactive process in which the new information changes slightly; the new information is subsumed. Similarly the existing concept (subsuming concept or subsumer) may change as well. As more information is assimilated, concepts (subsumers) become differentiated.

Development and elaboration of subsuming concepts or progressive differentiation occurs during meaningful learning. For example, two-year-old children often call everything with four legs and a tail "doggie" or "kitty," but soon learn to differentiate between dogs, cats, horses, cows, and all other four-legged animals.

Sometimes new information does not fit with existing concepts and cognitive dissonance results. Learners must use integrative reconciliation to assimilate or subsume the new information. For example, in the United States, 95 percent of the population conflates paleontology and archaeology, believing they are one and the same thing (Ramos and Duganne 2000). Many learners have difficulty in reconciling the new view of the two concepts—that is, paleontology and archaeology are not the same—and differentiating between the two disciplines. While Novak recognizes that each learner constructs his or her own knowledge, there is enough overlap in construction that knowledge and meaning can be shared.

> The almost infinite number of permutations of concept—concept relationships allows for the enormous idiosyncrasy we see in individual concept structures, and yet there is sufficient commonality . . . that discourse is possible, and sharing, enlarging and changing meanings can be achieved. It is this reality that makes possible the educational enterprise. (Novak 1993: 190)

Constructivism and Science Inquiry

Novak's Human Constructivism encompasses both a theory of learning and an epistemology of knowledge building and, at present, offers the most useful framework available for science teaching and for science curriculum development (Mintzes and Wandersee 2005). Constructivism is just as applicable to history and social studies (Davis 2005).

In the constructivist view of teaching and learning, "learners are seen as constructing meaning from input by processing it through existing cognitive structures, and then retaining it in long-term memory in ways that leave it open to further processing and possible reconstruction. Constructivists view learning as depending on the degree to which learners can activate existing structures or construct new ones to subsume the input" (Good and Brofy 1986: 229).

It follows, then, that teaching and training are not the same. The former focuses on student understanding, while the latter focuses on the students' observable actions. Knowledge is a network of conceptual structures and cannot simply be transferred from teacher to student; knowledge must instead be built by the student. Teaching is a social activity while learning is a private activity; therefore the teacher must have some idea of what the students already know in order to guide new learning. A teacher or researcher can only infer what students understand and cannot directly observe understanding. Language itself cannot transfer concepts or conceptual structure from one person to another; it can only call up representations of experiences that the listener (or reader) associates with what is said or written. In other words, the learner constructs his/her own knowledge and it may not be what the teacher thinks it is. For this reason, misconceptions should be of great interest in teaching because they represent what the learner thinks is correct at that moment in time.

Recent research in brain science and cognitive psychology shows that students learn best when knowledge is connected around broad concepts or "big ideas" (Bransford et al. 2000; Wiggins and McTighe 2005). Students must also have the opportunity to uncover these ideas for themselves through questioning, analyzing, and applying concepts in other domains. Disconnected facts or superficial coverage of a discipline do little to build understanding. Finally, learners need to reflect on their own learning and improve their work based on their own reflections and feedback from others.

The Understanding by Design model relies on this concept of learning and is sometimes called "backward design" because it begins with the end in mind. When using Understanding by Design, or UbD, the curriculum designer begins by identifying the desired learning results. These are broad concepts or "big ideas" such as the Rule of Law, or photosynthesis, which students should remember well into the future. Students uncover these big ideas, or enduring understandings, through a series of "essential questions." Next, the designer determines what constitutes evidence of understanding and designs assessments accordingly. Finally, the designer decides what knowledge and skills the student will need to uncover the enduring understandings, then plans the appropriate learning activities and events.

While the above may seem like common sense, Understanding by Design provides a rigorous process for ensuring that all elements are included and the resulting whole actually helps students achieve the desired results. It almost forces designers to employ many of the hallmarks of proven pedagogy, including interactive instruction, guided inquiry, advance organizers for learning, nonlinguistic representations of information, student reflection, transfer of knowledge to other contexts or domains, performance assessment, and constructivism. A rigorous application of Understanding by Design guided the development of *Project Archaeology: Investigating Shelter*.

Project Archaeology: Investigating Shelter consists of nine full lessons, a warm-up lesson, and a final performance of understanding. Each lesson teaches an enduring understanding and is guided by essential questions (Table 1.1).

Preconceptions and Misconceptions

In my case study (Moe 2011, 2016), I examined how twenty-seven 5th-grade students understood the concepts of scientific and archaeological inquiry. My primary question was: How do students understand the concepts of observation, inference, classification, context, and evidence as a result of instruction in archaeological inquiry? Do they misunderstand these concepts? If so, how?

The students received instruction with *Project Archaeology: Investigating Shelter* as part of their curriculum. Following each of the lessons, which covered the five basic inquiry concepts, the teacher administered a formative learning assessment probe and students responded in writing. The probes were designed to elicit student understanding of the concept in question, but not to assess correct or incorrect answers. I collected the written probes and then interviewed each of the students about their understanding of the concept. The probes served as good thinking prompts and the interviews allowed them to more fully express their understanding.

Table 1.1. Outline of *Project Archaeology: Investigating Shelter*

Enduring Understanding	Essential Questions	Learning Activity
		Warm-up Lesson: Thinking Like an Archaeologist
All people need shelter, but shelters are different from one another.	How are shelters the same and how do they differ? Why do they differ?	Lesson One: Knowing Shelter—Knowing People
We can learn about people by exploring how they build and use their shelter.	What does the study of shelter teach us about people? How important is this way of knowing?	Lesson Two: By Our Houses You Will Know Us
Everyone has a culture and our lives are shaped by culture in ways we may not even see.	How is culture expressed in the ways people meet basic human needs?	Lesson Three: Culture Everywhere
Using tools of scientific inquiry, archaeologists study shelters and learn how people lived in them.	How do archaeologists study the past?	Lesson Four: Observation, Inference, and Evidence Lesson Five: Classification Lesson Six: Context Lesson Seven: Every Picture Tells a Story
Studying a shelter can help us understand people and cultures.	How can investigating shelters help us understand people and cultures? How can we use what we learn about shelter in the present and the future?	Lesson Eight: Being an Archaeologist
All enduring understandings		Final Performance of Understanding: Archaeology under Your Feet

Source: Moe 2016, used with permission of Cambridge University Press.

All of the students except one were conversant in all five science inquiry concepts; they recognized the concept and could discuss it on some level either in writing or orally. One student did not seem to recognize the concept of "evidence," but he was, at least, minimally conversant on the other four concepts. While some students did seem to be conceptually confused on the written learning probes and in their interviews, their class work indicated some understanding of the concept. Without exception, all students performed reasonably well on a performance task in which they were asked to perform another investigation similar to the one they had done in class using another set of authentic archaeological data. In summary, all students, with the single exception noted above, had some level of understanding of each concept. Even students who struggled with the concepts and with expressing their understanding, either verbally or in writing, demonstrated moments of clear understanding.

While the bar graph (Figure 1.1) looks like a perfect bell curve, it is important to recognize that student understanding was idiosyncratic. Some students understood some of the concepts very well, but were confused by others. I found it unproductive to categorize students by "levels" of understanding and could not identify individual students who might represent a certain level of understanding. The more deeply I dug into student understanding, the more complex the picture of individual understanding became.

Misconceptions, misunderstandings, and incomplete understandings were of seminal importance in this study because they provided a picture of student understanding at that particular point in their learning process (Ausubel 1965; Novak 1977; Wiggins and McTighe 2005). All students except three showed at least one instance of misunderstanding a concept.

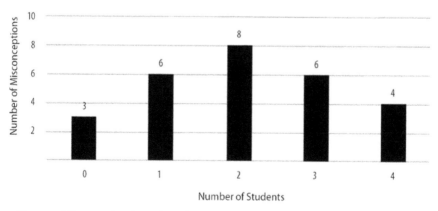

Figure 1.1. Misconceptions by students (Moe 2016). Used with permission of Cambridge University Press.

Learning Probe 5: Observations and Inference

(Adapted from *Intrigue of the Past: A Teachers Activity Guide Fourth through Seventh Grades*. Smith et al., 1996)

An Ancient Coin: This coin was found in an archaeological site. The drawings below show both sides of the coin. Look at the coin carefully and decide if each of the statements below is an observation or an inference.

Place an "O" before statements that are observations and an "I" before statements that are inferences.

_____ A. There is a picture of a face on one side of the coin. Explain your answer.

_____

_____ B. The coin tells us that these were deeply religious people. Explain your answer.

_____

_____ C. The words "We Trust the Gods" are printed on the coin. Explain your answer.

_____

_____ D. On one side of the artifact is a drawing of leaves. Explain your answer.

_____

_____ E. We can tell from the artifact that these were peace-loving people. Explain your answer.

_____

___F. The face on the coin is a picture of the nation's king. Explain your answer.

_____

Figure 1.2. Learning Assessment Probe: An Ancient Coin (Moe 2016). Used with permission of Cambridge University Press.

While the misconceptions detected in this study were mostly of a fairly minor nature, they indicated when students did not quite understand the concept. One of the clearest examples was Statement F on the observation and inference learning probe (Figure 1.2) "The face on the ancient coin is the nation's king." While almost all of the students handled the other five statements with ease, this statement tripped almost half of them. These students successfully used the skill of "observing," but because they did not have a complete understanding of the concepts of "observation" and "inference," they chose "observation" when "inference" was clearly the better choice. Moreover, when most of these students explained their reasoning, they described the skill of observing quite well, but still did not select the best possible choice.

Even practicing scientists and archaeologists may have difficulty in determining when an observation becomes an inference. In archaeology, for example, stones arranged in circles are ubiquitous on the Northern Plains of the western United States. Based on considerable research, they have long been thought to represent the presence of a tipi (a conical shelter) at some time in the past. Stone circles are so common that they are often referred to as "tipi rings" and the presence of tipi rings is often an observation rather than an inference when recording archaeological sites in the Northern Plains. If archaeologists did not think that stone circles commonly represented the presence of a tipi or other human-made structure, then researchers would not record them while in the field. Once a tipi ring is identified in the field, archaeologists begin making other observations such as size, number of stones, or the presence of other artifacts, and begin drawing further inferences from these observations.

In archaeological inquiry, classification and context are both useful and distinct conceptual tools. If archaeologists do not know exactly what these concepts are, they will not be able to use them effectively. In archaeological inquiry, the number of artifacts in a certain category sometimes needs to be separated from their location or their physical relationship to other artifacts. While locations of artifacts are routinely recorded in the field, archaeologists may want to group them by attributes such as material type, form, or function to answer research questions in the laboratory. In this study, a few students did not separate the two concepts, which led to confusing interpretations of the archaeological data in the performance task described above.

Similarly, some students did not differentiate between evidence as it is used in science and as it is used in legal contexts. These students used the terms "proof" or "prove" to describe the meaning of evidence in a scientific context while these terms more adequately describe the use of evidence in legal contexts.

Student conceptual understanding of science inquiry was clearly constructed by the students themselves, and sometimes it was constructed incorrectly, especially when pre-existing knowledge was faulty or incomplete (Bransford et al. 2000; Novak 1977; von Glaserfeld 1989). Conceptual knowledge is always under construction and concepts, like words, can change and grow in meaning as learners encounter them in different contexts (Brown et al. 1989). In the future, as these learners encounter each of the concepts in a new context or at a deeper level, their understanding may change again.

Most of the students were able to differentiate between the five concepts most of the time, but a few students conflated context and classification. Similarly, some students did not demonstrate a complete understanding of the difference between observation and inference, or the difference between evidence in science as opposed to evidence in legal contexts. These inadequacies in differentiation actually provide an excellent opportunity to expose flaws in reasoning and help students understand the differences between the concepts.

From a curriculum design standpoint, the misunderstandings and misconceptions detected in my case study were of seminal importance (Mintzes and Wandersee 2005; Wiggins and McTighe 2005). *Project Archaeology: Investigating Shelter* was designed to minimize misconceptions about archaeological inquiry and the nature of archaeological knowledge and includes a series of Misconception Alerts to help teachers identify and dispel common misconceptions and preconceptions.

While a large number of misconceptions, misunderstandings, and incomplete understandings were detected on the learning probes, in most cases these misconceptions could probably be dispelled and shifted to a more complete and accurate understanding of the concept. These misconceptions could be thought of as "teachable moments," but the teacher needs to know when misconceptions exist. Research shows that misconceptions need to be addressed directly, based on existing understanding (Bransford et al. 2000). Because these students already had a basic understanding of the concept, the shift might have been relatively easy to make.

Thirteen students thought that the statement, "The face on the ancient coin is the nation's king," was an observation when the statement is clearly an inference. A simple classroom discussion based on this statement would probably clarify the difference between observation and inference. A teacher could ask for a show of hands for "observation" and "inference" respectively, ask students to explain their reasoning, and then guide discussion to expose potential flaws in reasoning. During the interview phase of the study, two students exposed their own flaws in reasoning and, consequently, changed their answers to "inference." In this case, the difference between observation and inference is contextual—kings and queens are often represented on currency. Because context enters into explanation, observation and inference may also provide a good opportunity to examine the role of context in differentiating between the two conceptual tools.

Similarly, the difference between context and classification could be established through a simple differentiation exercise. A card-sorting activity in which students decide if each card is an example of classification or context might be sufficient for most students to differentiate the two concepts. Following the activity each student could write a brief description of each concept to make his or her understanding visible to the teacher for checking (Driver et al. 1994). A brief class discussion of the uses of evidence in science, as support for inferences or as a way to answer research questions, may have been sufficient to shift students to a better understanding of the concept. Students could also write a paragraph describing how evidence is used in science inquiry as opposed to how it is used in legal contexts to check for understanding. Again, context is highly relevant in differentiating between the two applications of the concept of evidence.

Misconceptions are persistent (Bransford et al. 2000), even in the face of direct instruction. Research shows that learners often revert to their original misunderstandings even following instruction—discouraging news for archaeology educators who usually have little time with learners and/or little control of the learning venue. As archaeology educators, the best we can do is identify common misconceptions such as the conflation of archaeology and paleontology, address the misconceptions directly with instruction, and assess conceptual understanding following the learning experience whenever possible. In other words, we cannot just throw learning activities and/or curriculum guides out to the public and expect them to grasp the concepts that we expect them to understand.

Stewardship

Early research (Levstik et al. 2005) showed that 5th-grade students of archaeology understood that they needed to protect archaeological sites and artifacts, but they did not understand why they should protect them. They did not understand that artifacts and sites have multiple stories to tell through evidence-based interpretation. When asked to interpret archaeological data uncovered at the Ashland Estate in Lexington, Kentucky, the students abandoned the archaeological evidence they had excavated from slave cabins and resorted to the well-known narrative of Henry Clay, Lexington's most famous historical figure. As Little and Shackel (2014: 63) point out, myths and accepted narratives are hard to change; these students of archaeology demonstrated the point very well.

Project Archaeology staff revised our educational materials to correct this problem through *Project Archaeology: Investigating Shelter* (Letts and Moe 2012). The use of authentic archaeological sites and artifacts seems to engage students more than do hypothetical archaeological contexts (for example, Smith et al. 1996). Through class discussion, they analyze the importance of archaeological sites as representations of the heritage of living descendant communities and of the shared heritage of the entire nation. The connection to living descendants seems to be a powerful feature of the shelter investigations. For example, summer camp students in Utah studied the Tinsley Homestead located in Bozeman, Montana. Sam Kirkley, Utah Project Archaeology Coordinator, reported that the students thought of Jackie Thompson, a Tinsley descendant, as a "rock star" and wanted to contact her personally about her memories of her ancestors and the place where they lived (Samantha Kirkley, personal communication 2013). These connections provide opportunities for students to connect history and historical places to real people in the present. They also learn that they can obtain information directly from people and do not have to "Google" everything. Additionally, students examine the laws protecting archaeological sites and engage in civic dialogue about historic preservation from the perspectives of developers, archaeologists, and members of the descendant communities. In sum, the curriculum guide puts a human face on archaeological sites and artifacts.

Judging from our research results (Brody et al. 2014), *Investigating Shelter* does a much better job of helping students understand the importance of protecting archaeological sites than did some of our earlier curriculum guides. Students (N=127) in this study showed a significantly better understanding of the need to protect archaeological sites, why they needed to be protected, and their personal responsibilities following instruction with *In-*

vestigating Shelter (Table 1.2). At this point we are not completely certain why this is the case, but we guess that it is because the students are engaged with real places, real descendants, and real archaeological data some of which has direct and immediate significance to descendant members. Further research on this aspect of the curriculum would certainly be warranted.

Other Research

Experience and anecdotal evidence show us that archaeology is well situated to teach cultural understanding. Unfortunately, we have not yet systematically researched the efficacy of archaeology to help teach cultural understanding, an important component of archaeological literacy (Franklin and Moe 2012), primarily because it is difficult to find funding for this type of research. In 2006, however, Project Archaeology received a grant from the American Honda Foundation to study the efficacy of archaeology as culturally relevant science curricula for underserved audiences (Brody et al. 2014). African American students in seven classrooms across the country learned about the lives of their enslaved ancestors through the archaeological study of the Poplar Forest Slave Cabin, at one of Thomas Jefferson's properties near Lynchburg, Virginia (Heath et al. 2009). The results of this small case study were promising and show that archaeology is a good vehicle for providing culturally relevant science education for underserved students. Students in this study were engaged in school science, some for the first time simply because the subject matter included their own heritage and their own ancestors. Specifically, several students reported that the content had an impact on them because of the personal connection. The majority of the students understood the importance of archaeological knowledge and knew what to do when finding or visiting an archaeological site, that is, be careful, do not touch or remove objects, and contact appropriate authorities (see Table 1.2). Additionally, these underserved students made gains in their understanding of science inquiry concepts such as observation, inference, context, evidence, and classification (Brody et al. 2014).

Project Archaeology staff members are working on materials that portray the heritage of living descendants of native populations in Montana. Examples include the Second Crow Agency at Absarokee, Montana (Doyle et al. 2016), the Clovis Child Burial near Wilsall, Montana (Agenten et al. 2014),

Table 1.2. Appropriate behavior at archaeological sites

Behavior	Pretest (N=127)	Posttest (N=118)
Study, Learn	16%	30%
Look Around	4%	0%
Take Pictures/Observe	4%	9%
Talk to Archaeologists/Work with Archaeologists	9%	6%
Leave Alone/Be Careful, Don't Touch	1%	24%
Dig or Take Things/Dig or Find Things	2%	2%
Nonrelated Answer	7%	3%
Don't Know/No Answer	47%	12%

Source: Brody et al. 2014.

and the descendants of enslaved people at both the Poplar Forest Slave Cabin in Virginia (Heath et al. 2009) and the Tabby Slave Cabin in Florida (James et al. 2010). We develop the materials collaboratively with members of the descendant communities and are researching the efficacy of these materials as culturally relevant science and social studies curricula for these underserved audiences.

Future Directions: Archaeology and Heritage Learning

Although my study focused on the conceptual understanding of science inquiry, its results have implications for teaching heritage concepts. It would be particularly interesting and productive to assess students' ability to grasp the role of archaeology and heritage in the development of sound public judgment, rather than relying on uninformed public opinion (Little and Shackel 2014).

Archaeology is potentially an excellent vehicle for providing "heritage learning" for underserved audiences. We are searching for more opportunities to provide culturally appropriate materials to underserved audiences and to assess their efficacy in both science and social studies education. Archaeology education can certainly be an important tool for historic preservation, a basic first step in democratizing archaeology (Little and Shackel 2014). While archaeology clearly can be a vehicle for teaching cultural understanding, little research has been conducted in this area.

Little and Shackel (2014: 63–64) show how "myth" usually trumps historical facts and how our myths often leave little room for new stories about the past. Yet stories about the past do change and grow with new questions and new interpretations. Archaeology education can be part of the, "Intentional effort . . . necessary to raise consciousness, work through meanings, and change cultural narratives, expectations, and reality" (Little and Shackel 2014: 64). For example, students studying the Poplar Forest Slave Cabin learned that their ancestors, despite the horrific institution of slavery, had some agency in choosing their work spaces, in providing a healthy diet through hunting and gathering in the nearby forest, and in gardening in their back yard. Similarly, students were required to deliberate about preservation of slave cabins versus the development of new homes for low-income families and arrive at reasonable and informed decisions. Research could be designed to elicit student conceptual understanding of these important concepts. Additionally, curriculum could be designed specifically to examine authentic heritage preservation issues within local communities and among Native Americans throughout the nation as, for example, Agenten et al. (2014) have done in Montana with *Investigating a Clovis Burial*.

Students and learners of all ages clearly need more exposure to open-ended inquiry and investigation to deal with real heritage issues as adults (Little and Shackel 2014; Shackel 2019). More research is needed to assess what people actually learn through archaeology education programs and instruction and how this learning can prepare them for meaningful and productive civic engagement in an increasingly pluralistic nation and world.

Conclusions

Misconceptions and preconceptions about archaeology are prevalent and may be strongly held. Misconceptions may be difficult to change, but not impossible to identify and alter in a classroom setting, especially if we think of them as "teachable moments." We can design our educational programs to assist learners with progressive differentiation of important concepts, such as the differences between archaeology and paleontology, and more importantly, the differences and similarities in the cultures and heritage of all Americans.

My study of conceptual understanding of science through archaeological inquiry (Moe 2011, 2016) demonstrates that learning and understanding basic science concepts was idiosyncratic for the twenty-seven participating students and, probably, dependent upon their existing structures of knowledge and experience (compare Novak 1977). While the study involved only a small sample, its implications are clear: as archaeology educators we cannot continue to throw educational materials out to the public without understanding how people learn and how they remember what they have learned. Archaeology educators need to have basic knowledge of how people learn and understand both concepts and content, how they store knowledge, and how they may reconstruct their conceptual understanding of archaeology and related information as they acquire new content and concepts.

We must also assess what people do learn about archaeology and its importance in the contemporary world at every opportunity. While assessment is difficult, both logistically and fiscally, it is essential to the long-term viability of archaeology education. Without knowing what people misunderstand, we have no way to help them correct their misconceptions and progressively differentiate knowledge for deeper conceptual understanding. Additionally, assessment data provides us with "teachable moments" that would be missed completely without knowing that misunderstandings exist. This point is especially critical as we work with increasingly diverse audiences and aim to craft more textured and democratic understandings with them.

Educating both teachers and their students is a long process. Merely gaining admittance to the vast and complicated world of education is an enormous undertaking, especially considering the limited resources available to archaeology educators. Nonetheless, the archaeological profession must commit to a long-term effort, heed the lessons learned, continually improve our offerings, adapt to teachers' ever-changing needs, and expand our support base wherever possible.

References Cited

Agenten, Courtney, Crystal Alegria, and Shane M. Doyle
2014   *Investigating the First Peoples.* Montana State University, Bozeman.
Ausubel, David P.
1965   Introduction. In *Readings in the Psychology of Cognition*, edited by R. C. Anderson and D. P. Ausubel, pp.3–17. Holt, Rinehart, and Winston, New York.

Ausubel, David P., and F. Robinson
1969   *School Learning: An Introduction to Psychology.* Holt, Rinehart, and Winston, New York.

Bransford, John D., Ann L. Brown, and Rodney R. Cocking (editors)
2000   *How People Learn: Brain, Mind, Experience, and School.* National Academy Press, Washington, D.C.

Brody, Michael, Jeanne M. Moe, Joelle G. Clark, and Crystal B. Alegria
2014   Archaeology as Culturally Relevant Science Education: The Poplar Forest Slave Cabin. In *Participation in Archaeology,* edited by Suzie Thomas and Joanne Lea, pp. 603–621. Boydell Press, Woodbridge, UK.

Brown, John S., Allan Collins, and Paul Duguid
1989   Situated Cognition and the Culture of Learning. *Educational Researcher* 18(1): 32–42.

Davis, M. Elaine
1997   *Making History: An Inquiry into How Children Construct the Past.* PhD Dissertation, University of North Carolina, Chapell Hill.
2005   *How Students Understand the Past: From Theory to Practice.* AltaMira Press, Walnut Creek, California.

Doyle, Shane M., Crystal B. Alegria, and Jeanne M. Moe
2016   *Changing Land, Changing Life: Investigating Archaeology in the Apsáalooke Homeland.* Draft. Montana State University, Bozeman.

Driver, R., A. Squires, P. Rushworth, and V. Wood-Robinson
1994   *Making Sense of Secondary Science: Research into Children's Ideas.* Routledge Falmer, London, UK.

Franklin, M. Elaine, and Jeanne M. Moe
2012   A Vision for Archaeological Literacy. In *The Oxford Handbook of Public Archaeology,* edited by Robin Skeates, Carol McDavid, and John Carman, pp. 566–580. Oxford University Press, Oxford, UK.

Good, T. L., and J. E. Brofy
1986   *Educational Psychology: A Realistic Approach.* 3rd ed. Longman, New York.

Heath, Barbara, Crystal B. Alegria, Harvey Bakari, and Michelle San Antonio
2009   Investigating the Poplar Forest Slave Cabin, Series no. 4. *Project Archaeology: Investigating Shelter.* Montana State University: Bozeman (www.projectarchaeology.org/teachers).

Henderson, A. Gwynn, and Linda S. Levstik
2016   Reading Objects: Children Interpreting Material Culture. *Advances in Archaeological Practice* 4(4): 503–516.

James, Pam, Mary Mott, and Dawn Baker
2010   Investigating a Tabby Slave Cabin, Series no. 13. *Project Archaeology: Investigating Shelter.* Montana State University, Bozeman (www.projectarchaeology.org/teachers).

Jewell, Elizabeth J., and Frank Abate (editors)
2001   *The New Oxford American Dictionary.* Oxford University Press, New York.

Kendall, John S., and Robert J. Marzano
2000   *Content Knowledge: A Compendium of Standards and Benchmarks for K-12*

Education, 3rd ed. Mid-continent Research for Education and Learning, Aurora, Colorado.

King, Eleanor M.

2019   African Americans, American Indians, and Heritage. In *History and Approaches to Heritage Studies*, edited by Phyllis Mauch Messenger and Susan J. Bender, pp. 59–86. University Press of Florida, Gainesville.

Letts, Cali A., and Jeanne M. Moe

2012   *Project Archaeology: Investigating Archaeology.* 2nd printing. Montana State University, Bozeman.

Levstik, Linda, A. Gwynn Henderson, and Jennie S. Schlarb

2005   In *Understanding History: Recent Research in History Education, Volume 4: International Review of History Education*, edited by Rosalyn Ashby, Peter Gordon, and Peter Lee, pp. 37–53. Routledge-Falmer, London.

Little, Barbara J., and Paul A. Shackel

2014   *Archaeology, Heritage, and Civic Engagement: Working toward the Public Good.* Left Coast Press, Walnut Creek, California.

Mintzes, J. J., and J. H. Wandersee

2005   Research in Science Teaching and Learning: A Human Constructivist Approach. In *Teaching Science for Understanding: A Human Constructivist View*, edited by J. J. Mintzes, J. H. Wandersee, J. D. Novak, pp. 59–92. Elsevier Academic Press, Burlington, Massachusetts.

Moe, Jeanne M.

2011   *Conceptual Understanding of Science through Archaeological Inquiry.* PhD dissertation, Montana State University, Bozeman.

2016   Archaeology Education for Children: Assessing Effective Learning. *Advances in Archaeological Practice* 4(4): 441–453.

2019   Best Practices in Archaeology Education: Successes, Shortcomings, and the Future. In *Public Engagement and Education: Developing and Fostering Stewardship for an Archaeological Future,* edited by Katherine M. Erdman, pp. 215–236. Berghahn Books, New York.

National Governors Association Center for Best Practices (NGA Center), Council of Chief State School Officers (CCSSO)

2010   *Common Core State Standards for English Language Arts & Literacy in History/Social Studies, Science, and Technical Subjects.* NGA Center, Washington, D.C.

National Research Council

1996   *National Science Education Standards.* National Academy Press, Washington, D.C.

Novak, Joseph D.

1977   *A Theory of Education.* Cornell University Press, Ithaca, New York.

1993   Human Constructivism: A Unification of Psychological and Epistemological Phenomena in Meaning Making. *International Journal of Personal Construct Psychology* 6: 167–193.

Ramos, Maria, and David Duganne

2000   *Exploring Public Perceptions and Attitudes about Archaeology.* Society for American Archaeology, Washington, D.C.

Shackel, Paul A.

2019   Civic Engagement, Representation, and Social Justice: Moving from CRM to Heritage Studies. In *History and Approaches to Heritage Studies*, edited by Phyllis Mauch Messenger and Susan J. Bender, pp. 9–23. University Press of Florida, Gainesville.

Simon, Rebecca L.

2013   *Teaching with Broken Glass: A Portfolio of Historical Archaeological Research, Curriculum Development, and Public Outreach*. Unpublished master's portfolio, Department of Anthropology, Colorado State University, Fort Collins.

Smardz, Karolyn E., and Shelley J. Smith (editors)

2000   *The Archaeology Education Handbook: Sharing the Past with Kids*. Altamira Press, Walnut Creek, California.

Smardz-Frost, Karolyn E.

2004   Archaeology and Public Education in North America. In *Public Archaeology*, edited by Nick Merriman, pp. 59–84. Routledge, New York.

Smith, Shelley J., Jeanne M. Moe, Kelly A. Letts, and Danielle M. Paterson

1996   *Intrigue of the Past: Investigating Archaeology*. Bureau of Land Management, Dolores, Colorado.

von Glaserfeld, Ernst

1989   Constructivism in Education. In *The International Encyclopedia of Education*, supplement vol. 1, pp. 162–163. Pergamon Press, Oxford and New York.

Wiggins, Grant, and Jay McTighe

2005   *Understanding by Design, Expanded Second Edition*. Association for Supervision and Curriculum Design, Alexandria, Virginia.

2

Archaeology in School

Tapping into Histories and Historical Inquiry

CHARLES S. WHITE

Archaeology, History, and the Social Sciences in School

The discipline of archaeology, whether alone or as a subdiscipline of anthropology, enriches our understanding of human history and seeks to preserve the evidence of material culture that is the fruit of archaeologists' labors. Whereas historians focus on writing and documentary evidence as the basis for drawing conclusions about the past, archaeologists draw from the objects humans use and leave behind for future generations to ponder. From these resources, we seek to acquire historical knowledge, which "is no more and no less than carefully and critically constructed collective memory. As such, it can make us both wiser in our public choices and more richly human in our private lives" (McNeil 1991: 103). Not only does history embrace our collective memory; it also captures our personal story and the multiple stories of our historical space.

For some time, however, scholars and opinion leaders have expressed deep concern about the state of history and social science teaching and learning in the United States. The issue spanned quantity and quality. Beginning in 1994, the National Assessment of Educational Progress (NAEP) has tracked student knowledge of history, geography, and civics. In its most recent study, undertaken in 2014, 73 percent of 8th graders scored below proficiency in geography, 77 percent below in civics, and 82 percent below in history. Only 3 percent scored in the advanced level for any of these three subjects. According to Terry Mazany, chairman of the NAEP Governing Board:

> Geography, U.S. history and civics are core academic subjects that must be a priority. They represent knowledge and skills that are fundamental

to a healthy democracy. The lack of knowledge on the part of America's students is unacceptable, and the lack of growth must be addressed. As a country, we must do better. (National Assessment Governing Board 2015: para. 5)

As knowledge of history among the young is at risk, so too are sites that could reveal new knowledge of our cultural heritage. Some are now lost to the ages. An iconic example is the ancient Library of Alexandria. Built around 300 B.C. under Ptolemy II, the library became the pre-eminent repository of works by ancient Greek philosophers and many others from the eastern Mediterranean. We wonder, for example, what knowledge we might have gleaned from the ancient Library of Alexandria in Egypt had people preserved its contents. Walking across a parking lot, we wonder what cultural artifacts might be slumbering under the pavement, just below our feet, lost in our haste to meet a transitory need. Many more sites, uncovered and admired, crumble where they stand. Perhaps we need new approaches to teaching history and to preserving the rich sources of cultural knowledge revealed by archaeologists.

Many educators believe that we have been teaching history the wrong way (Conway 2015; Levstik and Barton 2011; Schippers 2013; Wineburg 1991). We have treated the subject matter as a commodity and students as consumers. To enliven the study of history and social sciences—what is collectively referred to "social studies"—we need to engage students as "doers" of history and social science and to teach them to work and think like historians, archaeologists, geographers, and effective democratic citizens. We see this perspective reflected more and more in national and state content and curriculum standards that demand more fluency in communication, skill in numeracy, and sophistication in thinking skills. For disciplines like archaeology to enjoy a more central place in the social studies curriculum and to be embraced by young people as a call to preservation, they must demonstrate that they can help schools achieve the higher standards for which they are being held accountable.

Opening the School House Door

Where are the contact points where archaeology can make strong contributions to the schools' education mission? Examining the following definition suggests that the field of social studies may provide a considerable number of contact points:

> [Social studies is] the integrated study of the social sciences and humanities to promote civic competence. Within the school program, social studies provides coordinated, systematic study drawing upon such disciplines as anthropology, archaeology, economics, geography, history, law, philosophy, political science, psychology, religion, and sociology, as well as appropriate content from the humanities, mathematics, and natural sciences. The primary purpose of social studies is to help young people develop the ability to make informed and reasoned decisions for the public good as citizens of a culturally diverse, democratic society in an interdependent world. (Anderson 1993: 2)

The social studies curriculum draws especially from the content of history, along with social sciences, which are well represented in the collection of voluntary national standards documents commissioned in the early 1990s by the United States Department of Education. These include history (National Center for History in the Schools 1996), geography (Heffron and Downs 2012), and civics (Center for Civic Education 1994).

Shaping archaeology's outreach to schools to support history and social science goals and to meet rigorous standards is essential for getting in the schoolhouse door. Successful curriculum integration, however, is in the hands of the classroom teacher, whose needs and interests must also be met.

Partnering with Teachers

Archaeologists and school teachers have different agendas. The road of well-meaning outreach initiatives is strewn with projects that ignored or undervalued or misunderstood what teachers need to accomplish, even when those teachers were genuinely interested in what the field of archaeology could offer. Zimmerman's experience working with middle school teachers on an archaeology education project yielded a significant lesson. "We have learned that in any archaeology education project . . . we must engage teachers as professional equals and that the first goal of our programme must be to set an agenda that is mutual and negotiated" (Zimmerman et al. 1994: 371). Listening is a good way to start.

One item sure to come up in conversation is learning standards, both local and state. National standards have an influence on local practice to the extent that they are reflected in course development, textbook selection, and student-testing regimes (Sykes and Wilson 2016: 865). Since higher order–thinking skills, along with literacy and numeracy, take center stage in current school accountability assessment (Porter et. al. 2011), providing opportunities for students to practice and improve in these areas should be a top priority. Added to that should be a careful review of the specific content the teacher is charged with conveying. The greater the deviation from current practice and content, the stronger the lessons, projects, or experiences in archaeology must be to make the change worthwhile.

Teacher buy-in requires more than simply making an eloquent case and dropping off some instructional materials. Curriculum alignment without classroom usability produces frustration and, inevitably, failure. Three questions can gauge the usability of classroom content and pedagogy. First, has the teacher had enough time, exposure, and support to understand the content, methodology, and intent of the lessons or projects? This question is of particular importance for elementary teachers, whose academic background may lie outside of history and social science. Second, has the teacher had the chance to observe a model of best practice in implementing the material? Description only goes so far. Watching skillful models is a powerful aid to improving practice. Third, has the teacher been able to implement the material and receive feedback needed to mold the material to meet the needs of students? In short, a one-time session at a teachers' conference or after-school workshop might be adequate for information dissemination but is not likely to produce robust and sustainable implementation (White and White 2000). Sustainable outreach to classrooms requires a commitment to sustained engagement with teacher partners (Bruce et al. 2010; Desimone 2011).

What makes teachers persist in trying something new, even if it takes a good deal of effort to shape it for the classroom? They persist because the innovation captures their interest, curiosity, and imagination; it taps the learner in the teacher. Moreover, teachers will persevere in implementing new ideas if they believe these ideas will also capture the interest, curiosity, and imagination of their students.

Engaging Students

Few things engage students in learning more powerfully than a personal connection and a stake in the process. Fortunately, archaeology and history bring several advantages in this regard: (1) tangible artifacts and places of material culture to examine, (2) the power of narrative, (3) mysteries to unravel and problems to solve, and (4) actions to take.

Touching the Past

Over the years of preparing new teachers, I have recounted the story of my first visit to the Coliseum in Rome. Years ago, my wife and I had an unexpected layover in Rome. We arranged for a hotel and made our way by bus into the city. It was still early enough in the day to cram in as much as we could see in the Eternal City, so we figured out the metro system and found the "Coliseum" stop. As we emerged from the underground station, there it was—the Coliseum. At this point in the story, I asked my students, "What is the first thing I did?" Rarely did they hit on the correct answer. "I touched it." They instantly understood the reason, because most had done the same.

Figure 2.1. Marble just quarried in Carrara, Italy. Prized by sculptors like Michelangelo for its sublime whiteness. Photograph by Charles S. White, used with permission.

Touch connects us to the past in a unique way, as we imagine people of the distant past placing their hands on the same spot (see Moe, this volume). Placing our hands on a slab of marble from a quarry in Carrara, Italy, connects us to the marble drawn from the same quarry, more than half a millennium ago, that Michelangelo sculpted into a gleaming *David* (see Figure 2.1). Walking through historic places, we get the sensation of "being there," walking paths we know were walked by generations of fellow humans like us (Bhatawadekar 2017). This is the beginning of historical empathy (Baron 2012) and of engagement with narratives of history.

The Power of Narratives and Stories

When we step onto an archaeological site, we enter a stage upon which past lives played out. How did they meet their basic needs? What did they value? What ideas occupied their minds? How did they think about the past? What did they wonder about the future? Parenthetically, we should recognize as well that we are actors on our own stage, making our own history with our own stories to tell. Using the evidence that archaeology uncovers, we can begin to reconstruct or elaborate on the stories of those who left behind artifacts from their time and place (see Messenger, this volume).

Narratives as history need to be approached with some caution, of course. In Chapter 1, Jeanne Moe emphasized the importance of addressing students' archaeological knowledge. According to Epstein (2012), young people also entertain several misconceptions about historical narratives. They tend to view narratives as statements of objective truth; history is simply a description of what "really" happened. Moreover, they have little experience or skill at judging the credibility of primary resources, accepting them uncritically. This would extend to interpretation of artifacts in a vacuum without considering context or information about similar finds elsewhere. Students tend to be poor judges of human motivation and action in their historical context, applying present-day standards and conditions to the past. Finally, the effects of large-scale social or economic forces on historical change tend to be underestimated and the role of individuals, overestimated. Overall, then, the attraction of "story" must yield to an understanding of history as interpretive and our knowledge tentative, incomplete, and subject to change (Levstik and Barton 2011; Levstik et al. 2014; Zimmerman 2019).

Figure 2.2. An outdoor restaurant in ancient Herculaneum, with modern-day Ercolano's street level above. Photograph by Charles S. White, used with permission.

As engaging as a story can be, however, it is still only *one* story. Across the stage of any place, many feet have trod. Crossing paths are many people who have their own stories—stories told in their own ways from their unique perspectives. As archaeologists engage in excavation, they uncover history in layers, and a single place may have many stories. We can see this clearly in the photo from Herculaneum, which fell victim to Mount Vesuvius' wrath on the day following Pompeii's destruction (Figure 2.2). At camera level, we see the remains of an outdoor restaurant in A.D. 79. Looking at the top of the photo, we look up to street level of the current city of Ercolano, built on top of the ancient city that was swallowed up in the disaster.

Finally, we recognize that there may be multiple narratives represented by a single site. For every antebellum plantation house, there are slave quarters. For many cities, a neighborhood now part of one group's narrative was once a part of another group's story. When one asks "Who owns history?" the answer often is that history must be shared rather than claimed by a single dominant group (see MacDonald 2019).

Narratives and our connections to them remain powerful contact points for engaging students as long as we view them as a product of inquiry. Gaps in our knowledge of past peoples can serve as mysteries to be explored. Few people can resist a good mystery, especially if they can be drawn into seeking answers.

Mysteries and Problem Solving

Noted historian Sam Wineburg has reflected on school history and the work of historians:

> Over the years I've met many [students], for whom the life has been sucked out of history, leaving only a grim list of names and dates. When confronted with the term "historical thinking," many students scratch their heads in confusion, stumped by an alleged connection. . . . The funny thing is that when you ask historians what they do, a different picture emerges. They see themselves as detectives searching for evidence among primary sources to a mystery that can never be completely solved. Wouldn't this image be more enticing to a bored high school student? It would, and that is one reason why thinking like a historian deserves a place in the American classroom, the sooner the better. (Wineburg 2010)

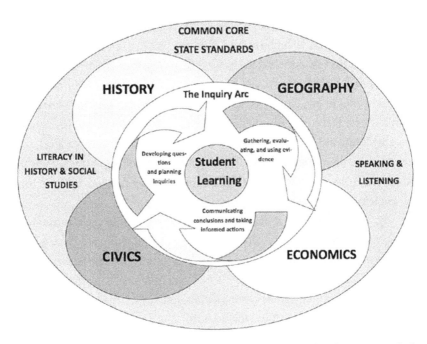

Figure 2.3. *College, Career, and Civic Life (C3) Framework for Social Studies State Standards,* aligned with the Common Core State Standards and organized around an Inquiry Arc. Used with permission of the State of Connecticut Social Studies Framework Project.

To capture the key role that problem solving and inquiry should play in the social studies curriculum, the National Council for the Social Studies (NCSS) published *The College, Career, and Civic Life (C3) Framework for Social Studies State Standards* (NCSS 2013). Importantly, the framework aligns with the *Common Core State Standards* (CCSS) in mathematics and English language arts/literacy, which have guided changes in content and skill requirements (and testing programs) in more than forty states and the District of Columbia (NGA Center and CCSSO 2010). Most distinctively, however, the *C3 Framework* features an "Inquiry Arc" that spans the study of discipline-based subject matter (see Figure 2.3).

For problem-solving involving historical thinking, Wineburg's (1991) study identified three key heuristics for interrogating a primary source, reflected in the following questions: (1) What is the document's *source*, its author and how was the document created? (2) What was the *context* in which the document was created? and (3) What other sources can we use to *corroborate* the information in this document, to reinforce or call into

Table 2.1. Comparing Wineburg and Baron: Analyzing 2D vs. 3D primary sources

Wineburg (1991)	Baron (2010, 2012)	Rationale
Sourcing—Who was the author? How did it come to be written?	Origination—Why is this [building, landscape] located in this place?	Authorship is a collective activity over time, rather than single authorship at a single moment.
Corroboration—How do other documents support or call into question the contents of the document?	Intertectonality—How does this place compare to other similar places (in design, in use of space)?	Veracity of an account is not relevant, only how the place compares to other comparable places.
Contextualization—What was the context in which the document was created?	Stratification—What are the layers of context for this place over time?	The place has many layers, used and altered in many contexts over time.
	Supposition—applying informed historical imagination to generate hypotheses and plausible explanations about the place	(in the absence of sufficient evidence to reach a firm conclusion)
	Empathetic Insight—marshaling the results of structured inquiry to achieve a sense of what the actors in the place believed and experienced in a specific context.	An understanding of history requires grasping the motivations and actions of people in their time and in that place.

question the contents therein?[1] This kind of critical analysis of history's raw material lies at the heart of historical thinking. Wineburg's heuristics, of course, apply to the analysis of two-dimensional primary sources. What if the primary source is three-dimensional, like a historic building, district, or landscape?

Baron (2010) tackled this issue of analyzing historic places in her 2010 dissertation and proposed a modification and extension of Wineburg's heuristics that would be better suited to "place" as document. Based on her more recent update (Baron 2012), Table 2.1 summarizes Baron's heuristics in comparison to Wineburg's, with a brief explanation for each. Of interest is how the questions emerging from Baron's work might apply to the primary sources of material culture uncovered by archaeologists. What similar questions do archaeologists pose? How should the heuristics formulated by

Wineburg and Baron be adapted and applied to outreach materials, projects, and experiences for schools?

Archaeologists capitalizing on the motivation and skill potential of problem solving and inquiry in the classroom can multiply these effects by ensuring that the learning that occurs is "authentic"—that it parallels closely the work of professional archaeologists. This doesn't mean that the work should simply be "relevant" or "hands-on." "Identifying the nature of intellectual work in [relevant professions] can help to define criteria for performance necessary for success in contemporary society" (King et al. 2009: 43). Research suggests that a program considered "authentic" engages students in the construction of knowledge through disciplined inquiry, has value beyond the classroom, and is connected to students' lives and the community around them (King et. al. 2009).

Two implications of authentic learning criteria seem particularly relevant for archaeological outreach to schools. First, students should "do archaeology," to the extent possible. Yes, this does include hands-on work akin to what one might find at field schools, modified to accommodate school realities (Sokol-Margolis 2016). Beyond the value of authenticity, such work also activates the force that "touching the past" provides. Second, authentic learning extends meaning beyond the student and classroom into the community around them (City of Alexandria 2016; *Coventry Telegraph* 2014), both local and global. It invites students to service, and to taking action.

Taking Action

In the National Council for the Social Studies' *C3 Framework* summarized in Figure 2.2, the final step in the Inquiry Arc calls for "communicating conclusions and taking informed actions." In the words of the framework's authors, "individual mastery of content often no longer suffices; students should also develop the capacity to work together to apply knowledge to real problems" (2013: 19). This view undergirds the definition of the field cited earlier in the chapter.

The civic dimension of education is most often reflected in schools' service learning programs. Service learning is one of six "proven practices" for civic learning and engagement (Gould et al. 2011: 29–32). It links the school curriculum to work in the community. "Service learning is distinguished from community service or volunteerism in two ways. First, the service activity is integrated with academic skills and content. Second, students engage in structured reflection activities on their service experiences" (National Council for the Social Studies 2000).

Service learning is a natural match for heritage preservation efforts, especially where students' efforts have been informed by instruction consistent with the pedagogical methods described in this chapter. The instinct to preserve arises from direct interaction with the fruits of the archaeological enterprise and a sense of historical ownership, not only from a general sense of social responsibility (see Shackel 2019). Service learning is also a potentially productive link between school outreach and community archaeology (Marshall 2002). Student research can become a useful resource for community groups interested in preserving a local historic site.

Taking action sometimes means tackling public policy issues relating to preservation (see MacDonald 2019). For example, convinced that an oil pipeline company in North Dakota will damage ancestral homeland, the Standing Rock Sioux Tribe has blocked excavation. They claim, in part, that the company's hired archaeologists "do not have the knowledge and cultural sensitivity" to adequately assess the area. The tribe has asked the state archaeologist to evaluate the site (Hand 2016). In another example, the mayor of Pensacola, Florida, has been criticized for failing to support a moratorium on demolishing historic buildings. Supporters of the moratorium want to "give city officials and the community the chance to reevaluate our processes and improve them if necessary" (*Pulse* 2016; see also Hayward 2016). When conflicts between progress and preservation arise, opportunities for research, problem solving, informed decision making, and service come to the fore. As discussed below, archaeologists' outreach to schools can set the stage for this kind of civic action through the schools' service learning programs.

Preserving tribal homelands is one example of archaeology's role in achieving social justice. Archaeologists help give voice to peoples whose history is disappearing and whose contributions to the human story merit protection (see King 2019). Forensic archaeologists apply their methods to medical and legal issues, which might include uncovering evidence of genocide hidden from the world's approbation (Ferllini 2007). In short, archaeology can be a tool of civic engagement (Little and Shackel 2007).

"Teaching with Historic Places" as an Example of School Outreach

Many history and social science professional organizations recognize the potential benefits of school outreach (American Association of Geographers 2016; Archaeological Institute of America 2016; Council for Economic Education 2016; National Council for History Education 2016; SAA 2016), not least of which is to engender long-term public appreciation of and support for their particular fields. There is a lot of variation in the depth, extent, and quality of those outreach efforts. One project of note has endeavored to address standards, teacher preparation, inquiry, and civic engagement. This example may be instructive for outreach efforts in other fields.

In the early 1990s, the National Register of Historic Places (NRHP), a department within the National Park Service, recognized that they possessed a largely untapped repository of historic places rich in source materials generated as part of their nomination process. The National Trust for Historic Preservation (NTHP) serves as stewards for historic places that are often overlooked and underappreciated by the public at large. The two organizations collaborated on a project called "Teaching with Historic Places" (Shull and Hunter 1992).

Given the rich database at their disposal, the most logical initial foray into the classroom for both organizations was to develop lesson plans based on a template that tapped the empathetic and inquiry potential of these historic places (National Park Service 2016a). Appreciating the need to engage teachers as partners and to better address their accountability responsibilities, the project commissioned *Teaching with Historic Places: A Curriculum Framework for Professional Training and Development of Teachers, Preservationists, and Museum and Site Interpreters* (White and Hunter 1995). The publication aimed to bring together these varied constituencies to forge bonds with schools.

To support professionals partnering with teachers who are interested in integrating historic places into their classrooms, the Teaching with Historic Places website provides professional development resources for teachers, offering sample outlines for workshops of varying durations (National Park Service 2016b). The project also encourages students in teacher education programs to explore historic places as part of their college methods course (National Park Service 2016c). Finally, the National Park Service website offers ideas for civic engagement through service learning (National Park Service 2016d). On that page, visitors can read a number of case studies of individuals and communities taking action, in collaboration with the National Park Service, to rescue cultural treasures from obscurity or loss. Archaeological outreach initiatives should capitalize on opportunities to support students in preservation efforts. Indeed, depending on local circumstances, service learning can extend to policy advocacy to save endangered cultural resources. Such activities exemplify the "informed action" culmination of the *C3 Framework*'s "Inquiry Arc" described earlier. Moreover, action civics is one element of recommendations for civic renewal (Levine and Kawashima-Ginsburg 2017). More importantly for the field of archaeology, this kind of civic engagement is central to public outreach goals.

Conclusion

Successful archaeology outreach to schools is a challenge. It requires understanding the goals of schools and teachers, as well as the constraints under which they operate. Effective outreach encourages young people to see themselves in the material culture that surrounds them. It engenders pride in the human labors that shaped the cultural ground on which they now stand. It fosters a commitment to preserve the past and their own stories for future generations to admire, emulate, and aspire to surpass.

At the beginning of this chapter, I referred to the Library of Alexandria as a lost repository of cultural knowledge. Most of us learned in school, and at the movies, that the Library of Alexandria was burned down by Julius Caesar during the siege of the city in 48 B.C. As it turns out, history is a bit more complicated, since blame has been cast on several other calamities and culprits up to the seventh century A.D. Calamities and culprits obscure the most likely cause of the library's demise, however:

> It is hard to give up villains, but it looks as if we must abandon the search for some individual or small group to blame. The disappearance of the Library is the inevitable result of the end of the impetus and interest that brought it into being and of the lack of the kind of sustained management and maintenance that would have seen it through successive transitions in the physical media by means of which the texts could have been transmitted. (Bagnall 2002)

What is instructive in this story is that it reveals the multiple ways in which material culture can be lost (Bokkem 2017). Yes, we lose historic temples when they are exploded by extremists (Westcott 2015), but we also lose archaeological sites through neglect, washed away through erosion (Kennedy 2015), or by failing to control access (*Salt Lake City Tribune* 2011). A measure of how much we value history is our willingness to preserve the evidence of our diverse pasts, whether represented in paper or stone. To the extent that young people are drawn into the story, the artifact, the inquiry, and the challenges of interpretation, they will be prepared to take action emblematic of responsible stewardship (Shapiro 1997).

Note

1. In the course of answering these questions, Wineburg recommends engaging in *close reading* (to discern both what is written and how it is expressed), applying relevant *background knowledge*, and *reading the silences*; that is, looking for what is missing from the document (Wineburg 2010).

References Cited

Anderson, Charlotte
1993   President's Message. *The Social Studies Professional*, January/February: 2.
American Association of Geographers
2016   *Education.* Electronic document, http://www.aag.org/cs/education, accessed October 27, 2016.
Archaeological Institute of America
2016   *Education.* Electronic document, https://www.archaeological.org/education, accessed October 27, 2016.
Bagnall, Roger S.
2002   Alexandria: Library of Dreams. *Proceedings of the American Philosophical Society* 146(4): 348–362.
Baron, Christine
2010   *Encouraging Historical Thinking at Historic Sites.* Unpublished PhD dissertation, Boston University, Boston, Massachusetts.
2012   Understanding Historical Thinking at Historic Sites. *Journal of Educational Psychology* 104(3): 833–847.
Bhatawadekar, Shraddha
2017   Heritage Walk as a Tool for Engaging Youth in Heritage. */encatcSCHOLAR.* March 20. Electronic document, http://blogs.encatc.org/encatcscholar/?p=1753, accessed February 13, 2018.

Bokkem, Rachel Van

2017   History in Ruins: Cultural Heritage Destruction around the World. *Perspectives on History*. April. Electronic document, https://www.historians.org/publications-and-directories/perspectives-on-history/april-2017/history-in-ruins-cultural-heritage-destruction-around-the-world, accessed February 7, 2018.

Bruce, Catherine D., Indigo Esmonde, John Ross, Lesley Dookie, and Ruth Beatty

2010   The Effects of Sustained Classroom-Embedded Teacher Professional Learning on Teacher Efficacy and Related Student Achievement. *Teaching and Teacher Education* 26(8): 1598–1608.

Center for Civic Education

1994   *National Standards for Civics and Government*. Center for Civic Education, Calabasas, California.

City of Alexandria

2016   *Family Dig Days*. March 2. Electronic document, https://www.alexandriava.gov/historic/archaeology/default.aspx?id=38960, accessed August 3, 2016.

Conway, Michael

2015   The Problem with History Classes. *Atlantic*, May 16. http://www.theatlantic.com/education/archive/2015/03/the-problem-with-history-classes/387823/, accessed October 27, 2016.

Council for Economic Education

2016   *Programs*. Electronic document, http://councilforeconed.org/programs-2/, accessed October 27, 2016.

Coventry Telegraph

2014   Budding Archaeologists Invited to Join Warwick Dig This Weekend. July 25. Electronic document, http://www.coventrytelegraph.net/news/coventry-news/archaeological-dig-st-johns-house-7506457, accessed August 10, 2016.

Desimone, Laura M.

2011   A Primer on Effective Professional Development. *Phi Delta Kappan* 92(6): 68–71.

Epstein, Terrie

2012   Preparing History Teachers to Develop Young People's Historical Thinking. *Perspectives on History* (American Historical Association) 50(5): 36–39.

Ferllini, Roxana

2007   *Forensic Archaeology and Human Rights Violations*. Charles C. Thomas, Springfield, Illinois.

Gould, Jonathan K., Kathleen Hall Jamieson, Peter Levine, Ted McConnell, David B. Smith

2011   *Guardian of Democracy: The Civic Mission of Schools*. Lenore Annenberg Institute for Civics of the Annenberg Public Policy Center and the Campaign for the Civic Mission of Schools, Philadelphia, Pennsylvania, available at http://civicmission.s3.amazonaws.com/118/f0/5/171/1/Guardian-of-Democracy-report.pdf, accessed August 10, 2016.

Hand, Natalie

2016   Support Grows Despite Arrests at Dakota Access Pipeline Protest, *Indian Coun-*

try Today Media Network. August 15. Electronic document, http://indiancountrytodaymedianetwork.com/2016/08/15/support-grows-despite-arrests-dakota-access-pipeline-protest-165472, accessed August 23, 2016.

Hayward, Ashton

2016   Grow Pensacola While Preserving History. *Pensacola News Journal,* August 18. Electronic document, http://www.pnj.com/story/opinion/2016/08/19/Mayor:mayor-grow-pensacola-preserving-history/88972640/, accessed August 23, 2016.

Heffron, Susan Gallagher, and Roger M. Downs (editor)

2012   *Geography for Life: National Geography Standards.* 2nd ed. National Council for Geographic Education, Washington, D.C.

Kennedy, Maev

2015   Volunteers and Drones to Survey Sites at Risk on British Coast. *Guardian,* August 4. Electronic document, https://www.theguardian.com/environment/2015/aug/03/drones-british-coast-volunteers, accessed on August 11, 2016.

King, Eleanor M.

2019   African Americans, American Indians, and Heritage. In *History and Approaches to Heritage Studies,* edited by Phyllis Mauch Messenger and Susan J. Bender, pp. 59–86. University Press of Florida, Gainesville.

King, M. B., Fred M. Newmann, and Dana L. Carmichael

2009   Authentic Intellectual Work: Common Standards for Teaching Social Studies. *Social Education* 73(1): 43–49.

Levine, Peter, and Kei Kawashima-Ginsberg

2017   *The Republic is (Still) at Risk—and Civics is Part of the Solution.* Jonathan M. Tisch College of Civic Life, Tufts University, Medford, Massachusetts. Electronic document, http://www.civxsummit.org/documents/v2/SummitWhitePaper.pdf, accessed January 15, 2018.

Levstik, Linda S., and Keith C. Barton

2011   *Doing History: Investigating with Children in Elementary and Middle School.* Routledge, New York.

Levstik, Linda S., A. Gwynn Henderson, and Youngdo Lee

2014   The Beauty of Other Lives: Material Culture as Evidence of Human Ingenuity and Agency. *Social Studies* 105: 184–192.

Little, Barbara J., and Paul A. Schackel (editors)

2007   *Archaeology as Tool of Civic Engagement.* AltaMira Press, Lanham, Maryland.

MacDonald, Robert I.

2019   Public Issues Anthropology as a Framework for Teaching Archaeology at the University of Waterloo. In *History and Approaches to Heritage Studies,* edited by Phyllis Mauch Messenger and Susan J. Bender, pp. 154–167. University Press of Florida, Gainesville.

Marshall, Yvonne

2002   What is Community Archaeology? *World Archaeology* 34(2): 211–219.

McNeil, William H.

1991   Why Study History? Three Historians Respond. In *Historical Literacy: The Case* for *History in American Education*. Paperback ed., edited by Paul G. Gagnon and Bradley Commission on History in the Schools, pp. 103–118. Houghton Mifflin, Boston.

National Assessment Governing Board

2015   News Release: No Change in Eighth-graders' Performance in U.S. History, Geography, Civics since 2010, *National Assessment Governing Board*. Available at https://www.nagb.org/newsroom/naep-releases/2014-history-geo-civics.html, accessed December 20, 2017.

National Center for History in the Schools

1996   *National Standards for History*. National Center for History in the Schools, Los Angeles, California.

National Council for History Education

2016   *Professional Development*. Electronic document, http://www.nche.net/professionaldevelopment, accessed October 27, 2017.

National Council for the Social Studies (NCSS)

2000   *Service-Learning: An Essential Component of Citizenship Education. A position statement of the National Council for the Social Studies*. Electronic document, http://www.socialstudies.org/system/files/publications/se/6504/650408.html, accessed August 3, 2017.

2013   *The College, Career, and Civic Life (C3) Framework for Social Studies State Standards: Guidance for Enhancing the Rigor of K-12 Civics, Economics, Geography, and History*. NCSS, Silver Spring, Maryland.

National Governors Association (NGA) Center for Best Practices & Council of Chief State School Officers (CCSSO)

2010   *Common Core State Standards*. National Governors Association Center for Best Practices, Council of Chief State School Officers, Washington, D.C.

National Park Service

2016a   *Teaching with Historic Places*. Electronic document, https://www.nps.gov/subjects/teachingwithhistoricplaces/index.htm, accessed March 31, 2017.

2016b   *Professional Development*. Electronic document, https://www.nps.gov/subjects/teachingwithhistoricplaces/professional-development.htm, accessed by January 30, 2018.

2016c   *A Social Studies Methods Course in the Power of Place*. Electronic document, https://www.nps.gov/subjects/teachingwithhistoricplaces/prof-dev_methods-course_outline.htm, accessed February 1, 2018.

2016d   *Civic Engagement*. Electronic document, https://www.nps.gov/civic/, accessed August 10, 2016.

Porter, Andrew, Jennifer McMaken, Jun Hwang, and Rui Yang

2011   Common Core Standards: The New U.S. Intended Curriculum. *Educational Researcher* 40(3): 103–116.

Pulse

2016   Our View: On Historic Preservation, Hayward Just Doesn't Get It. *Pulse*, August 23. Electronic document, http://pulsegulfcoast.com/2016/08/view-historic-preservation-hayward-just-doesnt-get, accessed on August 23, 2016.

Salt Lake City Tribune

2011   An Illegal Trail. Electronic document, http://archive.sltrib.com/article.php?id=
        51215299&itype=CMSID, accessed August 11, 2016.

Schippers, Vicky

2013   Let's Overhaul How We Teach History. *Education Week* 32(19): 25.

Shackel, Paul A.

2019   Civic Engagement, Representation, and Social Justice: Moving from CRM to
        Heritage Studies. In *History and Approaches to Heritage Studies*, edited by Phyl-
        lis Mauch Messenger and Susan J. Bender, pp. 9–23. University Press of Florida,
        Gainesville.

Shapiro, Anne-Louise

1997   Whose (Which) History is it Anyway? *History and Theory*, Theme Issue 36: Pro-
        ducing the Past: Making Histories Inside and Outside the Academy 36(4): 1–3.

Shull, Carol D., and Kathleen Hunter

1992   Teaching with Historic Places. *Social Education* 56(5): 312.

Society for American Archaeology (SAA)

2016   *Archaeology for the Public.* Electronic document, http://www.saa.org/publicftp/
        PUBLIC/home/home.html, accessed October 27, 2016.

Sokol-Margolis, Nathan

2016   *Malcolm X: Digging Up Artifacts, Stories, and Questions about the Truth.* Elec-
        tronic document, http://www.meridianacademy.org/news/2016/5/12/malcolm-
        x-digging-up-artifacts-stories-and-questions-about-the-truth, accessed August
        8, 2016.

Sykes, Gary, and Suzanne M. Wilson

2016   Can Policy (Re)Form Instruction? In *Handbook of Research on Teaching*, edited
        by Drew H. Gitomer and Courtney A. Bell, pp. 851–916. American Educational
        Research Association, Washington, D.C.

Westcott, Lucy

2015   What is Lost with Isis's Destruction of Syria's Temple of Bel. http://www.news-
        week.com/what-lost-isiss-destruction-syrias-temple-bel-367721, accessed Au-
        gust 11, 2016.

White, Charles S., and Kathleen Hunter

1995   *Teaching with Historic Places: A Curriculum Framework for Professional Training
        and Development of Teachers, Preservationists, and Museum and Site Interpret-
        ers.* National Trust for Historic Preservation, Washington, D.C.

White, Charles S., and Deborah J. D. White

2000   Preparing Teachers to Teach with Historic Places. *CRM*, National Park Service
        8: 28–30.

Wineburg, Samuel S.

1991   Historical Problem Solving: A Study of the Cognitive Processes Used in the
        Evaluation. *Journal of Educational Psychology* 83(1): 73–87.

2010   Thinking Like a Historian. *Teaching with Primary Sources.* Library of Congress
        3(1). Electronic document, http://www.loc.gov/teachers/tps/quarterly/histori-
        cal_thinking/article.html, accessed August 22, 2016.

Zimmerman, Larry J.

2019   Help Needed! Reflections on a Critical Pedagogy of Heritage. In *History and Approaches to Heritage Studies*, edited by Phyllis Mauch Messenger and Susan J. Bender, pp. 215–236. University Press of Florida, Gainesville.

Zimmerman, Larry J., Steve Dasovich, Mary Engstrom, and Lawrence E. Bradley

1994   Listening to the Teachers: Warnings about the Use of Archaeological Agendas in Classrooms in the United States. In *The Presented Past: Heritage, Museums, and Education*, edited by Peter G. Stone and Brian Molyneaux, pp. 359–371. Routledge, New York.

3

Assessing Student Learning in Heritage Studies

What Does it Mean for Students to "Understand" Archaeological Ethics?

ALICIA EBBITT MCGILL

Balancing Skills-Based Education and Critical Reflection

Skills-based training, assessment, and "authentic" learning experiences (for example, realistic and career-relevant) have become key components of education in many Western collegiate institutions. Recent critiques of higher education address the relationship between skills-based pedagogy and neoliberal economic values and practices. These critiques argue that corporate models in collegiate education focus primarily on products over process with an emphasis on the transfer and acquisition of knowledge, development of marketable skills, and competencies that can be easily defined, measured, and assessed (Aronowitz 2000; Hamilakis 2004; Shackel 2019). This is an educational structure "that ruptures the link between knowledge and the self, denigrating the ability to make ethical judgments and develop a wider vision about the world. It is a definition of knowledge as a commodity to be sold and exchanged, rather than as a life-transforming, experiential process" (Hamilakis 2004: 289). Such an educational focus can severely limit social critique and self- and disciplinary reflection. Heritage educators can confront these issues by examining the politics of heritage pedagogy, implementing educational practices centered on processes in addition to outcomes, and incorporating critical dialogue into educational contexts.

Following Harrison (2013) and Smith (2006), I define heritage as the myriad ways people engage with and utilize the past, and heritage studies as the recognition and analysis of the constructed, dialogical, political, and processual nature of heritage. Heritage practitioners (for example, academics, resource managers, museum professionals, and politicians who engage in heritage practices on a professional level) have an important role to play in conversations about contemporary higher education structures and values, for while we can diversify interpretations of the past and address inequalities through heritage programs, we are also a part of an industry with embedded power dynamics (Chilton 2019). We must be careful not to reinforce hegemonic knowledge structures about the management of the past or uncritically support free market approaches to education as we train future heritage practitioners (see Hamilakis 2004; Little and Shackel 2014; Shackel 2019). Growing concern about the limitations of skills-based higher education begs for deep reflection about how we define "skills" and "critical thinking" in heritage education.

Concerns about how to define and assess "critical thinking" exist throughout higher education. Scholars of teaching and learning across the globe are involved in efforts to balance disciplinary needs and content, critical thinking skills, and liberal philosophies of education with pressures placed on them by university administrators and politicians to produce data that quantifies what students have learned. The North Carolina State University (NC State) TH!NK initiative is one such effort working toward this balance (TH!NK Program 2018). TH!NK faculty have developed ways to assess critical thinking in qualitative and quantitative ways and are working toward embedding critical and creative thinking approaches throughout the NC State curriculum (Vila-Parrish et al. 2016).

This chapter explores how research ethics education and meaningful assessments about heritage learning can foster complex thinking processes and reflection, while also honing valuable and measurable skills in decision making and communication. Through an intentional emphasis on skill development and assessment, this approach helps to integrate with higher education systems focused on skills and utilitarian applications. In an era when the humanities and social sciences are frequently charged with demonstrating their contemporary relevance, ethics education that involves realistic case studies can highlight the applications of studying the past in the present. I demonstrate the applicability of research ethics education and assessments through examples from three sections of a Human Origins and Prehistory class I taught in the 2010–2011 academic year, and highlight the ways that analysis of student activity responses can broaden understandings of student learning.

Heritage Research Ethics Education

Although not unique to heritage studies, research ethics education and the use of case studies and role playing are becoming part of the signature pedagogy[1] (Calder 2006; Gurung et al. 2009) in collegiate-level heritage studies education. The establishment of ethics education as a signature approach has been influenced by changing practices in heritage fields such as intensified heritage politics, a diversification of practitioners, expansion of cultural resource management work, and increases in collaborative and community-based research. Many scholars acknowledge the ways the past is political and the ways heritage scholarship and industries are connected to and even embedded in these politics (Chilton 2019; Hamilakis 2012; Smith 2006; Trouillot 1995). Training in research ethics is now considered a professional responsibility to introduce future heritage practitioners to the range of interests and issues they might encounter in their work (for examples, see Sievert et al. 2019; Watkins 2019). On a philosophical level, through the introduction of diverse stakes in interpretations and uses of the past, heritage ethics education can help integrate multiple ways of knowing and connecting with the past, as advocated by Atalay (2008) and Nicholas (2010).

Changes in approaches to heritage studies have inspired scholarship on heritage pedagogy and ethics education (for example, Bender and Smith 2000; Colwell-Chanthaphonh et al. 2008; Pyburn and Smith 2015; Zimmerman et al. 2003). Linking ethics education and heritage studies enables heritage practitioners to understand heritage as a dynamic process connecting and affecting a variety of people and institutions. In ethics education, students learn about strategies to address ethical dilemmas, including the application of laws, history, professional principles, cultural values, and moral philosophies. On a disciplinary level, through heritage-based ethics education, students can examine strategies within heritage studies used to address ethical considerations and understand the meanings of specific ethical principles within the social sciences and humanities.

The benefits of using case studies and role playing in ethics education are well documented (Colwell-Chanthaphonh et al. 2008; Connolly et al. 2009). These approaches provide authentic learning experiences and enable students to develop broadly applicable skills in critique, evaluation, communication, argumentation, and debate. Moreover, as ethics education and working through case studies are "method[s] of discovery" (Card 2002: 20), they can enhance critical reflection in students. Such skills are applicable to a range of fields.

Through ethical scenarios about heritage research and discussion with classmates, students learn to examine and consider multiple viewpoints, helping them better understand and articulate ideas and practices of people who are different from them. Working through case studies, students cultivate decision-making skills and problem-solving strategies as they critique decisions made by others, evaluate impacts, articulate their own positions and those of others, and propose alternative solutions. Students learn that ethical dilemmas are not "black and white" situations with explicitly right and wrong answers, but through critical reflection, they recognize that there are sometimes better answers. Through these processes, students can also explore and confront their own values, biases, experiences, and misunderstandings. Additionally, through heritage-based case studies, students learn about the power dynamics involved in heritage work.

The rise of popular discourse about "alternative facts" in news media and politics adds to the sensitivity of and need for caution in the ways heritage practitioners teach about diverse perspectives regarding cultural heritage. It is essential for heritage practitioners to emphasize both the positivist potential of scientific approaches to understanding the past and the ways humanistic scholarly approaches can help us recognize how human biases and agendas influence engagements with the past, as well as how and why misunderstandings and misuses of the past have developed and persist. The persistence of discourse about "alternative facts" adds to the importance of the role of heritage practitioners in teaching students and others to use critical thinking and disciplinary knowledge and skills to evaluate diverse scholarly and cultural understandings of heritage. Exposure to multiple ways of connecting with cultural heritage and diverse points of view about heritage research also helps students to understand that all interpretations of the past are not necessarily equally appropriate or valid.

Students with limited familiarity with heritage research are often particularly struck by the contemporary relevance of studying the past. Working through hypothetical and actual heritage scenarios in the classroom broadens students' understanding of the relevance of heritage research, as suggested by a student comment following ethics activities in one of my classes: "Before this class I thought archaeology was just about dead people and digging things up. I was unaware of the broader impacts of archaeology and the ways it related to modern issues." Students in fields like nursing, education, journalism, social work, business, and communication are often encouraged or even required to take introductory anthropology, archaeology, and history courses to increase their cultural competence and develop skills in cross-cultural interaction. As such, introductory level courses often include many students who will not pursue heritage-related careers. Heritage educators can use this trend as an opportunity to emphasize the social, political, and economic significance of understanding diverse perspectives about the past and to link skills-based instruction with critical reflection.

Assessing Learning and Skills Development in Ethics Education

While the benefits of ethics education are clear, evaluating student learning can be complicated, which is why developing meaningful assessments is so important. Assessment tools enable educators to determine whether or not their students are reaching identified learning objectives. Moreover, by exploring data collected through assessments, educators can reflect on the implications and efficacy of certain pedagogical approaches. In addition to traditional assessments (quizzes, tests, and papers), instructors should utilize assessments that incorporate authentic tasks so that students can understand the relevance of what they are learning and apply knowledge and skills in ways that emulate professionals' practices in the field. To assess authentic learning activities, instructors must identify what they want students to know and be able to do after the activity. The concept of assessment can understandably make instructors apprehensive in an age of accountability, efficiency, and standardization in education. However, authentic learning assessments can satisfy student, university, and disciplinary needs by providing data on student skill development and knowledge retention while also providing insight into student knowledge processing and critical thought.

Collecting manageable and meaningful data about student learning can be difficult, especially when teaching about sensitive issues that involve multiple opinions, epistemologies, and values, such as those involved in heritage research ethics. In addition, instructors often offer vague instructions on what it means to think critically and do not provide examples of what kinds of products exemplify deep reflection (Fitzgerald and Baird

2011: 6–24). These limitations increase the difficulties in assessing students' thought processes in various activities. Consequently, it is important to design purposeful activities to foster and apply critical thinking, consider what we mean by critical thinking, assess the effectiveness of these activities and revise accordingly, and share results with fellow educators.

For the rest of this chapter, I discuss my efforts to assess student learning about heritage research ethics and critical thinking in three sections of an introductory Human Origins and Prehistory course, and I describe data collected from student activities.[2]

From August 2010 to May 2011, I was a graduate fellow in the Teagle Collegium on Inquiry and Action at Indiana University (Teagle), a multidisciplinary research project focused on the ways junior scholars learn to teach. Teagle brought together cohorts of upper-level graduate students teaching in biology, communication and culture, and anthropology to learn from each other and senior colleagues in these disciplines and reflect upon their teaching practices. Over the course of one academic year, Teagle fellows implemented projects designed to revise their teaching practices based on scholarship of teaching and learning and evidence of student learning in their specific courses.

During my tenure as a Teagle fellow, I taught three sections of A103: Humans Origins and Prehistory (A103) at Indiana University, Purdue University, Indianapolis (IUPUI) (two sections in Fall 2010 and one section in Spring 2011). In A103, students learn about the mechanisms of evolution, archaeology and paleoanthropology methods, primate characteristics and behaviors, modern human variation, and heritage concerns and research ethics. A103 has no prerequisites, is required for anthropology majors, is open to majors and nonmajors, and satisfies a general education requirement. A total of 102 students were enrolled in my three sections and only 12 were majors.

In my classes, I introduced students to ethical considerations in heritage practices, including: debates about cultural resource management (CRM), the existence of diverse heritage stakeholders, preservation concerns, effects of development on historical sites, and representations of archaeology and past cultures in popular culture. Students also learned about guidelines, principles, and codes used by heritage practitioners to address and respond to ethical issues in their research. Card suggests that ethics is "a critically reflexive morality aimed at identifying, examining, and addressing practical problems" (2002: 20). To provide A103 students opportunities to hone analytical skills, examine various perspectives about heritage issues, and apply what they learned about heritage research ethics to practical problems, they worked through case studies. For my Teagle project, I wanted to evaluate student learning about heritage research ethics and diverse perspectives about the past. In order to do this, I developed classroom assessment techniques (CATs) (Angelo and Cross 1993) with case studies and role playing, and identified specific forms of knowledge and actions that would demonstrate that students "understood" heritage research. I discuss the results from two CATs in detail below.

Learning about Stakeholders and Decision Making
in a Case Study Activity

In one activity, students worked through a case study and completed a "Pro-Con Grid" (Angelo and Cross 1993: 168–171) in which they evaluated the decisions made by an archaeologist in a situation, answered questions about the scenario, and shared responses. The case they were given involved Rebecca, a CRM firm project director in an area with a history of tensions between landowners, government agencies, and archaeologists. While conducting a survey on federal land, Rebecca and her crew take a road through private land to access the project area. Rebecca is instructed not to examine the private lands for cultural resources. While driving through the private property, however, Rebecca discovers a large ancient site and she and her crew decide to record the site on their own time. At the end of the project, Rebecca contacts the landowner to ask him some questions, and he becomes very upset. Rebecca must decide what to do with the information she collected and eventually decides to destroy her notes (see Colwell-Chanthaphonh et al. 2008: 92 for the complete case).

For the CAT, A103 students completed the following tasks: identified potential stakeholders and related Society for American Archaeology (SAA) Principles of Archaeological Ethics (SAA 1996), listed advantages and disadvantages of Rebecca's decisions, and identified potential alternative solutions. To systematically evaluate whether students grasped targeted concepts and skills related to decision making and heritage research ethics and analyze student responses in assessment terms, I identified a series of action-based learning objectives tied to specific knowledge-processing dimensions (following Anderson and Krathwohl 2001). Learning objectives for students included the following: (1) recall, recognize, and identify stakeholders who are affected by and interested in cultural heritage and archaeological research and differentiate the needs and interests of different stakeholders; (2) recall SAA Principles of Archaeological Ethics, recognize their meaning, and apply the principles to different scenarios; (3) recognize that many ethical issues do not have right or wrong answers, but there are often better answers. The first two objectives involved processing factual and conceptual knowledge, and the last involved processing procedural and metacognitive knowledge and critical reflection. I expected students to accomplish the third objective by critiquing Rebecca's decisions and assessing the consequences.

The case study activity had several benefits for heritage research ethics education and introduced students to a variety of stakeholders interested in and affected by archaeology. Applying the SAA Principles of Archaeological Ethics to the case helped students think about ways archaeologists work through ethical dilemmas. And assessing consequences of Rebecca's actions helped students hone analytical and decision-making skills.

When I analyzed the data collected from the activities, I assessed student success in fulfilling the learning objectives based on the number of SAA Principles of Archaeological Ethics, diversity of stakeholders, the types and range of advantages and disadvantages they listed, and the depth of alternative solutions they provided.

The task of listing stakeholders was relatively easy for students to complete; they listed a broad range of stakeholders and even mentioned stakeholders who were not explicitly addressed in the case study: community members, schools, other scientists, and descendant communities (see Table 3.1). Additionally, students exhibited an ability to differentiate interests within groups, recognizing that communities and scholars are not homogenous. Students identified subgroups of people within the community (for example, local political actors, educators, other landowners) and subgroups of scholars (such as museums and the archaeologist's team).

Overall, the A103 students had a good grasp of the names of the SAA Principles of Archaeological Ethics (see Table 3.2), but it was not always clear whether they fully understood the meanings and complexities of each principle. The fact that all the principles were mentioned at least once suggests, however, that students understood the complexity of the case study

Table 3.1. Most common stakeholders identified with number and percentage of students who listed them

	Semester and No. of Students	
	Fall 2010 (26)	Spring 2011 (37)
Rebecca	18 (69%)	16 (43%)
Landowner	17 (65%)	31 (84%)
Government	20 (77%)	26 (71%)
CRM Firm	14 (54%)	21 (57%)
Other Landowners or Farmers	13 (50%)	10 (27%)
Descendants/Indigenous People	7 (27%)	20 (54%)
Local Community	12 (46%)	13 (35%)
Other Archaeologists	10 (38%)	15 (41%)

Source: Table created by Alicia Ebbitt McGill based on activities conducted in A103: Human Origins and Prehistory at Indiana University–Purdue University–Indianapolis, during the Fall 2010 and Spring 2011 semesters.

and did not see it as solely a preservation issue. "Records and Preservation" and "Stewardship" were two of the most commonly listed principles indicating that students realized the strong stewardship and preservation ethics in archaeology and that these principles influence how archaeologists make decisions. As this case involved an archaeologist choosing to destroy records, the fact that so many students identified preservation and stewardship as relevant principles also suggests they understood that these ethical approaches should extend beyond the protection of archaeological sites and objects to information and notes gathered through research as well.

Angelo and Cross (1993: 168–171) suggest that relatively balanced lists

Table 3.2. SAA Principles of Archaeological Ethics identified by students with number and percentage of students who listed them

	Semester and No. of Students	
	Fall 2010 (26)	Spring 2011 (37)
Stewardship	18 (69%)	24 (65%)
Accountability	21 (81%)	31 (84%)
Commercialization	8 (31%)	10 (27%)
Public Education	8 (31%)	17 (46%)
Intellectual Property	9 (35%)	23 (62%)
Public Reporting	14 (54%)	21 (57%)
Records and Preservation	23 (88%)	36 (97%)
Training	10 (38%)	5 (14%)

Source: Table created by Alicia Ebbitt McGill based on activities conducted in A103: Human Origins and Prehistory at Indiana University–Purdue University–Indianapolis, during the Fall 2010 and Spring 2011 semesters.

of advantages and disadvantages in student responses in a "Pro-Con Grid" demonstrate their grasp of the range of implications and complexities of a situation and decisions that are made. In both semesters, A103 students provided many disadvantages and advantages, representing breadth and depth in their knowledge processing. They recognized that many people were affected by the scenario they read about and that there were complex heritage dynamics at play.

In the fall, students listed twenty-seven different disadvantages; in the spring, students listed forty-four. Some of the most common disadvantages identified included: loss of knowledge, the site not being preserved, Rebecca's decisions potentially limiting future work, Rebecca wasting time and resources, and a missed opportunity for Rebecca to work with and teach the landowner. The fall students listed twenty-five different advantages to Rebecca's decisions, and the spring students listed thirty. Commonly listed advantages were: the landowner's individual rights were protected, conflicts were avoided, the site and artifacts were protected, and Rebecca did not waste time and money. There were almost as many different disadvantages listed as advantages, which was interesting because most students agreed that Rebecca made poor decisions to trespass and to destroy her notes, and they proposed many options for addressing the situation differently. The somewhat balanced list of impacts demonstrated that students understood that heritage issues are usually neither "black and white" nor easy to solve. The fact that they identified advantages and disadvantages that affected a variety of stakeholders shows critical reflection and efforts to weigh multiple pros and cons, an important decision-making skill.

After analyzing results of this activity, I had some concerns about its format and the student responses. Because I did not ask students to define the principles they listed or explain how they related to the case, I do not know whether or not they understood the meanings of each principle. Moreover, I did not ask students to interpret, assess the utility of, or address the limitations of the ethical principles. It is problematic to consider ethical principles as established sets of rules to be passively accepted, memorized, and uncritically applied to solve ethical issues in heritage work (Smith and Burke 2003: 191). Card suggests that case studies enable students to "raise important philosophical questions about how to interpret and test ethical principles themselves" (2002: 27). Reflection on the ways ethical principles might privilege certain perspectives and forms of knowledge about heritage has been recommended by many scholars (Lynott 1997; Smith and Burke 2003). To involve students in critical thought about the utility of ethical principles and codes and disciplinary biases embedded in professional ethical principles, and to assess this learning in ethics activities, educators can facilitate discussion about the values and implications connected to professional principles of ethics before working through case studies, then ask students to explain why they think certain principles apply to a scenario. It would also be worthwhile to explicitly identify what we mean by critical thinking in activities and provide students examples of responses that demonstrate deep thought and critical reflection. In the context of ethics education, from my perspective, critical thinking is characterized by evaluating and critiquing diverse perspectives.

In the case study activity in A103, I was also concerned with how students' cultural backgrounds and American value systems about land ownership and cultural resources influenced their perspectives. In their responses, many students referenced economic concerns and the sanctity of private property. Several students were particularly concerned about potential wastes of money, and some suggested the situation could have been assuaged if Rebecca had compensated the landowner for working on his land. These responses demonstrate capitalist values about land, archaeological resources, and knowledge, and they provide insight into how such preconceptions might affect various publics' interactions with heritage research. This information can be used to help us think about ways to challenge such preconceptions, problematize the commodification of the past, and engage in dialogue about how the "values" of heritage are defined.

Learning about "The Ancient One" in a Role-Playing Activity

Another way A103 students participated in critical reflection about heritage research ethics and the politics of the past was through a role-playing activity about the discovery and treatment of The Ancient One (also known as Kennewick Man) (see Burke et al. 2009), which incorporated multiple interests, ideas, and concerns about the finding and treatment of this ancient individual. The role-playing activity was influenced by two different CATs ("Invented Dialogues" and "Everyday Ethical Dilemmas" [Angelo and Cross 1993: 203–207, 271–274]).

In preparation for the activity, students read articles about The Ancient One and also about research on human remains written from a variety of perspectives. In the activity, students were provided with a description of a hypothetical town hall meeting in Kennewick, Washington, shortly after The Ancient One was found, and each student was assigned the role of a concerned stakeholder who attended the hypothetical meeting. Examples of stakeholders in the activity were: anthropologists who authored the students' readings (that is, Clement Meighan [1996] and Larry Zimmerman [1996]), a member of the Umatilla Indian Tribe, forensic anthropologist Jim Chatters, Director of the Burke Museum (the Washington State Museum of Natural History and Culture), a Kennewick community member, and an

Army Corps of Engineers representative. Students had to prepare a brief statement for the meeting with proposed solutions regarding the treatment of The Ancient One from the perspectives of their stakeholder. Students also wrote a paragraph about their own opinions and how these changed (if at all) after their readings and the activity. I again identified a series of action-based learning objectives tied to specific knowledge-processing dimensions (following Anderson and Krathwohl 2001) in order to analyze student responses in assessment terms, and systematically evaluate whether they grasped the targeted concepts and were able to think critically about the treatment of The Ancient One. Learning objectives for the students included the following: (1) recall the readings and remember details of The Ancient One situation and potential stakeholders affected by it; (2) differentiate the possible opinions and positions of different stakeholders involved in or affected by this situation; (3) produce a position statement from their stakeholder and generate a conversation with their fellow classmates; (4) interpret the situation based on their own knowledge and perspectives, critique the decisions made, and articulate their own ideas and opinions. The first objective involved processing factual knowledge, the second involved processing conceptual knowledge, and the last two objectives involved processing procedural knowledge and metacognition.

The role-playing activity had several benefits for heritage research ethics education. Students again considered a variety of stakeholder connections with cultural heritage as well as their interests in and concerns about heritage research. Through the production of position statements about the treatment of The Ancient One, students practiced communication and argumentation skills. And having students discuss their own opinions about The Ancient One also created a link between personal-experiential and academic knowledge, which Hamilakis suggests is key to critical reflection (2004: 298).

I assessed student success in fulfilling the learning objectives based on their ability to incorporate information from the readings into their responses, the relevance and appropriateness of the arguments and position statements they constructed, and the breadth and depth in the alternative solutions they identified.

Students quite successfully remembered people from their readings, recalled details, and differentiated concerns about the treatment of The Ancient One. However, they had difficulties producing position statements for individuals not explicitly mentioned in their readings. In the fall semester, students identified a rather narrow range of alternative solutions for the treatment of The Ancient One. I thought perhaps if students knew more about the history of the treatment of Native Americans in anthropological science, they might better understand the complex social and political dynamics that influenced debates about The Ancient One. In the spring semester, I added a chapter from *Skull Wars: Kennewick Man, Archeology, and the Battle for Native American Identity* (Hurst Thomas 2000) to the reading list and students subsequently did indeed list a greater range of alternative solutions. In addition to those listed in Table 3.3, students also suggested other alternatives for the treatment of The Ancient One, such as: allowing

Table 3.3. Alternative solutions for the treatment of The Ancient One

	No. of Students Who Did the Activity		
	Fall 2010a (30)	Fall 2010b (24)	Spring 2011 (38)
Repatriate The Ancient One	5 (17%)	1 (4%)	2 (5%)
Study The Ancient One	13 (43%)	12 (50%)	14 (37%)
Compromise of Some Sort	9 (30%)	3 (12.5%)	3 (12.5%)
Original Decision Good	0	1 (4%)	6 (16%)
Study Then Repatriate or Rebury	0	Some	4 (10.5%)
Consultation with Native Americans	0	0	3 (8%)
Out of the Public Eye	0	0	1 (3%)
No Response	2 (7%)	1 (4%)	0

Source: Table created by Alicia Ebbitt McGill based on activities conducted in A103: Human Origins and Prehistory at Indiana University–Purdue University–Indianapolis, during the Fall 2010 and Spring 2011 semesters.

Native Americans to make the final decision, getting permission from Native American groups to study him, dividing him up among many groups, and developing a policy limiting how far back people could claim ancestry.

Several students were quite critical of the results following the 2004 court decision in which The Ancient One was studied and then kept at the Burke Museum.[3] Their critiques and specific ideas for alternative solutions demonstrated critical thought about the implications of heritage research.

However, the activity results also led me to think more about the learning effectiveness of role playing. While students tried to relate to the experiences of other people in their conversations, ultimately their knowledge of others' perspectives was limited by what they read. Without deeper knowledge and broader experiences, role playing can lead to generalizations about peoples' opinions and essentialization of groups. I also wonder to what extent role playing can help people develop empathy. Although students were asked to argue positions they thought other people would feel strongly about, I am not sure it is possible to do this fully if they are unable to identify with epistemologies and value systems different from their own.

Limited extant student knowledge, the ways The Ancient One has been represented as a controversy between two "sides" in some popular and academic discourse, student perceptions about science, and disciplinary value systems also influenced student interpretations of and responses to the treatment of The Ancient One. I had hoped that introducing students to diverse perspectives from scholars, Indigenous peoples, and other members of the public in their readings would help them acknowledge heterogeneity among academics and Indigenous peoples and avoid dichotomies like "science vs. religion" or "tradition vs. modernity." But students tended to homogenize the opinions of groups (for example, Native Americans opposed to science and scientists in opposition to religious beliefs) and reinforced dualisms in their position statements. The most prevalent dichotomy in student responses was one between science and religion. Additionally, over 35 percent of the A103 students felt that The Ancient One should absolutely be studied and suggested that the knowledge that could be gained outweighed the claims and interests of Native American groups. These responses were possibly influenced by the fact that the activity was conducted in a course focused on bioanthropology and archaeology as well as by student preconceptions about scientific authority and the values of scientific knowledge. Engaging students in conversations about diverse definitions and implications of science and biases, and limitations in scientific practices, may help to address these limitations, demystify science, and unpack value systems.

I was surprised and disappointed that students did not engage with the town hall discussion as actively as I thought they would. Several A103 students were usually very animated and opinionated and I expected their role-playing discussions to be more intense than they were. Moreover, the position statements students wrote were quite fact-driven, and the town hall discussion felt contrived and more focused on regurgitating details than on dialogue and debate. I had hoped this activity would be poignant and heated for students, but I think because it was being graded, students were concerned about demonstrating their knowledge of specific details. Based on this finding, I recognize that I need to be more aware in future activities of how power dynamics and assessment structures influence student learning and engagement.

Despite my concerns about shortcomings of The Ancient One activity and my perceptions of limited student reflection evidenced by their responses in the town hall discussion, when I read the questions students posed about The Ancient One readings in their notes, I realized I underestimated them and the assignment. Student questions highlighted complex, critical, reflective, and perhaps even transformative learning processes and demonstrated student efforts to evaluate and understand multiple perspectives. Examples of particularly provocative questions include: Where does this entitlement of "academic freedom" come from? In what ways will collaborating efforts contribute to a greater understanding of human history? Do archaeologists take real efforts of reconciliation with Indigenous people to overcome the heavy past of mistrust? To build trust between archaeologists and Native Americans, are the laws and courts enough? At what point can scientists say ancestry is not relevant in a particular study? Why is it so difficult for some scientists to come to some kind of compromise with the repatriation movement? How does the government decide which groups' beliefs will be respected? Are bones tucked away in museum drawers and cabinets really of scientific value? Evidence of sophisticated knowledge, critical thinking, and reflection may not always be explicit in student responses in assignments and on tests, but may be demonstrated by the questions they ask. This emphasizes the fact that we need to look in multiple places to assess learning processes.

Since conducting the research discussed in this chapter, I entered a faculty position in the Department of History at NC State, where I teach undergraduate history courses and graduate-level public history courses in cultural heritage and CRM. I continue to include lessons about heritage research ethics in my classes and I have revised my teaching practices to address some of the concerns raised in this chapter.

I still use heritage-based case studies and role-playing activities in undergraduate and graduate classes. I also developed "Frauds and Mysteries of the Past" (inspired by Anne Pyburn's Indiana University "Lost Tribes and Sunken Continents" course) in order to teach NC State undergraduate students critical thinking concepts and anthropological and historical analytical skills through the lens of myths, misconceptions, and manipulations of the past. In a role-playing activity about subsistence digging in this course, I recently added a reflective component with questions about student perspectives on the topic and their decision-making processes in the activity. I posed questions like: What do you see as the main problem in this situation? What did you find to be the most and least compelling positions in the scenario and why? How did your lens of experience influence your perspectives about this topic? Did you feel differently about the topic after the activity? What did you think about the decision your group came to at the end of the activity? Incorporating reflection into an assignment like this enables instructors to diversify the ways they assess student thinking and learning, and engages students in metacognitive practices about content and learning activities.

Discussions about pedagogy and assessment techniques help heritage educators explore the ways students learn, address politics and ideologies embedded in heritage education, and, through such practices, improve teaching methods. Although Western higher education systems centered on accountability, knowledge transfer, and skill development may limit transformative learning opportunities, ethics education and dialogue based on case studies can foster skill development applicable to careers in a global political economy, while also facilitating critical reflection and the development of a "wider vision about the world" (Hamilakis 2004: 289). Although the assessment of learning processes and critical thinking is difficult, classroom assessment techniques can be valuable tools for collecting analyzable data. Evaluation of activity results may inspire us to think more deeply about how we define and identify evidence of critical thinking.

Research ethics training for heritage practitioners should not be limited to cultural anthropology and archaeology students. Integrating sister disciplines such as museology, public history, and tourism studies into conversations about heritage research ethics education could be valuable to scholars and students by revealing shared concerns, innovative approaches to heritage issues, and disciplinary differences and tensions. A model of research ethics education that incorporates case studies and role-playing activities is especially useful in public history.

Heritage practitioners are finding themselves interacting with increasingly diverse groups of people. And fields like public history strive to incorporate more diverse narratives about the past into interpretations of the past (see Filene 2012; Kaufman 2004; Russell-Ciardi 2008). My public history graduate students frequently express interest in learning about minority groups' connections to heritage, collaborative heritage research practices, alternative epistemologies about the past, and community engagement initiatives. Within public history, as in heritage studies, there are debates about how to balance stakeholder interests in the past with historical expertise. The concept of "shared authority" is encouraged as a model for how to reach this balance (see Adair et al. 2011, for example). Case studies and role-playing exercises can be used in public history courses to teach the applications, benefits, and limitations of shared authority, by complicating the concept of heritage and incorporating varied perspectives and epistemologies about the past. As I venture into new disciplines in my scholarship and teaching, I have learned more about disciplinary differences and tensions tied to the concept of "heritage." Historian and geographer David Lowenthal famously highlighted the ways the past has been manipulated as "heritage" to malign and dispossess groups of land, rights, historical recognition, and cultural dignity (Lowenthal 1996). Such heritage "misuses," combined with the ways heritage is invoked in myths about U.S. history (for example, the Lost Cause myth of the Civil War), make the wariness of even a scholarly utilization of the term heritage understandable. The introduction of heritage concepts and stakes through case studies is helpful in unpacking the diverse ways individuals, groups, and disciplines think about the concept of heritage.

My graduate students are also interested in and concerned about the utility and implications of professional research ethics in their work. As many public history graduates pursue careers outside academia in contexts like museums, site interpretation, historic preservation, and community activism, training in research ethics from a broad range of fields is particularly important in public history training. And it is important to explore the ways perspectives on research practices involving living people and interactions with institutional review boards are different within history and anthropology, especially with regards to oral history (see Shopes 2007 for a discussion of this). In my public history graduate classes, students read disciplinary ethical codes and principles from a range of social sciences and humanities disciplines, and we discuss ideological differences and potential tensions between fields. Dialogue about differences related to disciplinary ethics across the humanities and social sciences fields is invaluable for students and academics in heritage fields, as they will likely increasingly be involved in interdisciplinary work. Interdisciplinary consideration about the concept of heritage and heritage research ethics can broaden conversations and critical reflection among heritage practitioners about how we study the past, how heritage knowledge is used, the power dynamics in heritage research, and academic freedom.

Notes

1. Signature pedagogies are educational practices used to teach fundamental knowledge, values, skills, and behaviors within a specific discipline (Calder 2006).

2. Data discussed in this chapter were collected for Indiana University (IU) Bloomington study #08-13645, which was reviewed and approved by the IU Institutional Review Board.

3. In February 2017, the remains of The Ancient One were returned to the tribes who claimed ancestral connections to him.

References Cited

Adair, Bill, Benjamin Filene, and Laura Koloski (editors)
2011   *Letting Go?: Sharing Historical Authority in a User-Generated World.* Pew Center for Arts and Heritage, Philadelphia, Pennsylvania.
Anderson, Lorin W., and David R. Krathwohl (editors)
2001   *A Taxonomy for Learning, Teaching, and Assessing: A Revision of Bloom's Taxonomy of Educational Objectives.* Abridged ed. Longman, New York.
Angelo, Thomas, and K. Patricia Cross
1993   *Classroom Assessment Techniques: A Handbook for College Teachers.* 2nd ed. Jossey-Bass, San Francisco, California.

Aronowitz, Stanley

2000   *The Knowledge Factory: Dismantling the Corporate University and Creating Higher Learning.* Beacon Press, Boston.

Atalay, Sonya

2008   Multivocality and Indigenous Archaeologies. In *Evaluating Multiple Narratives: Beyond Nationalist, Colonialist, Imperialist Archaeologies,* edited by Junko Habu, Clare Fawcett, and John M. Matsunaga, pp. 29–44. Springer, New York.

Bender, Susan, and George Smith (editors)

2000   *Teaching Archaeology in the Twenty-First Century.* Society for American Archaeology Press, Washington, D.C.

Burke, Heather, Claire Smith, Dorothy Lippert, Joe Watkins, and Larry Zimmerman (editors)

2009   *Kennewick Man: Perspectives on the Ancient One.* Taylor & Francis Group, Abingdon, UK.

Calder, Lendol

2006   Uncoverage: Toward a Signature Pedagogy for the History Survey. *Journal of American History* 92(4): 1358–1370.

Card, Robert F.

2002   Using Case Studies to Develop Critical Thinking Skills in Ethics Courses. *Teaching Ethics,* Fall, 19–27.

Chilton, Elizabeth S.

2019   The Heritage of Heritage: Defining the Role of the Past in Contemporary Societies. In *History and Approaches to Heritage Studies,* edited by Phyllis Mauch Messenger and Susan J. Bender, pp. 24–31. University Press of Florida: Gainesville.

Colwell-Chanthaphonh, Chip, Julie Hollowell, and Dru McGill

2008   *Ethics in Action: Case Studies in Archaeological Dilemmas.* Society for American Archaeology Press, Washington D.C.

Connolly, Peggy, David R. Keller, Martin G. Leever, and Becky Cox White

2009   *Ethics in Action: A Case-Based Approach.* Wiley-Blackwell, Malden, Massachusetts.

Filene, Benjamin

2012   Passionate Histories: "Outsider" History-Makers and What They Teach Us. *Public Historian* 34(1): 11–22.

Fitzgerald, Jennifer, and Vanessa A. Baird

2011   Taking a Step Back: Teaching Critical Thinking by Distinguishing Appropriate Type of Evidence. *PS: Political Science and Politics* 44(3): 619–624.

Gurung, Regan A. R., Nancy L. Chick, and Aeron Haynie (editors)

2009   *Exploring Signature Pedagogies: Approaches to Teaching Disciplinary Habits of the Mind.* Stylus, Sterling, Virginia.

Hamilakis, Yannis

2004   Archaeology and the Politics of Pedagogy. *World Archaeology* 36(2): 287–309.

2012   Are We Postcolonial Yet? Tales from the Battlefield. *Archaeologies* 8(1): 67–76.

Harrison, Rodney

2013   *Heritage: Critical Approaches.* Routledge, London.

Hurst Thomas, David

2000   *Skull Wars: Kennewick Man, Archaeology, and the Battle for Native American Identity.* Basic Books, New York.

Kaufman, Ned

2004   Historic Places and the Diversity Deficit in Heritage Conservation. *CRM: The Journal of Heritage Stewardship* 1(2): 68–85.

Little, Barbara J., and Paul A. Shackel

2014   *Archaeology, Heritage, and Civic Engagement.* Left Coast Press, Walnut Creek, California.

Lowenthal, David

1996   *The Heritage Crusade and the Spoils of History.* Cambridge University Press, New York.

Lynott, Mark J.

1997   Ethical Principles and Archaeological Practice: Development of an Ethics Policy. *American Antiquity* 62(4): 589–599.

Meighan, Clement W.

1996   Burying American Archaeology. In *Archaeological Ethics*, edited by Karen D. Vitelli, pp. 209–213. AltaMira Press, Walnut Creek, California.

Nicholas, George P.

2010   Seeking the End of Indigenous Archaeology. In *Bridging the Divide: Indigenous Communities and Archaeology into the 21st Century*, edited by Caroline Phillips and Harry Allen, pp. 233–252. Left Coast Press, Walnut Creek, California.

Pyburn, K. Anne, and George S. Smith

2015   The MATRIX Project (Making Archaeology Teaching Relevant in the XXIst Century): An Approach to the Efficient Sharing of Professional Knowledge and Skills with a Large Audience. In *Sharing Archaeology: Academe, Practice, and the Public*, edited by Peter Stone and Zhao Hui, pp. 132–140. Routledge, London.

Russell-Ciardi, Maggie

2008   The Museum as a Democracy-Building Institution: Reflections on the Shared Journeys Program at the Lower East Side Tenement Museum. *Public Historian* 30(1): 39–52.

Shackel, Paul A.

2019   Civic Engagement, Representation, and Social Justice: Moving from CRM to Heritage Studies. In *History and Approaches to Heritage Studies*, edited by Phyllis Mauch Messenger and Susan J. Bender, pp. 9–23. University Press of Florida, Gainesville.

Shopes, Linda

2007   *Oral History, Human Subjects, and Institutional Review Boards.* Electronic document, http://www.oralhistory.org/about/do-oral-history/oral-history-and-irb-review/, accessed February 13, 2018

Sievert, April, Teresa Nichols, K. Anne Pyburn, and Jayne-Leigh Thomas

2019   Learning NAGPRA and Teaching Archaeology. In *History and Approaches to Heritage Studies*, edited by Phyllis Mauch Messenger and Susan J. Bender, pp. 87–106. University Press of Florida, Gainesville.

Smith, Claire, and Heather Burke

2003   In the Spirit of the Code. In *Ethical Issues in Archaeology,* edited by Larry J. Zimmerman, Karen D. Vitelli, and Julie Hollowell-Zimmer, pp. 177–200. AltaMira Press, Walnut Creek, California.

Smith, Laurajane

2006   *Uses of Heritage.* Routledge, London.

Society for American Archaeology (SAA)

1996   *Principles of Archaeological Ethics.* Electronic document, http://www.saa.org/AbouttheSociety/PrinciplesofArchaeologicalEthics/tabid/203/Default.aspx, accessed February 13, 2018.

TH!NK Program

2018   About TH!NK. Electronic document, https://think.dasa.ncsu.edu/about/, accessed February 13, 2018.

Trouillot, Michel-Rolph

1995   *Silencing the Past: Power and the Production of History.* Beacon Press, Boston.

Vila-Parrish, Anita, T. Baldwin, Lina Battestilli, Sara Glee Queen, Jessica Young Schmidt, and Sue Carson

2016   *TH!NK: A Framework to Assess and Support Critical and Creative Thinking,* American Society for Engineering Education Proceedings 123rd Annual Conference. Electronic document, *https://peer.asee.org/th-nk-a-framework-to-assess-and-support-critical-and-creative-thinking,* accessed February 13, 2018

Watkins, Joe

2019   Teaching Indigenous Archaeology to Multiple Constituencies. In *History and Approaches to Heritage Studies,* edited by Phyllis Mauch Messenger and Susan J. Bender, pp. 107–126. University Press of Florida, Gainesville.

Zimmerman, Larry J.

1996   Sharing Control of the Past. In *Archaeological Ethics,* edited by Karen D. Vitelli. pp. 214–218. AltaMira Press, Walnut Creek, California.

Zimmerman, Larry J., Karen D. Vitelli, and Julie Hollowell-Zimmer (editors)

2003   *Ethical Issues in Archaeology.* AltaMira Press, Walnut Creek, California.

4

The Challenges of Curriculum Change
and the Pedagogy of Public Archaeology and CRM
at the University of South Florida

THOMAS J. PLUCKHAHN

Curricula are notoriously slow to change. One study published in the 1960s suggested that it could take as many as 50 years for educational innovations to become widely established in schools (Miles 1964). This estimate may be overly pessimistic for the pace of curriculum change in contemporary colleges and universities, but the persistence and severity of conservatism is evidenced by a vast literature on the impediments to, and strategies for, curriculum reform (for example, Roy et al. 2007). Barriers to curriculum change operate at multiple levels, from university to college or school to departmental governance (Roy et al. 2007). Faculty, too, are frequently an impediment to reform, not because they lack the desire or capacity to improve, "but because, collectively, teachers value their autonomy, worry about their ever-increasing workload and time constraints, and are, by nature, averse to risk and change" (Jorgenson 2006).[1]

Curriculum change may be particularly challenging where there is discontinuity between disciplinary theory and practice. As Kandiko and Blackmore note, "There are continuing debates about the relative merits of theory-based academic or disciplinary knowledge in contrast to practical or mission-oriented knowledge . . . the organisation of content varies dramatically in these two orientations, and this difference is a key inhibitor of university-wide curriculum change, as the inherent tension is played out by staff who may take strong positions on what they value" (2012: 7).

Anthropology curricula exemplify these challenges (Mills 2006). With regard to the last impediment, it is by now axiomatic that the vast majority of anthropologists in the United States earning a graduate degree will either not seek, or not find, employment in academia (for a recent summary of the competition for academic jobs in archaeology, see Speakman et al. 2017). The number of doctorates granted annually in anthropology has remained steadily in the range of 350 to 450 for the past few decades, while the number of academic positions advertised on the American Anthropological Association (AAA) website and newsletter is generally only about half this total (Neumann and Sanford 2010: 23). The AAA (2017) notes that over half of all the new PhDs in anthropology since 1985 have taken nonacademic positions.

The problem is particularly acute—or at least more often acknowledged—in archaeology, perhaps because the nonacademic employment sector for this subfield is comparatively large, thanks to the industry of cultural resource management (CRM) that has developed around compliance with the National Historic Preservation Act and National Environmental Policy Act (Green and Doershuk 1998; Patterson 1998). Summarizing the results of a survey of archaeologists undertaken by the Society for American Archaeology (SAA), Zeder (1994) noted "a strong tendency for government and private sector archaeologists to feel that the training they received prepared them poorly for their current careers and that these careers are not consistent with their original expectations." Indeed, as a standard textbook for CRM notes (Neumann and Sanford 2010: 23), it is entirely possible—if not common—for an archaeologist to graduate with a PhD in anthropology from any one of the highest-tier anthropology programs with only a rudimentary understanding of the legal framework undergirding CRM, where the vast majority of archaeological research is conducted and where they are most likely to find employment (see also Bender and Smith 2000; Fiske et al. 2010; Green and Doershuk 1998; McAndrews 2007; Vawser 2004; White et al. 2004; Whitley 2004; Yu et al. 2006).

For several decades, representatives of CRM firms have complained publicly that the newly minted graduate students they hire are poorly trained for the type of work they do (for example, Schuldenrein 1995, 1998). As one such commentator bluntly opined, "It is patently absurd that the vast majority of departments continue to train archaeologists for traditional academic careers at a time when opportunities for secure tenure track lines are at the lowest ebb since the 1960s and costs for such training are absolutely prohibitive" (Schuldenrein 1995). The poor prospects for academic employment are well known to the many of us who have either applied for an academic position or served on a search committee for such a position, or both. And yet, many anthropology programs implicitly deny this reality and encourage their students to believe that they are exceptional in regard to academic employment by not adapting their curricula to meet the realities of employment their students will face upon graduation.

But while the problem is plain, the solution is less so. Blanton (1995) calls for CRM tracks with curricula that include traditional core classes, as well as courses covering essential topics such as "legislation and official guidelines, ethics, CRM field strategies, resource evaluation (that is, application of National Register criteria), proposal writing, personnel management, and business practices." Similar appeals have been offered by Green and Doershuk (1998: 139–140) and Schuldendrein (1995), among others. Still, as Green and Doershuk (1998: 139) observe, the development of programs focused narrowly on CRM "would not help in the long run because the discipline does not need practitioners with an overly specialized CRM-only orientation and with limited cognizance of the larger issues of anthropological and archaeological method and theory" (see also Ebbitt 2006; Mills 2006; Neusius 2009; Sebastian 2006; Shackel and Mortensen 2006; G. Smith 2006; Weisman 2006). Hayes and colleagues (2019) address the need for broad training and critical thinking in this volume's companion.

Perhaps as important as the need for anthropological and archaeological theory is the fact that CRM has expanded to include much more than just the mechanics of compliance (see King 2013). As mandated by NAGPRA, amendments to the NHPA, and NPS technical bulletins (for example, Parker and King 1990), the practice of CRM now requires greater coordination with descendant communities and other stakeholders, and thus a wider range of skills and concepts—a point clearly articulated by Shackel (2019).

Public archaeology has likewise expanded. Where four decades ago CRM and "public archaeology" were largely synonymous, with the former perhaps expanded to include working with avocational archaeologists to promote site preservation (for example, Davis 1972; McGimsey 1972; see also Jameson 2004, and Wurst and Novinger 2011), public archaeology now considers a more diverse public, employs more democratic models of engagement, and reaches out through a wider variety of media and methods. Industry trends may be tracking this change.

Indeed, Moore (2006: 33) has argued that CRM has already begun a decline and "will likely shrink to a minimum level," to be replaced by public archaeology. He notes that federal compliance policy is unlikely to expand, and that the compliance industry created around the existing legislation is overly competitive. According to Moore, this industry cycle is reinforced by a value shift: "a new ethic is emerging that involves Public Archaeology and multivocal interpretive discourse" (2006: 32).

How can academic programs, still struggling to catch up to changes in the workforce that began forty years ago, keep pace with these more recent developments in CRM and public archaeology? In this essay, I provide a personal narrative of the evolution of the public archaeology curriculum at the University of South Florida (USF). In contrast with the vast majority of graduate programs, the Department of Anthropology at USF has a longstanding commitment to training graduate students in applied anthropology, including CRM. However, as with almost any university curriculum, the program struggles to adapt to changes in archaeological practice, as a result of both institutional structural limitations and the dispositions of faculty.

Public Archaeology at USF

In 1974, USF established the first graduate degree program[2] in applied anthropology, offering M.A. degrees in Applied Anthropology and Public Archaeology. Kushner and Angrosino, writing of the newly formed program, observed:

> The members of the Department felt that yet another traditional M.A. program was emphatically not what the discipline needed, nor what we wanted to be involved in. . . . We found no reason why we should help turn out more anthropologists who would, regardless of the quality of their training, be unable to secure employment related to their professional qualifications. (1974: 34)

The original M.A. program included three tracks: Medical Anthropology, Urban Anthropology, and "Field Archaeology" (sometimes labeled Public or Salvage Archaeology) (Kushner and Angrosino 1974: 35). The authors summarized the focus of the Public Archaeology track:

Instead of the emphasis on long term process characteristic of archaeology in general, this subfield is devoted to locating, preserving, and disseminating information about previous habitation in a given location under conditions of impending physical change or destruction of the archaeological resources. Recent and probably forthcoming environmental impact legislation at local, state, regional, and federal levels requires that this kind of archaeology be done prior to clearing and construction activities. (1974: 35)

With the benefit of hindsight, the decision to found a public archaeology program of this sort seems both remarkably prescient (given that it began the same year as Moss-Bennett and only eight years after the NHPA was enacted) and naive (considering the expanding scope of CRM and public archaeology in the years since).

More specific descriptions of the program from its early years are scant, but consistent with the use of the term "public archaeology" by archaeologists like McGimsey (1972) and Davis (1972), the emphasis was on "cultural resources management and contract archaeology . . . but also including public education, historic preservation, and museology" (White et al. 2004: 26; see also White 2000a, 2000b; White and Williams 1994). Since its founding, the curriculum has included a required course in Public Archaeology/Cultural Resource Management, as well as the more typical general courses in archaeological method and theory and more specialized electives.

In addition to their normal coursework, students in the graduate program at USF have been required to complete an internship to gain practical experience in the field or with an agency. Over the years, many students have worked for governmental or nongovernmental organizations, sometimes producing a needs assessment or a program evaluation for their hosts that would become the basis for their master's thesis or doctoral dissertation. Alternatively, students would write their theses or dissertations conforming to traditional academic standards and produce a separate "Agency Report" (Angrosino 1976; Kushner 1978, 1994; Kushner and Angrosino 1974; Kushner and Wolfe 1993; Wolfe 1982, 1991). Historically, archaeology students often worked on small CRM projects under contract with local and state agencies (Weisman 2002; Weisman and White 2000).[3] The internship requirement continues today, but because of the difficulties in managing CRM projects on academic schedules, as well as other constraints, students more often complete the requirement by assisting with field schools or working under direct supervision of the faculty on field or laboratory research. A recent initiative seeks to reinvigorate the internship by allowing students to complete an internship and either write a technical report or create a public archaeology installation in lieu of a traditional thesis.

Adapting to the Changing Face of Public Archaeology

I came to USF as an assistant professor in 2006. I was hired partially for my experience in CRM, which included many years as a field technician and more than a decade working as a project archaeologist for various private firms in the southeastern United States; this resulted in the authorship or co-authorship of more than 100 technical reports.

I was asked to teach the required course in Public Archaeology in spring semester 2007. The class, which had not been taught in several years, retained a strong emphasis on the understanding of the term *public archaeology* as it had been defined three decades before. As described on a syllabus from a previous iteration, the course was titled "Cultural Resource Management (Public Archaeology)." True to the title, content leaned heavily to CRM, with major sections devoted to: (1) the legal framework of CRM; (2) method, theory, and ethics of CRM (with method and theory focusing primarily on significance and business); (3) resource preservation and protection; and (4) connecting to the public (with readings mainly focused on archaeology in the classroom).

In developing the syllabus for my own version of the class, I faced a dilemma. Clearly, the expectation of my faculty colleagues was that this course would provide our graduate students with the background knowledge and skills they would need for a career in CRM. But this was inconsistent with the contemporary understanding of the term public archaeology, as well as the growing possibility of employment in areas other than CRM. Indeed, our own department was at the time in the process of staffing a center of the newly formed Florida Public Archaeology Network (FPAN), a state-funded agency whose mission, in focusing on public outreach and assistance to state and local governments, explicitly excludes it from involvement with the enforcement of regulation or law, as well as work that is required by federal, state, or local preservation programs (FPAN 2017) (today, USF is the institutional home for two FPAN offices: the West and West-Central Regional centers).

Looking back at my notes for this period, I see that, whether by intuition or luck, I borrowed from the online syllabi of more senior colleagues, from Stephen Lekson to Richard Wilshusen to Carol McDavid. I elected initially to retain a primary focus on CRM, with standard readings on CRM law (for example, King 2013) and practice (for example, Neumann and Sanford 2010). However, I added readings on the concepts and legal framework for world heritage and cultural property (for example, Kersel 2004; Magness-Gardiner 2004; Omland 2006), encouraging students to consider many of the complications discussed by Elizabeth Chilton (2019). Moreover, I challenged the students to critically consider the historical development of public archaeology (for example, Jameson 2004), highlighting how the meaning of this term had changed from its original inception in the processual milieu of the 1970s (for example, Davis 1972; McGimsey 1972) to the critical and Indigenous archaeologies of the 1980s and beyond (for example, Potter 1994; L. Smith 2004; see also Shackel 2019). Similarly, I added readings on the newly emerging topic of community archaeology (for example, Ardren 2002; Marshall 2002; Moser et al. 2002). I also included public archaeology readings and exercises of a more methodological nature; for example, how to present archaeology for a popular audience in print (for example, Allen 2002; Fagan and Rose 2003), on the Web (for example, McDavid 2004; Young 2002; Zimmerman 2003), and in museums (for example, Merriman 2004; Stahlgren and Stottman 2007; Stone 2004; Swain 2007; Thomas 2002).

Since the first time in 2007, I have generally taught the required graduate seminar in Public Archaeology once each year. I have shifted the emphasis incrementally from CRM to more contemporary understandings of public archaeology. The syllabus has expanded accordingly, with additional readings on both the philosophy of interpretation (for example, Copeland 2004; Holtorf 2005; Little 2004; Lovata 2007; Tilden 1957) and best practices for interpretation in forums from museums to tours and signage (for example, Ham 1992; Serrell 1996). Perhaps the greater challenge has been keeping the syllabus up to date with the ever-expanding varieties of public archaeology that have emerged over the past decade. By this I refer to further developments in community archaeology (for example, Atalay 2012; Dawdy 2009), as well as "collaborative" and "indigenous archaeology" (for example, Lightfoot 2008), "participatory" and "engaged" archaeologies (for example, Little 2007), ethnographic archaeology (for example, Castañeda

2008), and archaeological ethnography (for example, Hollowell and Nicholas 2008; Meskell 2005).

Students in the course complete a project that ideally incorporates many of these insights. Most recently, students worked with FPAN, the Tampa Bay History Center, and History Bike Tampa to develop interpretive stations for a bike ride focused on the remnants of Fort Brooke, a Seminole War–era military installation now buried beneath Tampa's modern downtown (Figure 4.1). Over the years, students in the course have developed podcasts, websites, children's books, popular summaries of technical reports, signage, and museum displays. I encourage them to work with the personnel of state and local parks, where applicable, so that they encounter some of the constraints that frequently affect public interpretation in the real world, from

Figure 4.1. University of South Florida graduate students Colette Witcher (*left*) and Jean Lammie (*right*) at one of the stations in the public archaeology exhibit *Re-Placing Fort Brooke*, Spring, 2016. Photograph by Thomas J. Pluckhahn, used with permission.

such seemingly mundane matters as limitations on fonts, color, and paper size to broader limitations on content.

For several of the past few years, I have asked the students to direct their projects to the Crystal River Archaeological State Park, a famous Woodland-period (circa 1000 B.C. to A.D. 1050) mound complex north of the USF–Tampa campus. Their efforts complement my (with Brent Weisman and Victor Thompson) NSF-funded study at the site, the goal of which is to identify the role of competition and cooperation in the growth of early village societies (Pluckhahn and Thompson 2018; Pluckhahn et al. 2010; Pluckhahn et al. 2015; Pluckhahn et al. 2016; Thompson et al. 2015). Interpretation of the site, a National Historic Landmark, is currently lacking in many respects: signage is minimal, and the on-site museum has been little updated since it opened in the late 1960s.

One year, students completed a conceptual redesign of the museum and scripts for self-guided and directed tours, which I compiled into a technical report and submitted to the state park system (Pluckhahn et al. 2010). Most recently, students designed new interpretive signage for the park. They met with park personnel to develop an overarching theme (Little 2004) or "big idea" (Serrell 1996) to tie their work together, and were given a signage template that conformed to state requirements with regard to font sizes, and so on. The students' designs, although later considerably refined by myself and colleagues at FPAN, form the basis for signage soon to be implemented (thanks to a grant from the Florida Humanities Council, as well as matching funds from the Friends of Crystal River Archaeological State Park).

For several years, I asked students to also conduct a miniethnography of the visitor experience at the park, consisting of behavioral observation and structured interviews. Although the sample size was small, the ethnographic project produced useful insights regarding the potential placement of signage relative to the flow of visitors through the site. For example, the participant observation revealed that some of the features considered most interesting to archaeologists—including perhaps the earliest formal arrangement of platform mound and plaza—were often ignored by visitors because they were off the main path. The structured interviews highlighted the types of information visitors remembered from the current interpretation of the site, as well as the types of questions they had that were not addressed. Regarding the former, many of the visitors who were interviewed seemed to recall the general period of occupation but less often the reasons the archaeologists find the site unusual or exceptional, for instance, its role in the Hopewell Interaction Sphere. The information that visitors found lacking included the explanation of basic archaeological terms like "midden" and "stelae," as well as larger concepts like the nature of regional interaction. Thus, in addition to providing these insights toward improving the interpretation of the site, the project presented the graduate students with a brief introduction to ethnographic methods, a point I return to below.

Pedagogical Challenges and Opportunities

The widening scope of public archaeology, coupled with the inevitable syllabus and mission "creep," have made it increasingly difficult to maintain the dual focus on both CRM and public archaeology, both in terms of the Public Archaeology course and the overall graduate curriculum. In some years, I have taught an additional graduate seminar on CRM that included more advanced readings and exercises on topics like scoping, budgeting, and research design (for example, McGimsey 2004; Metcalf and Moses 2011); significance determination (for example, Butler 1987; Sebastian 2009; Tainter 2004); alternative mitigation strategies (for example, Chandler 2009); ethics and standards for CRM (for example, Bergman and Doershuk 2003; Fowler 1984; Bridges 2009); fair labor practices and workplace safety (for example, Berggren and Hodder 2003; Langley and Abbott 2000; McGuire and Walker 1999; Wagers and Nicholson 2008; Wright 2003); press relations (for example, Kuhn 2002); and more recent calls for reforming the compliance process (for example, Barker 2009; Cushman and Howe 2011; King 2002; Sebastian 2011; Lipe and Sebastian 2009; Mackey 2009). We visited local CRM firms, the Florida Division of Historical Resources in Tallahassee, and the Seminole Tribe of Florida's Tribal Historic Preservation Office.

Having a second, CRM-focused class provides more flexibility with regard to the topical coverage in Public Archaeology. However, only the latter course is required of graduate students in our program, and thus the only certain forum for imparting at least the basics of CRM; for this reason, the dual focus must continue to an extent. One might argue, as I have several times, that the curriculum should be expanded to include separate required classes, one focused on CRM and the other on public archaeology (more broadly defined). Colleagues have countered, perhaps rightly, that additional required classes lengthen the time to graduation and reduce the flexibility of the graduate curriculum. Of course, there are also structural obstacles, such as the time and effort it takes—a minimum of one year at USF, and revisions to the graduate handbook, plus submission of proposals to college and university committees—to make substantive changes to our graduate program.

Given our increased accountability to living communities, one might argue that a graduate curriculum in public archaeology should also include a required course in ethnographic methods. My colleague Rebecca Zarger and I (2013) have argued this case elsewhere, suggesting that the growing use of ethnography by public archaeologists necessitates better training in this technique. The miniethnography I have required in my Public Archaeology class is an imperfect response to this need, in that the students are exposed to very limited range of ethnographic techniques by a professor (myself) with limited ethnographic training (supplemented by short courses offered by the National Science Foundation). Further, while I sought and obtained institutional review board (IRB) approval for the project, the constraints of the class did not permit students in the course to also complete IRB training. Preferably, students who are interested in research or work of this sort take an ethnographic methods class taught by one of the cultural anthropologists on our faculty, but they must do so as an elective.

Other elective coursework similarly helps to fill the gap in adapting our graduate curriculum to the changing face of public archaeology. My colleague Antoinette Jackson regularly teaches a graduate seminar on Heritage Tourism. Although the focus is not on archaeological sites, students in this course further develop the sort of critical perspective on heritage that Shackel (2019) and Zimmerman (2019) have called for, with deeper reflection on the issues of representation, inclusion, and multivocality than are permitted in the Public Archaeology course. New courses in Digital Heritage and Digital Antiquity may also touch on these themes. As a four-field program with an applied focus, our graduate students can also take classes such as applied anthropology and the anthropology of development, which further reinforce critical thinking with regard to public engagement and community partnerships.

Looking Ahead

The decision by my predecessors at USF to initiate an M.A. program in Public Archaeology in the early 1970s was a reaction to changes in both the discipline and the workplace. Although we think of it as a more recent problem, by this time the number of archaeologists with advanced degrees had already far outweighed the limited number of academic positions. However, many of the changes in archaeology were not yet fully formed; at the time the program was founded, some of the major pieces of CRM legislation were only recently enacted and the term "public archaeology" was just entering general discourse (McGimsey 1972). Rather than simply reacting, the founders of the program anticipated changes in the practice of archaeology that would take another decade to become firmly entrenched.

Continuing calls for more graduate training in CRM are well founded. The gap between traditional archaeological training and the realities of the job market arguably violates the ethical standards of most of our professional organizations to properly train students (see, for example, SAA's [2017] Principle 7). But perhaps, like the founders of the USF program, we would do well to try to anticipate, rather than react to, changes in disciplinary practice and the broader economy. If Moore (2006) is correct in his reading of industry trends, CRM is already in decline and public archaeology is ascendant.

There are signs that this is true in Florida. FPAN now has a full-time staff of around twenty, counting only those with degrees in archaeology or related fields. This is more than the combined full-time staff of three of the more prominent "home grown" CRM firms in the state.[4] Several of the graduates of the Public Archaeology program at USF work for FPAN or similar organizations, and more and more enter the program with this goal in mind.

As with those who plan to work in CRM, students who aspire to work in public archaeology of the sort practiced by FPAN need to understand historic preservation laws and practice, in order to assist local governments and educate and collaborate with the public. Of course, they also need to be trained in basic principles of interpretation. The reverse is also true, however. That is, students who intend to work in CRM increasingly need training not only in historic preservation law and practice, but also in communicating their work to a broader public. And of course students from both specialties need training in ethics.

A pioneer in the training of students for careers outside the academy, the Public Archaeology program at USF has struggled at times in adapting to the diversity of contemporary public archaeology and CRM. I have labored to transform the required seminar into something that reflects contemporary understandings of public archaeology, while also retaining the foundational knowledge necessary for a career in CRM.

Changing a syllabus is easy, in principle if less so in practice sometimes. Changing the curriculum has proved more difficult. Some of the challenges stem from the concerns of my colleagues, and many of these concerns are justified. There are real limitations on the skills and concepts students can master in a graduate program while still maintaining reasonable time to graduation. There are also larger structural limitations on curriculum change imposed by university bureaucracy. Notwithstanding these challenges, the graduate program at USF remains at the forefront in training archaeologists for careers in public archaeology and CRM. For this I am thankful to the vision of my predecessors and colleagues.

Notes

1. Jorgenson (2006), although not addressing an audience of archaeological educators specifically, employs a metaphor to which this cohort may easily relate when he compares instructional change to moving graveyards: "Nobody pays much attention until you try to do it!"

2. The Bureau of Applied Research in Anthropology at the University of Arizona was established much earlier, but does not grant degrees.

3. In many respects, the curriculum for the M.A. in Public Archaeology at USF resembles SAA's (2008) model curriculum for an M.A. program in Applied Archaeology. One exception is that the model curriculum calls for a two-semester sequence of required courses on CRM, where ours is only one semester.

4. Archaeological Consultants, Inc. (2017) has a staff that includes at least four permanent, full-time archaeologists; SouthArc (2017) has three; and Janus Research, Inc., has around eleven (Jim Pepe, personal communication 2017). SEARCH, Inc., is probably the largest CRM firm in Florida, with a full-time staff of archaeologists in the dozens, but it works a great deal outside the state.

References Cited

Allen, Mitch
2002   Reaching the Hidden Audience: Ten Rules for the Archaeological Writer. In *Public Benefits of Archaeology*, edited by Barbara J. Little, pp. 244–251. University Press of Florida, Gainesville.
American Anthropological Association (AAA)
2017   *Career Paths and Education: Anthropology: Education for the 21st Century.* Elec-

tronic document, http://www.americananthro.org/AdvanceYourCareer/Content.aspx?ItemNumber=1782, accessed December 19, 2017.

Archaeological Consultants, Inc.

2017   About. Electronic document, http://www.aci-crm.com/about.html, accessed December 19, 2017.

Angrosino, Michael V.

1976   The Evolution of the New Applied Anthropology. In *Do Applied Anthropologists Apply Anthropology?*, edited by Michael V. Angrosino, pp. 1–10. University of Georgia Press, Athens.

Ardren, Traci

2002   Conversation about the Production of Archaeological Knowledge and Community Museums at Chunchucmila and Kochol, Yucatán, Mexico. *World Archaeology* 34(2): 379–400.

Atalay, Sonya

2012   *Community-Based Archaeology: Research with, by, and for Indigenous and Local Communities.* University of California Press, Berkeley.

Barker, Pat

2009   The Process Made Me Do It: Or, Would a Reasonably Intelligent Person Agree that CRM is Reasonably Intelligent? In *Archaeology and Cultural Resource Management: Visions for the Future*, edited by Lynne Sebastian and William D. Lipe, pp. 65–90. School for Advanced Research Press, Santa Fe, New Mexico.

Bender, Susan J., and George S. Smith (editors)

2000   *Teaching Archaeology in the Twenty-First Century.* Society for American Archaeology, Washington, D.C.

Bergman, Christopher A., and John F. Doershuk

2003   Cultural Resource Management and the Business of Archaeology. In *Ethical Issues in Archaeology*, edited by Larry J. Zimmerman, Karen D. Vitelli, and Julie Hollowell-Zimmer, pp. 85–97. AltaMira Press, Walnut Creek, California.

Berggren, Åsa, and Ian Hodder

2003   Social Practice, Method, and Some Problems of Field Archaeology. *American Antiquity* 68(3): 421–434.

Blanton, Dennis B.

1995   The Case for CRM Training in Academic Institutions. *SAA Bulletin* 13(4): 40–41.

Bridges, Sarah T.

2009   Archaeology and Ethics: Is There a Shared Vision for the Future? In *Archaeology and Cultural Resource Management: Visions for the Future*, edited by Lynne Sebastian and William D. Lipe, pp. 223–251. School for Advanced Research Press, Santa Fe, New Mexico.

Butler, William B.

1987   Significance and Other Frustrations in the CRM Process. *American Antiquity* 52(4): 820–829.

Castañeda, Quetzil

2008   The "Ethnographic Turn" in Archaeology: Research Positioning and Reflexivity in Ethnographic Archaeologies. In *Ethnographic Archaeologies: Reflections on*

Stakeholders and Archaeological Practices, edited by Quetzil E. Castañeda and Christopher N. Matthews, pp. 25–61. AltaMira Press, Lanham, Maryland.

Chandler, Susan M.

2009   Innovative Approaches to Mitigation. In *Archaeology and Cultural Resource Management: Visions for the Future*, edited by Lynne Sebastian and William D. Lipe, pp. 115–139. School for Advanced Research Press, Santa Fe, New Mexico.

Chilton, Elizabeth

2019   The Heritage of Heritage: Defining the Role of the Past in Contemporary Societies. In *History and Approaches to Heritage Studies*, edited by Phyllis Mauch Messenger and Susan J. Bender, pp. 24–36. University Press of Florida, Gainesville.

Copeland, Tim

2004   Presenting Archaeology to the Public: Constructing Insights On-Site. In *Public Archaeology*, edited by Nick Merriman, pp. 132–144. Routledge, London.

Cushman, David, and Tony Howe

2011   National-Scale Cultural Resource Legislation. In *Archaeology in Society: Its Relevance in a Modern World*, edited by Marcy Rockman and Joe Flatman, pp. 45–56. Springer, New York.

Davis, Hester A.

1972   The Crisis in American Archeology. *Science* 175(4019): 267–282.

Dawdy, Shannon Lee

2009   Millennial Archaeology: Locating the Discipline in the Age of Insecurity. *Archaeological Dialogues* 16(2): 131–142.

Ebbitt, Alicia

2006   Successful Graduate Education: Coursework, Professional Development, Collaboration and Multidisciplinary Exchange. *SAA Archaeological Record* 6(5): 34–35.

Fagan, Brian, and Mark Rose

2003   Ethics and the Media. In *Ethical Issues in Archaeology*, edited by Larry J. Zimmerman, Karen D. Vitelli, and Julie Hollowell-Zimmer, pp. 163–176. AltaMira Press, Walnut Creek, California.

Fiske, Shirley J., Linda A. Bennett, Patricia Ensworth, Terry Redding, and Keri Brondo

2010   *The Changing Face of Anthropology: Anthropology Masters Reflect on Education, Careers, and Professional Organizations*. AAA/CoPAPIA 2009 Anthropology MA Career Survey. American Anthropological Association, Arlington, Virginia.

Florida Public Archaeology Network (FPAN)

2017   About Us, Overview. Electronic document, http://www.flpublicarchaeology.org/about/, accessed December 19, 2017.

Fowler, Don. D.

1984   Ethics in Contract Archaeology. In *Ethics and Values in Archaeology*, edited by Ernestine L. Green, pp. 108–116. Free Press, New York.

Green, William, and John F. Doershuk

1998   Cultural Resource Management and American Archaeology. *Journal of Archaeological Research* 6(2): 121–167.

Ham, Sam H.

1992   *Environmental Interpretation: A Practical Guide for People with Big Ideas and Small Budgets.* Fulcrum, Golden, Colorado.

Hayes, Katherine, Greg Donofrio, Patricia Emerson, Tim Hoogland, Phyllis Mauch Messenger, Kevin P. Murphy, Patrick Nunnally, Chris Taylor, and Anduin Wilhide

2019   Challenging the Silo Mentality: Creating a Heritage Studies and Public History Program at the University of Minnesota and Minnesota Historical Society. In *History and Approaches to Heritage Studies*, edited by Phyllis Mauch Messenger and Susan J. Bender, pp. 127–153. University Press of Florida, Gainesville

Hollowell, Julie, and George Nicholas

2008   A Critical Assessment of Ethnography in Archaeology. In *Ethnographic Archaeologies: Reflections on Stakeholders and Archaeological Practices*, edited by Quetzil E. Castañeda and Christopher N. Matthews, pp. 63–94. AltaMira Press, Lanham, Maryland.

Holtorf, Cornelius

2005   *From Stonehenge to Las Vegas: Archaeology as Popular Culture.* AltaMira Press, Walnut Creek, California.

Jameson, John H., Jr.

2004   Public Archaeology in the United States. In *Public Archaeology*, edited by Nick Merriman, pp. 21–58. Routledge, London.

Jorgenson, Olaf

2006   The Teaching Life: Why Curriculum Change Is Difficult and Necessary. *Independent School Magazine*, Summer. Electronic document, http://www.nais.org/Magazines-Newsletters/ISMagazine/Pages/Why-Curriculum-Change-Is-Difficult-and-Necessary.aspx, accessed September 28, 2014.

Kandiko, Camille B., and Paul Blackmore

2012   The Networked Curriculum. In *Strategic Curriculum Change: Global Trends in Universities*, edited by Paul Blackmore and Camille Kandiko, pp. 3–20. Routledge, New York.

Kehoe, Alice B., and Peter R. Schmidt

2017   Introduction: Expanding our Knowledge by Listening. *SAA Archaeological Record* 17(4): 15–19.

Kersel, Morag

2004   The Politics of Playing Fair, or, Who's Losing Their Marbles? In *Marketing Heritage: Archaeology and the Consumption of the Past*, edited by Yorke Rowan and Uzi Baram, pp. 41–56. AltaMira Press, Walnut Creek, California.

King, Thomas F.

2002   *Thinking about Cultural Resource Management: Essays from the Edge.* AltaMira Press, Lanham, Maryland.

2013   *Cultural Resource Laws and Practice.* 4th ed. AltaMira Press, Walnut Creek, California.

Kuhn, Robert D.

2002   Archaeology under a Microscope: CRM and the Press. *American Antiquity* 67(2): 195–212.

Kushner, Gilbert
1978   Applied Anthropology Training Programs. *Practicing Anthropology* 1(2): 23.
1994   Training Programs for the Practice of Applied Anthropology. *Human Organization* 53(2): 186–191.
Kushner, Gilbert, and Michael V. Angrosino
1974   Applied Anthropology at the University of South Florida. In *Training Programs for New Opportunities in Applied Anthropology*, edited by Eleanor Leacock, Nancie L. González, and Gilbert Kushner, pp. 34–38. American Anthropological Association and Society for Applied Anthropology, Washington, D.C.
Kushner, Gilbert, and Alvin W. Wolfe
1993   Applied Anthropology at the University of South Florida. *Practicing Anthropology* 15(1): 3–32.
Langley, Ricky L., and Lawrence E. Abbott Jr.
2000   Health and Safety Issues in Archaeology: Are Archaeologists at Risk? *North Carolina Archaeology* 49: 23–42.
Lightfoot, Kent G.
2008   Collaborative Research Programs: Implications for the Practice of North American Archaeology. In *Collaborating at the Trowel's Edge: Teaching and Learning in Indigenous Archaeology*, edited by Stephen W. Silliman, pp. 211–227. University of Arizona Press, Tucson.
Lipe, William D., and Lynne Sebastian
2009   Perspectives from the Advanced Seminar. In *Archaeology and Cultural Resource Management: Visions for the Future*, edited by Lynne Sebastian and William D. Lipe, pp. 283–297. School for Advanced Research Press, Santa Fe, New Mexico.
Little, Barbara J.
2004   Is the Medium the Message? The Art of Interpreting Archaeology in U.S. National Parks. In *Marketing Heritage: Archaeology and the Consumption of the Past*, edited by Yorke Rowan and Uzi Baram, pp. 269–286. AltaMira Press, Walnut Creek, California.
2007   Archaeology and Civic Engagement. In *Archaeology as a Tool of Civic Engagement*, edited by Barbara J. Little and Paul A. Shackel, pp. 1–22. AltaMira Press, Lanham, Maryland.
Lovata, Troy
2007   *Inauthentic Archaeologies: Public Uses and Abuses of the Past*. Left Coast Press, Walnut Creek, California.
McAndrews, Timothy L.
2007   Bridging the Great Divide: How Academic Archaeology Can Serve the Cultural Resource Management Industry. *SAA Archaeological Record* 7(3): 39–42, 60.
McDavid, Carol
2004   Towards a More Democratic Archaeology? The Internet and Public Archaeological Practice. In *Public Archaeology*, edited by Nick Merriman, pp. 159–187. Routledge, London.
McGimsey, Charles R. III
1972   *Public Archaeology*. Seminar Press, New York.

2004   CRM on CRM: One Person's Perspective on the Birth and Early Development of Cultural Resource Management. Arkansas Archaeological Survey Research Series 61, Fayetteville.

McGuire, Randall H., and Mark Walker
1999   Class Confrontations in Archaeology. *Historical Archaeology* 33(1): 159–183.

Mackey, Douglas P., Jr.
2009   Is the Same Old Thing Enough for Twenty-first Century CRM? Keeping CRM Archaeology Relevant in a New Millennium. In *Archaeology and Cultural Resource Management: Visions for the Future*, edited by Lynne Sebastian and William D. Lipe, pp. 195–222. School for Advanced Research Press, Santa Fe, New Mexico.

Magness-Gardiner, Bonnie
2004   International Conventions and Cultural Heritage Protection. In *Marketing Heritage: Archaeology and the Consumption of the Past*, edited by Yorke Rowan and Uzi Baram, pp. 27–39. AltaMira Press, Walnut Creek, California.

Marshall, Yvonne
2002   What Is Community Archaeology? *World Archaeology* 34(2): 211–219.

Merriman, Nick
2004   Involving the Public in Museum Archaeology. In *Public Archaeology*, edited by Nick Merriman, pp. 85–108. Routledge, London.

Meskell, Lynn
2005   Archaeological Ethnography: Conversations around Kruger National Park. *Archaeologies* 1(1): 81–100.

Metcalf, Michael D., and Jim Moses
2011   Building an Archaeological Business. In *Archaeology in Society: Its Relevance in the Modern World*, edited by Marcy Rockman and Joe Flatman, pp. 89–96. Springer, New York.

Miles, Matthew B.
1964   Educational Innovation: The Nature of the Problem. In *Innovation in Education*, edited by Matthew B. Miles, pp. 1–46. Bureau of Publications, Columbia Teachers' College, New York.

Mills, Barbara
2006   A Diversity of Curricula for Archaeology Graduate Programs. *SAA Archaeological Record* 6(5): 25–26, 31.

Moore, Lawrence E.
2006   CRM: Beyond Its Peak. *SAA Archaeological Record* 6(1): 30–33.

Moser, Stephanie, Darren Glazier, James E. Phillips, Lamya Nasser el Nemr, Mohamed Saleh Mousa, Rascha Nasr Aiegh, Susan Richardson, Andrew Conner, and Michael Seymour
2002   Transforming Archaeology through Community Practice: Strategies for Collaborative Archaeology and the Community Archaeology Project at Quseir, Egypt. *World Archaeology* 34(2): 220–248.

Neumann, Thomas W., and Robert M. Sanford
2010   *Practicing Archaeology: An Introduction to Cultural Resources Archaeology.* 2nd ed. AltaMira Press, Lanham, Maryland.

Neusius, Sarah W.

2009   Changing the Curriculum: Preparing Archaeologists for Careers in Applied Archaeology. *SAA Archaeological Record* 9(1): 18–22.

Omland, Atle

2006   The Ethics of the World Heritage Concept. In *The Ethics of Archaeology: Philosophical Perspectives on Archaeological Practice*, edited by Chris Scarre and Geoffrey Scarre, pp. 69–93. Cambridge University Press, Cambridge.

Parker, Patricia L., and Thomas F. King

1990   Guidelines for Evaluating and Documenting Traditional Cultural Properties. *National Park Service Bulletin* 38. U.S. Department of the Interior, Washington, D.C.

Patterson, Thomas C.

1998   The Political Economy of Archaeology in the United States. *Annual Review of Anthropology* 28: 155–174.

Pluckhahn, Thomas J., and Victor D. Thompson

2018   *New Histories of Village Life at Crystal River.* University Press of Florida, Gainesville.

Pluckhahn, Thomas J., Victor D. Thompson, and Alexander Cherkinsky

2015   The Temporality of Shell-bearing Landscapes at Crystal River, Florida. *Journal of Anthropological Archaeology* 37: 19–36.

Pluckhahn, Thomas J., Victor D. Thompson, and W. Jack Rink

2016   Evidence for Stepped Pyramids of Shell in the Woodland Period of Eastern North America. *American Antiquity* 81(2): 345–363.

Pluckhahn, Thomas J., Victor D. Thompson, and Brent R. Weisman

2010   A New View of History and Process at Crystal River. *Southeastern Archaeology* 29(1): 164–181.

Potter, Parker B., Jr.

1994   *Public Archaeology in Annapolis: A Critical Approach to History in Maryland's Ancient City.* Smithsonian Institution Press, Washington, D.C.

Roy, Dale, Paola Borin, and Erika Kustra

2007   Assisting Curriculum Change through Departmental Initiatives. *New Directions for Teaching and Learning* 112: 21–32.

Schuldenrein, Joseph

1995   The Care and Feeding of Archaeologists: A Plea for Pragmatic Training in the 21st Century. *SAA Bulletin* 13(3): 22–24.

1998   Changing Career Paths and the Training of Professional Archaeologists: Observations from the Barnard College Forum, Part I. *SAA Bulletin* 16(1): 31–33.

Sebastian, Lynne

2006   Building a Graduate Curriculum for CRM Archaeology. *SAA Archaeological Record* 6(5): 29, 35.

2009   Deciding What Matters: Archaeology, Eligibility, and Significance. In *Archaeology and Cultural Resource Management: Visions for the Future*, edited by Lynne Sebastian and William D. Lipe, pp. 91–114. School for Advanced Research Press, Santa Fe, New Mexico.

2011   Secrets of the Past, Archaeology, and the Public. In *Archaeology in Society: Its Relevance in a Modern World*, edited by Marcy Rockman and Joe Flatman, pp. 267–276. Springer, New York.

Serrell, Beverly

1996   *Exhibit Labels: An Interpretive Approach*. AltaMira Press, Walnut Creek, California.

Shackel, Paul A.

2019   Civic Engagement, Representation, and Social Justice: Moving from CRM to Heritage Studies. In *History and Approaches to Heritage Studies*, edited by Phyllis Mauch Messenger and Susan J. Bender, pp. 9–23. University Press of Florida, Gainesville.

Shackel, Paul A., and Lena Mortensen

2006   Some Thoughts about the Graduate Curriculum. *SAA Archaeological Record* 6(5): 23–24.

Smith, George S.

2006   Skills, Knowledge and Abilities: Archaeology in the 21st Century. *SAA Archaeological Record* 6(5): 30–31.

Smith, Laurajane

2004   *Archaeological Theory and the Politics of Cultural Heritage*. Routledge, New York.

Society for American Archaeology (SAA)

2008   *Recommended Model Curriculum: Masters in Applied Archaeology*. Electronic document, http://www.saa.org/Portals/0/SAA/new/MAA.pdf, accessed October 6, 2014.

2017   *Principles of Archaeological Ethics*. Electronic document, http://www.saa.org/AboutheSociety/PrinciplesofArchaeologicalEthics/tabid/203/Default.aspx, accessed December 19, 2017.

SouthArc, Inc.

2017   Staff. Electronic document, http://www.southarc.com/staff, accessed December 19, 2017.

Speakman, Robert J., Carla S. Hadden, Matthew H. Colvin, Justin Cramb, K. C. Jones, Travis W. Jones, Corbin L. Kling, Isabelle Lulewicz, Katharine G. Napora, Katherine L. Reinberger, Brandon T. Ritchison, Maria Jose Rivera-Araya, April K. Smith, and Victor D. Thompson

2017   Choosing a Path to the Ancient World in a Modern Market: The Reality of Faculty Jobs in Archaeology. *American Antiquity*, doi:10.1017/aaq.2017.36.

Stahlgren, Lori C., and M. Jay Stottman

2007   Voices from the Past: Changing the Culture of Historic House Museums with Archaeology. In *Archaeology as a Tool of Civic Engagement*, edited by Barbara J. Little and Paul A. Shackel, pp. 131–150. AltaMira Press, Lanham, Maryland.

Stone, Peter G.

2004   The Re-display of the Alexander Keiller Museum, Avebury, and the National Curriculum in England. In *The Presented Past: Heritage, Museums, and Education*, edited by Peter G. Stone and Brian L. Molyneaux, pp. 190–205. Routledge, London.

Swain, Hedley

2007   *An Introduction to Museum Archaeology*. Cambridge University Press, Cambridge.

Tainter, Joseph A.

2004   Persistent Dilemmas in American Cultural Resource Management. In *A Companion to Archaeology*, edited by John Blintiff, pp. 435–453. Blackwell, Malden, Massachusetts.

Thomas, David Hurst

2002   Roadside Ruins: Does America Still Need Archaeology Museums? In *Public Benefits of Archaeology*, edited by Barbara J. Little, pp. 130–145. University Press of Florida, Gainesville.

Thompson, Victor D., Thomas J. Pluckhahn, Oindrilla Das, and C. Fred T. Andrus

2015   Assessing Village Life and Monument Construction (cal. AD 65–1070) along the Central Gulf Coast of Florida through Stable Isotope Geochemistry. *Journal of Archaeological Science: Reports* 4: 111–123.

Tilden, Freeman

1957   *Interpreting our Heritage*. University of North Carolina Press, Chapel Hill.

Tully, Gemma

2007   Community Archaeology: General Methods and Standards of Practice. *Public Archaeology* 6(3): 155–187.

Vawser, Anne M. Wolley

2004   Teaching Archaeology and Cultural Resource Management. *SAA Archaeological Record* 4(2): 18–19.

Wagers, Scott J., and Chris Nicholson

2008   What Are Archaeological Field Technicians Paid? *SAA Archaeological Record* 8: 30–33.

Weisman, Brent R.

2006   The New Curriculum is More than Courses. *SAA Archaeological Record* 6(5): 27–28.

2002   Learning by Doing in Public Archaeology Training. *Practicing Anthropology* 24(2): 11–15.

Weisman, Brent R., and Nancy Marie White

2000   A Model Graduate Training Programme in Public Archaeology. *Antiquity* 74: 203–208.

White, Nancy Marie

2000a   Teaching Public Archaeology at the University of South Florida. In *Teaching Archaeology in the Twenty-first Century*, edited by Susan Bender and George Smith, pp. 111–115. Society for American Archaeology, Washington, D.C.

2000b   Teaching Archaeologists to Teach Public Archaeology. In *The Archaeology Education Handbook: Sharing the Past with Kids*, edited by K. Smardz and S. Smith, pp. 328–339. AltaMira Press, Walnut Creek, California.

White, Nancy Marie, Brent R. Weisman, Robert H. Tykot, E. Christian Wells, Karla L. Davis-Salazar, John W. Arthur, and Kathryn Weedman

2004   Academic Archaeology is Public Archaeology. *SAA Archaeological Record*, March, 26–29.

White, Nancy Marie, and J. Raymond Williams

1994   Public Archaeology in Florida, USA: A Review and Case Study. In *The Presented Past*, edited by P. Stone and B. Molyneaux, pp. 82–94. One World Archaeology Series, Routledge, London.

Whitley, Thomas G.

2004   CRM Training in Academic Archaeology: A Personal Perspective. *SAA Archaeological Record* 4(2): 20–25.

Wolfe, Alvin W.

1982   Internships in Applied Anthropology: Evaluation after Five Years. *Practicing Anthropology* 4(3–4): 12–13.

1991   Internships and Practica in Applied Anthropology. *Southern Anthropologist* (Summer): 22–35.

Wright, Rita P.

2003   Gender Matters—A Question of Ethics. In *Ethical Issues in Archaeology*, edited by Larry J. Zimmerman, Karen D. Vitelli, and Julie Hollowell-Zimmer, pp. 85–97. AltaMira Press, Walnut Creek, California.

Wurst, Louann, and Sue Novinger

2011   Hidden Boundaries: Archaeology, Education, and Ideology in the United States. In *Ideologies in Archaeology*, edited by Reinhard Bernbeck and Randall H. McGuire, pp. 254–269. University of Arizona Press, Tucson.

Young, Peter A.

2002   The Archaeologist as Storyteller. In *Public Benefits of Archaeology*, edited by Barbara J. Little, pp. 239–243. University Press of Florida, Gainesville.

Yu, Pei-Lin, Barbara Mills, and Anna Neuzil

2006   What Skills Do I Need to Get and Keep A Job in Archaeology? *SAA Archaeological Record* 6(3): 9–13.

Zarger, Rebecca K., and Thomas J. Pluckhahn

2013   Assessing Methodologies in Archaeological Ethnography: A Case for Incorporating Ethnographic Training in Graduate Archaeology Curricula. *Public Archaeology* 12(1): 48–63.

Zeder, Melinda A.

1994   The American Archaeologist: Results of the 1994 SAA Census. *SAA Bulletin* 15(2): 12–17.

Zimmerman, Larry J.

2003   *Presenting the Past*. Archaeologist's Toolkit 7. AltaMira Press, Walnut Creek, California.

2019   Help Needed! Reflections on a Critical Pedagogy of Heritage. In *History and Approaches to Heritage Studies*, edited by Phyllis Mauch Messenger and Susan J. Bender, pp. 215–236. University Press of Florida, Gainesville.

5

Teaching Heritage in the Field

An Example from Menorca, Spain

RICARDO J. ELIA, AMALIA PÉREZ-JUEZ,
AND MEREDITH ANDERSON LANGLITZ

Field Schools, Ethics, and Heritage

The archaeological field school is a traditional means of training students in the practical skills of survey, excavation, recording, and artifact processing. Field schools are not the only way to prepare students, of course, but their avowed goal of providing systematic, hands-on instruction in essential aspects of archaeological fieldwork makes them attractive both to aspiring professional archaeologists and to students in other disciplines who do not plan to work in the field professionally but wish to experience how archaeology is done. In this chapter we describe our experience in offering an archaeological field school in Menorca, Spain, where students learn traditional field methods through the perspective of heritage management, an emerging discipline that incorporates archaeology as one of a broader set of skills involving the study, valuing, interpreting, and preserving of the past.

Archaeological field schools provide valuable opportunities for experiential and interactive learning at real archaeological sites. They have also engendered considerable discussion about ethics and ethical practice. For example, field schools where students pay to participate are commonly used to help finance archaeological research as well as to provide a labor force, and the potential ethical problems created by this situation have been the subject of concern for some time. In 1974 the Society for American Archaeology passed a resolution condemning the practice of excavation of sites "solely or primarily for 'teaching' purposes," equating it with indiscriminate excavation (RPA 2015). In 1998, shortly before it became the Register of Professional Archaeologists (RPA), the Society for Professional Archaeologists (SOPA) established a certification program for archaeological field schools that required field schools to be part of established research projects or cultural resource management programs with a demonstrated record of conservation, curation, and publication. The RPA's ongoing field school certification program offers detailed guidelines for training in survey, excavation, recording, and laboratory analysis (Bernadini 2012; Register of Professional Archaeologists 2015).

Contemporary discussions about field school ethics often focus on issues relating to stewardship, public outreach, and relations with Indigenous and local peoples. Anne Pyburn (2003), for example, has championed the "priority of stewardship" in the conduct of field schools, arguing that students need to learn more than the mere nuts and bolts of digging. She advocates for a more reflexive approach that balances method and theory within a clearly defined research design, and encourages field school students to engage actively in the process of research and to think about what stewardship means—not only to the field school participants themselves, but also to local communities and to the preservation and interpretation of archaeological resources. James VanderVeen and Jeanette Repczynski (2010) have also called for stewardship training in field schools, arguing that students need to learn about the social and political contexts in which archaeology is conducted— for example, identifying stakeholders and learning the local laws—in order to become not just field technicians but effective stewards of the past.

Much of the discussion about the need to incorporate training in stewardship into archaeological field schools has been generated by archaeologists working at sites associated with Indigenous populations, especially in the Americas, where archaeologists explore the past among living people who may or may not be culturally affiliated with the archaeological sites under study and who may or may not welcome archaeologists working in their midst (for example, Atalay 2008; Silliman 2008). Many of these field schools have included some aspects of heritage management training under the pedagogical rubric of stewardship, primarily in the areas of incorporating stakeholders into the project, developing relationships with Indigenous peoples, and engaging in public outreach and community archaeology efforts directed toward both Indigenous and non-Indigenous communities (Mitchell et al. 2013). These efforts stem from a concern not only for practicing and teaching best practices in archaeological field research, but also an interest in promoting the sustainable conservation of the archaeological resource base. The main focus of stewardship training in these field schools appears to be involving students in the projects' efforts to work with Indigenous people rather than a broad-based effort to teach students practical skills in heritage management.

Recent studies have also focused on the pedagogy of archaeological field schools (for example, papers in Mytum 2012), as well as practical considerations of running field schools; this includes planning, personnel, and logistics; the challenge of attracting paying students during times of economic downturns; and making field schools more responsive to heritage-related skills such as conservation, field recording of threatened and looted sites, and other necessary cultural resource management activities (for example, Baxter 2009; Doelle and Huntley 2012; Hunter 2008; Morrison 2012; Thomas and Langlitz 2013).

Construed very broadly, the growing discipline of heritage management is concerned with the identification, preservation, and stewardship of cultural heritage in the public interest. Cultural heritage, including archaeological heritage, embraces a broad range of values and meanings; it comprises the cultural expressions of humanity, whether tangible or intangible, movable or immovable, old or new, and includes archaeological objects, sites, buildings, monuments, landscapes, documents, and archives. Cultural heritage is finite, nonrenewable, and frequently threatened (Elia and Ostovich 2011). Heritage management, with its concern for conservation, stakeholders, preservation, and interpretation, is in many ways the practical embodiment of an ethic of stewardship.

Incorporating formal training in heritage management into archaeological field schools is one way to introduce both future professional archaeologists, as well as other students who will find careers in different, perhaps related, fields, to the theory and practice of managing the past. In this paper we describe our experience in training students in heritage management as an integral component of Boston University's Menorca Field School in Archaeology and Heritage Management, held on the island of Menorca (Spain) during the summers of 2009 through 2014. We also advocate for the need to approach field training from a holistic perspective so that it includes not only a broad range of skills related to excavation, recording, and artifact processing, but also practical skills relating to preservation, management, interpretation, and public outreach.

Ricardo J. Elia, Amalia Pérez-Juez, and Meredith Anderson Langlitz

Boston University Field School in Archaeology and Heritage Management

Since 2002, Boston University has conducted an archaeological field school at different sites on the island of Menorca, Spain. Boston University's Department of Archaeology requires all undergraduate majors to participate in a field school, and many BU archaeology students attend our field school to fulfill this requirement. The Menorca program is also open to all Boston University students regardless of their major concentration as well as those from other colleges and universities. The six-week field school has been teaching certain aspects of heritage management since the beginning, and in 2009 the heritage component was expanded. By that point, it was clear that students were requesting more training in various aspects of heritage, including stewardship, cultural tourism, museology, and threats to heritage such as looting. Many of these students were majors in fields like anthropology, art history, political science, or international relations and were not planning a career in archaeology. They were interested in archaeology, but also wanted to learn more than how to dig, and they saw the broader area of heritage studies as relevant to their own future careers.

Instruction in field methods on Menorca includes survey, geophysical remote sensing, excavation, and site mapping. In addition to learning standard methods of excavation, recording, and artifact processing, our field school students receive instruction and participate in various analytical techniques, including paleoethnobotany, geoarchaeology (with micromorphology), zooarchaeology, and experimental archaeology. Our field school has always included trips to museums, sites, and monuments, and encouraged the students—through a number of exercises—to think about these spots not just as old sites but as cultural places that survived and hold meaning in the present (and often multiple or even conflicting meanings). We challenge our students to think about more than the cultural history presented on the interpretive signage and to ask: Who cares about these sites? Why should they be preserved? What is the state of conservation? What kind of security is there? How accessible and informative is the interpretation offered?

Menorca is an ideal setting for students to grapple with and engage in the past, present, and future of heritage management. The easternmost of Spain's Balearic Islands, Menorca is a small island with a rich and diverse archaeology and history. It is also a UNESCO Biosphere Reserve (since 1993), a candidate for nomination as a World Heritage site, and a popular Mediterranean summer tourist destination for many Europeans. As a result, heritage management on the island must go beyond interaction with local stakeholders and address issues that have arisen especially in the past few decades as a result of globalization, such as increased cultural tourism, threats to preservation, and development. Exposure to a wide variety of heritage management topics is a valuable experience for our students, and our field school alumni have gone on to pursue careers not only in archaeology, but also in conservation, tourism, museums, art and cultural heritage law, education, and even documentary filmmaking.

Field School Sites

In recent years the field school has worked at two archaeological sites: Torre d'en Galmés and Isla del Rey. The sites correspond to two different time periods and have singular and specific problems that can be approached differently, making them ideal case studies to teach heritage management in the field (in 2013 and 2014 all students worked on both sites). Although the island was first settled in the fourth millennium B.C.E., it is best known for its distinctive Iron Age Talayotic Culture, characterized by megalithic architecture and large settlements (Pérez-Juez 2013). The Talayotic culture dates to the first millennium B.C.E.; its settlements feature large, tower-like structures called *talayots*, enclosures with prominent T-shaped monuments known as *taulas*, and a variety of house forms and storage features (Figure 5.1). Torre d'en Galmés is the largest Talayotic site on Menorca, an urban center that flourished in the Iron Age during the periods of Carthaginian and later Roman control. Later, the site was reinhabited during the Middle Ages as Menorca's population surged with Muslim groups fleeing mainland Spain as a result of the *Reconquista*.

Isla del Rey, a small island in Menorca's Mahon Harbor, is best known today for its distinctive architectural heritage in the form of the surviving buildings of an eighteenth-century British naval hospital. The hospital was built in 1711, shortly after the British gained control of Menorca. The U-shaped naval hospital on Isla del Rey served for decades as the most important installation of its type for the British Navy outside of England.

Figure 5.1. View of the Talayotic site of Trepuco, with taula in foreground and conical talayot in background. Photograph by Amalia Pérez-Juez, used with permission.

Figure 5.2. Students excavating in front of the naval hospital on Isla del Rey. Photograph by Ricardo J. Elia, used with permission.

The British used the naval hospital during its three periods of dominion over Menorca (1708–1756, 1763–1782, and 1798–1802). France and Spain also controlled the island during intermediary periods. Spain took possession of Menorca in 1802 and continues to hold sovereignty over the island. The hospital was abandoned in 1964 and faced serious neglect and looting. Since 2004 the "Friends of Hospital Island" have been actively undertaking a project to "protect, preserve and restore its historical buildings, preserve the natural environment and provide a cultural use for the site, maintaining its public ownership and incorporating it in the historical, artistic, and cultural life of the Port of Mahon" (Espiau Espiau 2010: 287). In 2013 and 2014, Boston University's field school conducted a program of survey and limited testing as part of a study to develop an archaeological management plan for Isla del Rey in collaboration with the ongoing restoration program at the naval hospital (Figure 5.2). This was the first time the field school research was specifically designed from the outset as a heritage management project.

Teaching Heritage in the Field

Students attending the Menorca field school receive credits for two courses: Archaeology Field Methods and, since 2009, Studies in Archaeological Heritage Management. In order to design an entire course devoted to heritage management, we divided the program into lectures, field trips, and projects. In practice, on a day-to-day basis the heritage and methods courses were integrated without much distinction, as we tried to make thinking about heritage an overarching perspective at all times, whether we were digging or visiting a museum.

Heritage Lectures

Students were introduced to a number of heritage topics through classroom lectures held throughout the six-week program, usually given in the evening after fieldwork was done for the day. Most lectures required student preparation in the form of readings or worksheets designed to elicit thoughtful responses to the issues presented, but we tried to be realistic about what students could accomplish outside of class when most days were busy with work in the field and lab. Lectures incorporated both local details from Menorca and case studies from around the world. Lectures on local archaeology (for example, Talayotic culture, Roman Menorca, eighteenth-century Menorca, and so on) and geoarchaeology introduced students to the rich cultural and archaeological legacy of the island. Heritage-specific lectures typically included:

- Introduction to Archaeological Heritage Management
- Why We Care: Stakeholders and Values
- The UNESCO World Heritage Convention and Biosphere Program
- Site Management: Principles and Practice
- Cultural Tourism
- Archaeological Site Looting and the Antiquities Market
- Museums and Acquisitions Policies
- Introduction to Spanish and Local Policies and Patrimony Laws
- Elements of Site Preservation: Conservation, Sustainability, and Outreach

Field Trips

In 1993, the island of Menorca was listed as a UNESCO Biosphere Reserve for, among other reasons, the amazing preservation of its archaeological heritage in a sustainable developed territory. The combination of natural and cultural sites makes the island a perfect laboratory to introduce students to key aspects of heritage management. Field trips are a critical part of the field school and are designed to present the students with these situations as well as the challenge of managing sites in a touristic island. They include visits to natural and cultural sites, ethnographic landscapes, museums, and historic towns (and beautiful beaches). As students encounter these places, they are encouraged to think about issues related to security, presentation, facilities, conservation, and management of these diverse sites. On many of these trips, students complete a worksheet that invites them to record observations about the management of heritage in Menorca. Questions on the worksheet cover state of preservation and conservation, site security, amenities, signage, brochures, and other information provided to visitors. We ask our students to observe the other visitors at the site, describe the amenities available and the site layout, record what cultural periods are being interpreted, make observations about the nature of the signage and any site literature, and take note of any evidence of previous archaeological excavations. One field school class participated in a "scavenger hunt" while exploring the historic city of Ciutadella on the west coast of Menorca. In this exercise, students were divided into groups of four and each group was given a map with a detailed list of cultural sites and places of interest that they had to locate, visit, and answer questions about. After returning to our base in Mahon, each group reported their results in slide presentations.

Heritage Projects

An integral part of the heritage management component of the field school is a major group project presented at the end of the session. Students gain real-world experience by working on practical applications relating to the heritage of Menorca. Past projects have included designing a museum exhibition, developing heritage management plans for archaeological sites on the island, and preparing itineraries and corresponding information on local sites. Examples are illustrated below.

Designing a Public Exhibit

Students in the 2010 field school participated, along with professional staff, in the design and production of an exhibit of a medieval building excavated at Torre d'en Galmés. The building represented a reoccupation of the Talayotic-period site and preserved intact the last occupation of a medieval Muslim settlement, likely abandoned in haste during the Christian conquest of 1287 C.E. Students conducted historical research on Muslim Menorca, and created a welcome video, exhibit panels, games for children, and a recreation of the medieval house that they excavated. Explanatory texts emphasized the importance of archaeology for understanding the history of Menorca and the need to preserve cultural sites on the island. The exhibit was mounted in the town of Alaior during the fall of 2010 and traveled throughout the island the following year (Pérez-Juez 2012).

British Heritage Trail Brochure

Menorca has a rich history of sites dating to the period of British military and naval control over the island in the eighteenth and early nineteenth centuries, including public buildings, roads, fortifications, and landscape features. In 2012, students researched and designed a brochure for tourists that presents surviving British buildings and monuments of this era. The British Heritage Trail brochure was designed especially for the many British tourists who come to Menorca each summer, and included a map, photo, and brief historical descriptions of key sites.

Heritage Management Plans

In different years, field school students have tackled the challenge of creating heritage management plans for archaeological sites on the island. For example, in 2009, students prepared an archaeological management plan for a small Talayotic site that had recently been excavated on the island (see Case Study box). In 2013, four teams of students worked on different aspects of a heritage management plan for Isla del Rey, the site of a British and Spanish naval hospital in the eighteenth to nineteenth centuries, where they had been conducting survey and excavations. At the end of the field school, the students gave presentations on their recommendations for research and public access; identification of stakeholders and their potential concerns; visitor management; and preservation issues, including conservation and restoration.

Case Study: Developing a Heritage Management Plan at Binisafullet

In 2009, we selected a small Talayotic site that our students had never seen or heard of at Binisafullet, near Menorca's capital of Mahon. This site, dating roughly from the fourth century B.C.E. through the Roman period, had been surveyed and minimally tested in 1988 (Plantalamor et al. 1990); additional work, including conservation, was carried out at the taula enclosure in 1990 (Isbert 1993). Although a protected site, that summer Binisafullet was largely overgrown, off the tourist routes, with no visitor facilities and only limited signage. In short, it was perfect for our project, which was to develop a concept for a management plan for Binisafullet that would allow for meaningful public interpretation and access to the site while ensuring the long-term preservation of its archaeological remains.

We divided up our field school students into five teams of three to four students each. Each team was responsible for one of the following components of heritage management at the site: (1) Identification; (2) Evaluation; (3) Preservation; and (4) Presentation. Each team was required to develop an outline or framework for use in a management plan and, because there is always overlap in studies of this type, the teams were encouraged to coordinate with one another. They were also free to consult with the project staff about technical issues or if they had questions relating to local preservation law, policy, and practice. The final result would be a series of presentations made by each group of students and illustrated with slides that together created an outline of a management plan for the site.

Students in each group were invited to think about a number of questions:

Identification Team:
- What kind of site is it—type of site, culture, time period, and so on?
- What are the existing conditions at the site?
- What is the archaeological potential of the site?
- What types of data need to be obtained for the site's Management Plan?

Evaluation Team:
- Who are the various stakeholders?
- What are their needs and interests?
- Do they conflict?
- Can you weigh the values of the various stakeholders and develop a statement of significance for the site?

Preservation Team:
- Who owns the site?
- Is it threatened?
- What is the physical condition of the archaeological remains?
- What are the preservation needs for the site?
- What are the security needs for the site?

Presentation Team:
- How is the site currently interpreted to the public?
- Based on other sites you have visited, what facilities, infrastructure, signage, and so on, do you recommend?
- Do you think the site (or part of it) should be restored and how?
- Can you suggest plans to deliver information about the site to nonvisitors, taking into account the multiple publics for the site and the kinds of information they want?

Ricardo J. Elia, Amalia Pérez-Juez, and Meredith Anderson Langlitz

- How would you improve access to archaeological data about the site for researchers?
- What types of media and approaches would you recommend for public outreach?

To make this assignment fun as well as challenging, we initially gave the students no information about the site, not even its location or name. We drove them to Binisafullet, dropped them off, and told them we would return in two hours. They were to explore together and figure out what kind of site they had (Figure 5.3). Everybody enjoyed this part of the project. The students got to explore and make sense of a site by themselves using the experience they had gained from their readings, lectures, excavation work, and previous visits to numerous archaeological sites on the island.

Figure 5.3. Students recording observations at Talayotic site of Binisafullet. Photograph by Ricardo J. Elia, used with permission.

The students quickly realized that Binisafullet was a small Talayotic settlement, based on the characteristic taula enclosure, talayot, houses, and walls. During their initial visit they took plenty of photos, sketched the site, and made observations on the visible remains, the state of preservation, and other aspects of the site, such as proximity to roads and availability of parking.

Over the next few weeks they worked on their projects, collaborating with the other teams, and regularly consulting the Internet for resources as well as talking with project staff. The students asked to be taken back to the site so they could look at the remains again and check on their initial observations.

Ultimately, the students produced the beginnings of a creditable and pragmatic management plan. Throughout the project, they applied much of their newly gained awareness of heritage management and Menorcan archaeology and observed and responded to the site through the eyes of knowledgeable visitors. Their plan recognized that a small site like Binisafullet, in an area off the beaten path and with little available parking, would not be a good candidate for touristic development. Instead, it would be best reserved for its archaeological research potential and for the occasional visitor who prefers to avoid the large, touristic sites. The students also identified other likely stakeholders, including the year-round residents who lived in close proximity to the site and the seasonal visitors who rented cottages in the vicinity.

Challenges and Prospects

Five years of combining training in heritage management with traditional archaeological field methods in Menorca have revealed many positive synergies and some clear challenges. Showing students that there is more to archaeology than survey, excavation, and lab work has encouraged them to explore questions of why cultural sites are important and how they should be studied, managed, and made accessible to the public. These questions become more critical in times of economic stress, social unrest, and armed conflict when cultural heritage is vulnerable to appropriation, neglect, and destruction, both deliberate and unintentional. Most students who participate in archaeological field schools probably will not become professional archaeologists, but some will doubtless move into related careers in the

Ricardo J. Elia, Amalia Pérez-Juez, and Meredith Anderson Langlitz

areas of government, management, culture, and the arts where their time learning archaeology and heritage may prove useful.

Field training in heritage management offers many of the same experiential and interactive learning opportunities for students as does field training in archaeology. First-hand encounters with real sites and real problems, from bulldozers carving through archaeological features to crumbling architecture, offer unique experiences to students. So does being confronted by an angry landowner, or surveying a looted landscape. Of course, many experiences are positive, too, such as the pleasure of describing one's excavation to a visitor, the thrill of archaeological discovery, or the satisfaction of recording a site for posterity.

At the same time, integrating heritage management and all its various aspects into a traditional archaeological field school is challenging. It is difficult to survey, excavate, and do labwork every day and still be able to include a full suite of heritage-related activities. But digging less is not necessarily a bad thing; indeed, it is a trend that has been developing for a long time in most parts of the world, where more heritage management and less digging is the general rule.

Another pedagogical challenge, especially working in a foreign country, is how to develop and implement practical field projects in heritage survey, documentation, and management planning that will be authorized by, and of use to, local preservation agencies. Involving students in heritage management projects will be more effective if students realize that the projects will have practical application in the real world. Our two years of survey and testing at the site of the British naval hospital on Isla del Rey, for example, was developed from the start as a heritage management project with the goal of identifying the nature, extent, and sensitivity of archaeological resources on the island. Knowing that the ultimate goal will be an archaeological management plan for the island has made the work there more interesting, and, we believe, more meaningful to our students.

Many, if not most, field schools would be amenable to adding heritage education to their programs; indeed, many already do to one degree or another (for example, Hunter 2008; Mills et al. 2008). Field schools normally include regular lectures in addition to fieldwork, and some of these lectures might cover heritage-related subjects. Fieldtrips to archaeological sites, historic buildings and monuments, and museums are frequently incorporated into field schools to expose students to the diversity of cultural heritage in the area. These traditional elements of field schools offer abundant opportunities for students to engage in thinking about heritage management and the practical challenges of putting our ethical duty of stewardship into action. Like stewardship itself, heritage management is as much a way of thinking about the material remains of the past as it is a set of skills. As we have noted earlier, it is likely that most of the students who participate in field schools will not go on to become professional archaeologists. We believe that the true measure of success for our field school will be that our students, the future stewards of the past, come away thinking that heritage values, preservation, and stewardship are just as integral to the practice of archaeology as using a trowel or a tape measure.

Postscript

In the summer of 2017, after a period of reassessment and retooling, the authors implemented a new version of the field school. The new Boston University Menorca Field School in Archaeological Heritage Management is a five-week field program focusing exclusively on heritage management without the traditional component of archaeological excavation. By dropping the daily excavation component, we have made it possible to devote our full-time efforts to teaching and engaging the students with heritage. We still rely on an interactive pedagogy of lectures, field trips, field surveys for heritage assessments, hands-on heritage projects, discussion, and debate, only now it is all heritage, all the time.

In its first iteration, we divided the five-week program into the following themes: (1) introduction to Menorca's archaeology, cultural heritage, and heritage management; (2) World Heritage and Biosphere; (3) collections management; (4) field survey and mapping for heritage sites (involving fieldwork at an archaeological site, exclusive of excavation); and (5) archaeological site management. We are currently in the process of reviewing and assessing our new, nondigging field school, but our initial reactions as well as student assessments are largely positive; we believe that a specialized field school of this type is perfectly viable and will be useful for many students, both archaeology majors and students in other fields who do not intend to pursue a professional career in field archaeology.

Acknowledgments

We are grateful to all the colleagues who participated in the BU field school over the years, especially Paul Goldberg, James Wiseman, and Norman Hammond. We are also indebted to all our teaching assistants in the field school for their hard work with the project and with training students: Alexander Smith, Marta Ostovich, Kevin Mullen, Ilaria Patania, Jonathan Ruane, Kathryn Ness, Allison Cuneo, Karyn Necciai, and Loren Sparling. We are grateful for support from the Amics de la Isla del Hospital, Consell Insular de Menorca, BU Study Abroad, and the BU Department of Archaeology. We also thank all of the wonderful field school students who participated in the field school and engaged in research with us; they were the reason we were there and it was a pleasure to share our love for the island, its people, and its culture with them. Finally, we thank Phyllis Messenger and Susan Bender for inviting us to contribute this chapter and for their careful editing.

References Cited

Atalay, Sonya
2008   Pedagogy of Decolonization: Advancing Archaeological Practice through Education. In *Collaborating at the Trowel's Edge: Teaching and Learning in Indigenous Archaeology*, edited by Stephen W. Silliman, pp. 123–144. University of Arizona Press, Tucson.

Baxter, Jane Eva
2009   *Archaeological Field Schools: A Guide for Teaching in the Field.* Left Coast Press, Walnut Creek, California.

Bernadini, Wesley
2012   Commentary: Perspectives on Field Schools from the Register of Professional Archaeologists. *SAA Archaeological Record* 12(1): 39–40.

Doelle, William H., and Deborah L. Huntley
2012   Teaching, Research, and So Much More through a Preservation Archaeology Field School. *SAA Archaeological Record* 12(1): 36–38.

Elia, Ricardo J., and Marta Ostovich
2011   Heritage Management. *Oxford Bibliographies Online: Classics*, edited by Dee Clayman. Electronic document, http://oxfordbibliographiesonline.com/view/document/obo9780195389661 /obo9780195389661-0019.xml, accessed May 22, 2015.

Espiau Espiau, Isabel
2010   Preview of the Plan of Action and Uses for the Isla del Rey in the Port of Mahon. *The Hospital on the Island del Rey: The King's Island: Port of Mahon*, 4th ed., p. 287. Amics de l'Illa de l'Hospital, Menorca.

Hunter, Andrea A.

2008   A Critical Change in Pedagogy: Indigenous Cultural Resource Management. In *Collaborating at the Trowel's Edge: Teaching and Learning in Indigenous Archaeology*, edited by Stephen W. Silliman, pp. 165–187. University of Arizona Press, Tucson.

Isbert, Francesc

1993   La taula de Binisafullet. Una interesante restauración. *RdA* 149. Zugarto Ediciones.

Mills, Barbara J., Mark Altaha, John R. Welch, and T. J. Ferguson

2008   Field Schools without Trowels: Teaching Archaeological Ethics and Heritage Preservation in a Collaborative Context. In *Collaborating at the Trowel's Edge: Teaching and Learning in Indigenous Archaeology*, edited by Stephen W. Silliman, pp. 25–49. University of Arizona Press, Tucson.

Mitchell, Myles, David R. Guilfoyle, Ron Doc Reynolds, and Catherine Morgan.

2013   Towards Sustainable Community Heritage Management and the Role of Archaeology: A Case Study from Western Australia. *Heritage and Society* 6(1): 24–45.

Morrison, Bethany A.

2012   More than Digging Square Holes: The New Role of Archaeological Field Schools. *SAA Archaeological Record* 12(1): 23–24.

Mytum, Harold (editor)

2012   *Global Perspectives on Archaeological Field Schools: Constructions of Knowledge and Experience*. Springer, New York.

Pérez-Juez, Amalia

2012   La exposición monográfica "Manurqa." Proyecto didáctico de Boston University sobre la excavación de una estructura andalusí en Torre d'en Galmés. In *IV Jornades d'Arqueologia de les Illes Balears*, pp. 179–186. Vessants, Arqueología i Cultura.

2013   Talayotic Culture. In *Encyclopedia of Ancient History*, edited by Roger S. Bagnall. Wiley-Blackwell, Malden, Massachusetts.

Plantalamor, Lluis, J. M. Gual, and F. Isbert

1990   *Informe preliminar de l'excavació arqueològica al recinte de Taula de Binissafullet (SanLluís)*. Informe sobre la restauració de la Taula de Binissafullet. Ajuntament de Sant Lluís.

Pyburn, K. Anne

2003   What Are We Really Teaching in Archaeological Field Schools? In *Ethical Issues in Archaeology*, edited by Larry J. Zimmerman, Karen D. Vitelli, and Julie Hollowell-Zimmer, pp. 213–223. AltaMira Press, Walnut Creek, California.

Register of Professional Archaeologists (RPA)

2015   *Guidelines and Standards for Archaeological Field Schools*. Electronic document, http://rpanet.org/?FieldschoolGuides, accessed May 22, 2015.

Silliman, Stephen W. (editor)

2008   Collaborative Indigenous Archaeology: Troweling at the Edges, Eyeing the Center. In *Collaborating at the Trowel's Edge: Teaching and Learning in Indigenous*

Archaeology, edited by Stephen W. Silliman, pp. 1–21. University of Arizona Press, Tucson.

Thomas, Ben, and Meredith Anderson Langlitz

2013   Sustainable Site Preservation: The Future of Saving the Past. In *Archaeology and Society in Daily Life: Challenges and Co-operation in the 21st Century*, edited by Ulla Lähdesmäki, SamiRaninen, and Kerkko Nordqvist, pp. 46–53. City of Tampere, Museum Services, Pirkanmaa Provincial Museum, Tampere, Finland.

VanderVeen, James M., and Jeanette Repczynski

2010   The Need for Stewardship Training in Archaeological Field Schools. *SAA Archaeological Record* 10(1): 26–28.

6

Educating Students about the Modern Realities of Exploring the Ancient Middle East

SANDRA SCHAM

To some observers, the attacks of September 11, 2001, exposed more gaps in our knowledge about the Middle East than in our security system. One of the weaknesses immediately perceived by experts was the woeful inadequacy of our education system in informing the younger generation about the Arab and Muslim worlds. The geography and history of the region had already fallen off the radar screen in most middle and high schools in the United States, and the number of young people who could even locate it on a map was a paltry 13 percent in 2002 (National Geographic 2002). (See the discussion of heritage and historical consciousness in White, this volume.) By 2006, that percentage had improved by almost 40 percent, which demonstrates what a little more attention, and a much publicized war, can accomplish (*National Geographic* 2006).

As an anthropologist working in what antiquarians (and the State Department) call the "Near East," I came to realize that our pedagogical approach to Middle Eastern archaeology was as much in need of adjustment as our grasp of its current affairs. Rather than simply examining the cultural history of the Middle East as a succession of mostly forgotten empires that may (or may not) have influenced the modern West, I was determined that my students and I would work toward developing a stronger connection between the events of the past and those of the present. Having lived in the Middle East for a number of years, I knew that collective memory there is the quintessential example of the continuing effects of long-term history. In order to be prepared for the new world disorder, we needed to better understand how the Middle Eastern present was a product not only of postcolonial history but of the much more distant past.

Most of the students who have taken my classes, always electives, do so because they are interested in antiquity, so they are surprised when the first assignment I give them is to read news stories on a biweekly basis to find information related to the cultures and areas we would be studying. Few of them had ever consistently done that before—tending to ignore the hard news in favor of more relatable material. Generally, they had little or no knowledge about the region other than its relationship to terrorism. More recently, the poignant images of refugees made homeless and stateless by extreme violence have only reinforced that connection.

Evolution of Middle East Heritage Pedagogy

In the beginning, my approach was to expand the curriculum to include the ancient and modern heritages of Syria, Turkey, and Iran, as well as those of Mesopotamia, Ancient Egypt, Jordan, Israel, and Palestine. With this much broader geographical focus, the way in which the course had been divided before (into chronological periods from the Neolithic to the Early Byzantine) suddenly seemed both overspecific for the intended audience and undertheorized. I needed an overarching conceptual framework. (Chilton 2019 provides a detailed discussion of heritage approaches.)

The Cultural Heritage of the Middle East, as recognized by its indigenous populations, explored and romanticized by Europe and the United States, and consistently misunderstood—tragically so for both the region itself and the West—effectively replaced the course that was once billed as "Biblical and Ancient Near Eastern Archaeology." I have not been particularly satisfied that the definitions of heritage (even critical heritage) that I have seen in the literature (for example, Harrison 2013; Smith 2006) are a good fit with the goals of my class. So I essentially put forth a "view," rather than a definition, of heritage that is more informed by Edward Said (1978 and 1993) than by heritage theorists. (For a comprehensive definition of heritage in general, see McGill, this volume; see Zimmerman 2019 for a discussion of critical pedagogy of heritage.) While I tell students that cultural heritage, in general, encompasses both the representation and comprehension of the past in the present, I advocate a critical approach that is, perhaps, unique to the challenge of understanding the multilayered history of the Middle East.

The vestiges of the intrusion of the West in the Middle East have influenced all of the interpretations of Middle East heritage that my students are likely to encounter. Thus, critique of the cultural heritage of the region, as it is characterized in most of the literature, cannot lead to absolute rejection of "the fruit of the poisonous tree" of orientalism and colonialism. To do so would leave us with very little to study. The goal of discussing the contribution of the various "isms" that have made the region what it is today is to recognize their influence for what it is. Many Orientalists were more appreciators than appropriators although their rapturous infatuation with the East may strike modern scholars as having insidious purposes (Scham 2009). Others in the Orientalist tradition (for example, Lewis 1990 and 2002) have more to answer for in contributing to current tragic events in the region.

My main goal has been to introduce, as soon as practicable, awareness of current events into my archaeological curriculum. It was not until I began to develop the syllabi for two interdisciplinary courses that overtly incorporated politics that I thought about "piloting" an entirely a new kind of Middle East Archaeology curriculum. Because the majority of my students would not train as archaeologists, it also occurred to me that many of them might never take another anthropology course as well.

From this I have extrapolated an "idea of heritage" that emphasizes the discursive relationship between various communities, the way that they represent their pasts and the way that it is represented by others. The eugenicist theories of nineteenth- and early twentieth-century European explorers, orientalism and its effects, postcolonial and neonationalist reactions to imperialism, and religious ideology have all affected these representations. Accordingly, the design of these courses incorporates certain themes specific to Middle East heritage discourse, such as the contested Iron Age (in Israel and Palestine); a critique of Mesopotamia as the cradle of civilization and Egyptomania; museums and cultural appropriation; the historic and recurring marginalization of certain ethnic and religious groups; and, of course, tourism, international development, and public diplomacy.

Emerging from this is the ultimate goal of the course—to shift the focus of the course from archaeological sites to local, and sometimes national, communities—tacking back and forth between the two as necessary. All of this is meant to lead students toward a recognition of how much they have been persuaded by what Smith refers to as "the authorized heritage discourse" (Smith 2006: 10), to understand that cultural heritage is one construct that very often supports another (identity) and that Western archaeology can sometimes be at cross purposes with that identity construction. While this kind of analysis has been done for years by archaeologists working in other regions, it is still (embarrassingly) novel in the Middle East, a place where one might argue it is most needed (Bernbeck and Pollock 2005).

In this way, my classes have become a journey into heritage from the point of view of its primary agents—constructors of "history" (that is, victorious imperialists), subalterns (the colonized), and insurgents (when "the subaltern speaks") (Morton 2007; Spivak 1988). The point of this shift is not only to demonstrate how people who use a particular discourse see the world, but also how discourses may "represent possible worlds which are different from the actual world . . . tied in to projects to change the world in particular directions" (Fairclough 2003: 124). The emphasis on agency is intended to counter the rigid categorization of Ancient Near Eastern and Modern Middle Eastern culture into sequential power struggles with varying degrees of success based upon whether or not the West remembers them.

Even though the Ancient Near East has been the subject of the world's first systematic archaeological explorations, it has also been the object of the world's most flagrant attempts to shape the past to serve the needs of the present. Smith envisions heritage as a performance (2006) that can either bolster or undermine the "authorized heritage discourse." Looking at the performance of heritage, "there is fertile ground for considering how far performance in the mundane can extend and leak into and across other values, relations, and significations through which individuals may act, feel, think and adjust" (Crouch 2003: 1958–9).

This description of the performative characteristics of heritage is intriguingly close to the theatrical notion of subtext—as drama majors in my class have pointed out. Along with the props (material culture), the scenery (the landscape), and the texts, it is actors (agents) who bring out the much-needed subtext—the "aspect of the uncontrolled" (Scham 2010: 450) that is most likely to engross the audience.

The Classroom Experience

The notion that heritage was about either conservation technologies or resource management "was never true," Logan asserts (2012: 241). In calling for a human rights centric view of heritage, he further exhorts heritage professionals to explore and challenge the politics of heritage and, in particular, teachers of heritage to consistently "reconsider what new knowledge and skills are needed" (Logan 2012: 241) in order for students to understand the implications of heritage for modern populations.

I decided that a consistent framework was needed to introduce students to a culture that most of them were unfamiliar with. I discovered that framework in literature on competence-based curriculum development (Barman and Konwar 2011; Kouwenhoven 2009; Ocampo and Delgado 2014). Using a modified competence-based approach, I did not begin by preparing a course syllabus outlining content and readings. Rather, I identified competencies and then selected content, readings, and assignments to support student attainment of those competencies. The objectives for the first classes I taught using this approach were for the student to attain a beginner-level grasp of: (1) cultural competence for advocating on behalf of and protecting the cultural heritage of the Middle East; (2) reflexive competence for isolating and confronting personal biases about the Middle East; and (3) narrative competence for grasping at least some elements of the dynamics of the past in the Middle East. (See Lerner and Effland, this volume, detailing a similar approach.)

Most instructors in the cultural heritage field will immediately recognize the barriers to conducting such a course. Finding a textbook for these classes that could add to our discussions was, and continues to be, a particular challenge. There are many books that adopt the time period–centric model, concentrate mainly on biblical archaeology, reconstruct engaging stories, or comprehensively cover archaeological or historical details, but these were not relevant to my particular emphasis. Books on the ancient world that reference the heritage of the entire region or the agents of the Middle Eastern past, beyond kings and emperors, are rare. Notable exceptions are two books that I have had occasion to use—Harmansah's (2013) examination of the physical shaping of culture and memory through urban spaces in Middle Eastern antiquity, and an edited volume (Steadman and Ross 2010) on agency and identity in the Ancient Near East.

Another challenge was formulating appropriate assignments and examinations for an "applied heritage" course on the Middle East, considering that most students had never been to the region. I assigned several tasks in addition to the readings and class participation to overcome this difficulty.

These assignments included two critical response papers on any two of the required articles and book chapters that incorporated students' own experiences as well as outside sources, and take-home midterm and final examinations that consisted of a combination of fieldwork assignments (looking for symbolic elements of Middle Eastern culture in public buildings and cemeteries and conducting interviews with tour guides) and questions about media coverage of the Middle East and its relationship to the Ancient Near East.

Cultural Competence

The remit to advocate for and preserve culture is one singular aspect of cultural competence (that is, the ability to interact with people from other cultures [Moule 2012]) that is important to archaeologists, and achieving this goal requires a deeper knowledge of the communities in which we work. While the classroom is not the ideal venue to demonstrate this competence, it is still possible to provide students with face-to-face encounters with material culture, and with other class members, to approximate the kinds of cultural challenges that archaeologists encounter in bridging the past and present.

In the first weeks of class, I introduce students to basic methods for analyzing material culture, including descriptive analysis, functional analysis, ethnographic analogy, and, most importantly, "reading" artifacts in order to convince them that one really can mine potsherds and stone tools for cultural information. This approach encourages students to think about connecting the concrete evidence of archaeological work with the hypothetical world of archaeological interpretation. Generally, after an introductory lecture on the physical analysis of artifacts, I give students free rein to form conjectures within randomly selected groups about the societies that produced these artifacts (pottery and stone tools) before plunging into the study of what we know about them from archaeological publications and what our knowledge of them means to modern populations.

First, we contemplate the story these artifacts could tell about the society that produced them. These connections also need to be couched in terms that do not call up the Orientalist fantasy of the "timeless and unchanging" Middle East. When reading the artifacts of pastoralist cultures, for example, we talk about how they evidence that particular subsistence economy. From stone tools identified with animal husbandry and a variety of "ad hoc" tools associated with nomadism, we use ancient sources on how humans and animals on the move have been a challenge to sedentary populations. We look at the way early towns in the Middle East began to be structured to exclusively serve the needs of farmers, sometimes to the exclusion of pastoralists. Because our goal is to comprehend the relationship between the past and the present in the Middle East and how our views of the region have been shaped by cultural assumptions, references to modern media continue throughout the course.

Another exercise centers on a discussion of statements from political and religious leaders that reference ancient history. The students are not made aware of who was responsible for these statements until they have analyzed them in accordance with several specific questions about their culture, politics, and religion. Most of the discussion groups come up with surprisingly accurate answers to these questions with the telling exception of those who have to analyze speeches by American diplomats. Following this, we discuss the field of Western professional foreign affairs and its maxim that one must avoid imparting personal information in diplomatic discourse. The contrast this presents to ancient Middle Eastern diplomacy, as best evidenced in the Amarna Letters (Sofer 2013), was a follow-up discussion to this exercise.

These discussions and exercises are useful in giving students tools (primarily based in discourse analysis) to enable them to approach Middle Eastern heritage not just on the concrete material level, as most archaeologists and tourists do, but on a deeper basis. As culturally competent practitioners, my students, whether they go on to study the archaeology of the Middle East or not, should become more critical of the "received wisdom" about the region and the sources of that knowledge. Of course, cultural competence involves more than critique, but thinking about the cultures of the region on a more personal level than they had theretofore done is an important first step.

Reflexive Competence

In initial classes concentrating on the material culture, we used artifacts to reflect upon what the physical evidence in students' own "residential complexes," both permanent and temporary, would say about their lifeworld (Habermas 1987), a term I introduce and explain in the initial classes. Later, more complex exercises encourage students to reflect on their biases and the extent to which such biases could be brought into the open. I also introduce various methods used by social scientists to "surreptitiously" determine real attitudes.

If a class is large enough, I have used, as one example of these methods, a modified "list experiment." Two groups are selected "at random" from the class. Both groups are given a list of nonsensitive items and asked how many they liked. These items include mostly normal activities. In addition, several "slightly sensitive" items are added to the list for one group only. The items included on the list are first generated by asking each student before engaging in the list experiment to write down on a slip of paper a fairly innocuous activity that they wouldn't really want to admit to doing if they were given a direct survey. For example, if they were asked on a survey how much time they spent streaming movies, how much they exercised, or how much junk food (or beer) they consumed, they might say one thing while knowing that their answer would represent what their ideal behavior should be rather than what their actual behavior was. The higher the proportion of respondents in that group who added any of these items to their list of likes, as determined by the mean differences between the control and experiment groups in number of items liked, the more positive their attitude toward that item was assumed to be (Arce et al. 2011).

To some extent, this exercise is reminiscent of the famous Tucson Garbage Project (Rathje 1992), except that it doesn't involve fieldwork. It is less revealing (and embarrassing considering the size of the group) than similar experiments conducted by researchers to determine racial or ethnic bias, which we discuss as a follow-up. The list experiment has been called a "statistical truth serum" and has even been used in the heritage field to evaluate the extent to which minorities in a population believe that their cultural heritage is respected both within and outside of their communities (USAID 2013). If the results of the exercise are communicated to the class (without of course identifying individual respondents), the two groups can interact on and discuss the question of how difficult it is for individuals to openly acknowledge behaviors and attitudes that may not be socially sanctioned.

In subsequent exercises, we explore the very complicated issue of "ethnicity" in the past by examining how ethnicities are evidenced in the present. Many students' ethnicities were complex and some had difficulty identifying the "artifacts" that could be found in their homes that could be used as a means to interpret their lives. Since ethnicity is a concept that anthropological archaeologists are not always comfortable with (Jones 1997), this result is interesting to note. In the subsequent discussion, students are positioned to understand the artificiality of this construct as well as its uses. While most students felt that their own multiple identities were beneficial to American society, the question of how we assimilate Middle Eastern populations today seemed very much dependent upon students' preconceived notions about the "flexibility" of Muslim cultures to adapt to modern life and their belief that these societies are rooted in the past.

Narrative Competence

Narrative is a much-discussed but ill-defined concept that has found its way into the parlance of government officials and the military as well as historians and archaeologists. As a historical concept, narrative lends itself generally to more traditional teaching methods, emphasizing chronological order, but it also raises the intriguing notion of looking at alternative narratives on the same event. Accordingly, we examined different accounts of the looting of the Baghdad Museum—one from an American archaeologist and one from an Iraqi archaeologist—and compared them in terms of their assumptions about the ties that Iraqis have with their ancient history.

I also ask students to provide their views on their own personal relationship with the Middle Eastern past by sorting, in order of their agreement, phrases about their attitudes toward several important subjects that have obsessed archaeologists for decades, including the Biblical Flood, the Exodus from Egypt, the monarchies of David and Solomon, the Islamic Conquest, and the Crusades. This exercise is based upon "Q methodology," a quantitative-qualitative technique for studying subjectivity by first eliciting a series of statements on a topic from students, reducing them to short phrases, and then providing them with a grid that enables the prioritization of those statements by number based upon their level of agreement or disagreement with them (Van Exel and de Graaf 2005).

Rather than simply examining this topic through unstructured discussion, I applied the principles of other social science methodologies to assess students' receptivity to messages about the Middle East in the past and the present. As a prelude to an in-class abbreviated integrative complexity exercise, we performed conflict-style assessments both before and after the demonstration of this approach, which is designed to measure individual abilities to think and reason about narratives outside of their own reference groups (Liht and Savage 2013).

We also discussed how individuals interact with and influence social networks. Social Network Analysis (SNA) has, interestingly, become a method of choice for counterterrorism analysts and archaeologists alike (see, for example, Knappet 2013) because it is useful in assessing the influence of narratives on individuals within a group and how those narratives become persuasive. I gave students an opportunity to select a certain topic among a list that contained items such as "the Exodus narrative," "the use of the Bible in archaeology," and "the relationship between the Ancient Near East and the modern Middle East," among others. They discussed their topic with three other members of the class and later analyzed their in-class "social networks" based upon demonstrated interactions (Perliger and Pedahzur 2010).

Students are then asked to determine which individual they would turn to for further information on the topic of the three that they spoke with. Because of the limited number of students (although this could not work with fewer than twenty), there were overlaps, as intended, and surprisingly there was a trend that could be discerned by both the frequency of the topic selected and the choice of individual in the class who had the most information about it. For example, at Catholic University, biblical topics were of greater interest, and the seminarians in the class received the most mentions as influential persons. At the University of Maryland, anthropology and history students (both male and female) tended to be singled out as being knowledgeable about the Modern Middle East but, because the university has a sizable Jewish population, the Exodus narrative was equally popular as a topic. The relationship between SNA and narratives hinges on the question of *who* an individual turns to for advice, the *characteristics* of that individual, and *which* of the narratives presented as topics was most discussed.

I asked my students to bring in samples of websites referencing the archaeology of the Middle East, critique them in groups, and determine what narratives these sites were intended to support or refute and how well they accomplished their agendas. The exercise was designed to enable students to think about the goals or agendas of the authors, what qualifications such authors had, whether they presented the information as objective and what the students thought about that objectivity, and, finally, whether the website provided useful information from the student's point of view.

Because this was an archaeology and heritage class, it was relevant for students to examine the historical narratives that inform modern extremist behavior in the Middle East and how leaders of major movements that Western governments have classified as "terrorist" often make use of these narratives. We discussed, for example, the Kurdish view that they are direct descendants of the ancient Medes and the tribal insurrections in Yemen that reflect the seventh-century rivalries among Christians, Jews, and the newly formed Islamic Caliphate (Scham 2018).

Class Requirements and Evaluation

My preliminary evaluation of the students' work was, like those of most educators, based upon their papers, presentations, and examinations. It was difficult to determine from most presentations the extent to which students had achieved competence objectives. A very few students in my classes have found the approach taken uncomfortably challenging to their beliefs. For example, one student who thought that the Bible was the most authentic source for the people and events of the Ancient Past in the Middle East was reluctant to examine that text in the light of archaeological discoveries and new interpretations. A few other students who expressed stronger affirmative views about the validity of their own perspectives in the initial exercises were more antagonistic than confused. An example of the latter was a student who chose to give his end-of-class presentation on Jerusalem as the "eternal and undivided capital of Israel" and who walked out of the class during our discussion of Islamophobia.

For formal evaluation of student views, I used three fairly standard methods—observations about the discussions both by other students and by me, a mid-course formative assessment soliciting anonymous student views on the direction of the class, and a final survey via SurveyMonkey. At the end of each course, I added several questions to the student evaluations required by the universities and the departments, and conducted my own survey relating to each of the core competencies as a follow-up online. The class sizes were small and the numbers of students who responded to the survey even smaller. Therefore, none of these methods yielded enough evidence to provide anything more than a preliminary notion of whether or not the pedagogy was meaningful or relevant.

Most students answered questions concerning the potential for the course and similar ones to expand their cultural competence affirmatively. One student who responded to the "why?" question on the cultural competence framework for the course seems to have had a fairly good idea of this course objective. He stated that comprehending "both how History does and (perhaps more importantly) does not relate to the current geopolitical situation" was a valuable insight. Other students referred to the importance of increasing respect and knowledge concerning the cultures of the Middle East.

The extent to which the students understood the course as an "alternative" to traditional chronological approaches, however, was another matter. While most students (over 60 percent) agreed that they found the teaching approach instructive, an even larger majority answered "yes" to the leading (and, admittedly, not well phrased) question on the survey, "Do you believe that traditional historical approaches to teaching about the cultural heritage of the Middle East, such as examining the characteristics of successive empires, are relevant to the region today?" This certainly implies that at least that particular critique of the field was lost on them.

Asking students directly on a survey whether or not a class changed their personal perspective (reflexivity) is difficult but, in terms of recognizing the effects that biases have on interpretations of the past, most students indicated that they were aware that these sometimes matter more in the Middle East than elsewhere. One of them noted that "ancient history is constantly subject to political/social appropriation to further the agenda of relevant parties." Another stated, in answer to the question, "Do you believe the course is relevant to your understanding of the Middle East?," that this approach was a good one for "raising awareness and opening the mind." Most students who responded to the survey replied that the course had increased their understanding, and one of them noted that being "able to incorporate their own interests into the course work" made the course more valuable to them.

I hoped that, even though the course approach was different, students would still come away from the class with a better idea of the Middle East, both ancient and modern. I also expected that they would find the nonsequential presentation of the archaeological material an issue. As it turned out, few objected to this approach and most indicated that explorations of a multivocal past were enlightening.

In at least one case, a student was disappointed that the course did not cover "more contemporary issues in the Middle East that are connected to heritage and archaeology, as opposed to the earlier material about the Bronze Age, Iron Age, biblical stuff, etc.," which surprised me as I thought that we had focused too much on the present. One student found the course a useful supplement to another that dealt with the Modern Middle East going back to the eighth century A.D. The student wrote that "the combination of the two [courses] was critical and in my opinion essential." Overall, the evaluations, flawed as they were, did confirm that students accepted the relevance of the archaeology of the Ancient Near East to the modern Middle East.

Conclusion

Archaeologists in the Middle East have now come to accept that artifacts and sites belong to the countries they were discovered in, but we need to go further. We need to include nonpractitioners in our discourse and make it relevant to achieving a greater understanding of the region today. Can enhanced insights into how the past affects the present provide students with any useful grounding in the world in which they are expected to function? My students, for the most part, have *not* been in the archaeology field. Therefore, the question of whether this approach is just an attempt to introduce trendy relevance into the rather hidebound field of Near Eastern Archaeology is a valid one.

Many of the exercises and classroom activities described above may seem to be a rather complicated way to teach the archaeology of the Middle East. Once I had made the decision to introduce critical heritage into the classroom, however, I recognized the necessity to also introduce applied social science techniques beyond a simple analysis of material culture or even the fieldwork assignments. The logistical challenges of conducting a course like this were considerable. Absences in small classes created issues depending upon the number of people needed to accomplish each activity and could limit discussion in groups. A number of students found the required assignments unusual and needed fairly detailed explanations.

Despite all of these problems and concerns, it seems that students, for the most part, came away from the class with what I thought was the required information—whether or not they agreed that this knowledge was, in fact, needed or even applicable to their lives is another matter. My ideal scenario was that at least some of them would elect to continue to study *both* heritage and archaeology and others would go into professions that required cultural, reflexive, and narrative competence on Middle Eastern affairs—a group that should encompass anyone who contemplates working in the Middle East or with people of Middle Eastern origin. Of course, I hear from certain students periodically and have discovered that this scenario has been realized to an extent.

Outside of professional goals, another important effect I hoped the class would help to achieve has to do with the nature of our system of government. More than a few political surveys have indicated that Americans vote based on domestic issues (Pew Research Center 2015) and, because of this, foreign policy debates such as international trade agreements, treaties with Iran, the Wars in Iraq and Afghanistan, the Arab Revolutions, and the Civil War in Syria only influence the process at the highest level. Therefore, the more we can educate our future citizens about the Middle East past, present, and future, the better prepared they will be to act on the policies that are being carried out in their names in this part of the world.

Beyond discussions of terrorism, civil war, and eternal conflict, beyond even the dreams of the return of the Caliphate or the claim of rights to land based on history that is over two millennia old, perceiving the Middle East on a deeper level could even serve to enable students to become citizens of the world (Nussbaum 2007)—once, arguably, the goal of higher education in this country.

References Cited

Arce, Daniel, Rachel Croson, and Catherine Eckel
2011   Terrorism Experiments. *Journal of Peace Research* 48(3): 373–382.
Barman, Arup, and Jothika Konwar
2011   Competence Based Curriculum in Higher Education: A Necessity Grounded by Globalization (English version). *Journal for Multidimensional Education* 03/2011; 6(April): 7–15.
Bernbeck, Reinhard, and Susan Pollock
2005   Introduction. In *Archaeologies of the Middle East: Critical Perspectives,* edited by Reinhard Bernbeck and Susan Pollock, pp. 1–10. Blackwell, Oxford, UK.

Chilton, Elizabeth

2019   The Heritage of Heritage: Defining the Role of the Past in Contemporary So-
        cieties. In *History and Approaches to Heritage Studies*, edited by Phyllis Mauch
        Messenger and Susan J. Bender, pp. 24–31. University Press of Florida, Gaines-
        ville.

Crouch, David

2003   Space, Performing, and Becoming: Tangles in the Mundane, *Environment and
        Planning* 35: 1945–1960.

Fairclough, Norman

2003   *Analysing Discourse: Textual Analysis for Social Research*. Routledge, London.

Habermas, Jurgen

1987   *Lifeworld and System: A Critique of Functionalist Reason*. Beacon Press, Boston,
        Massachusetts.

Harrison, Rodney

2013   *Heritage: Critical Approaches*. Routledge, London.

Harmansah, Omur

2013   *Cities and the Shaping of Memory in the Ancient Near East*. Cambridge Univer-
        sity Press, Cambridge, UK.

Jones, Sian

1997   *The Archaeology of Ethnicity: Constructing Identities in the Past and Present*.
        Routledge, New York.

Knappett, Carl (editor)

2013   *Network Analysis in Archaeology: New Approaches to Regional Interaction*. Ox-
        ford University Press, New York.

Kouwenhoven, Wim

2009   Competence-based Curriculum Development in Higher Education: A Glo-
        balised Concept? In *Technology Education and Development*, edited by Alek-
        sandar Lazinica and Carlos Calafate. Electronic document, http://www.
        intechopen.com/books/technology-education-and-development/competence-
        based-curriculum-development-in-higher-education-a-globalised-concept, ac-
        cessed 10/21/16.

Lewis, Bernard

1990   The Roots of Muslim Rage. *Atlantic* 266/3: 47.

2002   *What Went Wrong? Western Impact and Middle Eastern Response*. Oxford Uni-
        versity Press, Oxford.

Liht, Jose, and Sara Savage

2013   Preventing Violent Extremism through Value Complexity: Being Muslim Being
        British. *Journal of Strategic Security* 6: 44–66.

Logan, William

2012   Cultural Diversity, Cultural Heritage and Human Rights: Towards Heritage
        Management as Human Rights-based Cultural Practice. *International Journal of
        Heritage Studies* 18(3): 231–244.

Morton, Stephen

2007   *Gayatri Spivak: Ethics, Subalternity and the Critique of Postcolonial Reason*.
        Wiley-Blackwell, Oxford.

Moule, Jean

2012   *Cultural Competence: A Primer for Educators.* Wadsworth/Cengage, Belmont, California.

National Geographic

2002   *Roper Geographic Literacy Survey.* Electronic document, http://www.national-geographic.com/geosurvey2002/download/RoperSurvey.pdf, accessed 10/21/16.

2006   *Geographic Literacy Survey/Roper.* Electronic document, http://www.nation-algeographic.com/roper2006/pdf/FINALReport2006GeogLitsurvey.pdf, accessed 10/21/16.

Nussbaum, Martha

2007   Cultivating Humanity and World Citizenship. *Forum for the Future of Higher Education.* Cambridge, Massachusetts.

Ocampo, Mercedes, and Pauline Delgado

2014   Basic Education and Cultural Heritage: Prospects and Challenges. *International Journal of Humanities and Social Science* 4/9: 201–209.

Perliger, Arie, and Ami Pedahzur

2010   Social Network Analysis in the Study of Terrorism and Political Violence. Political Networks *Working Papers, 48.* http://opensiuc.lib.siu.edu/pn_wp/48, accessed March 4, 2018.

Pew Research Center

2015   *State of the Union 2015: How Americans See the Nation, Their Leaders and the Issues.* Electronic document, http://www.pewresearch.org/fact-tank/2015/01/20/state-of-the-union-2015/, accessed 10/21/16.

Rathje, William

1992   *Rubbish! The Archaeology of Garbage.* HarperCollins, New York.

Said, Edward

1978   *Orientalism.* Pantheon Books, New York.

1993   *Culture and Imperialism.* Vintage Books, New York.

Scham, Sandra

2009   "Time's Wheel Runs Back." Conversations with the Middle Eastern Past. In *Cosmopolitan Archaeologies,* edited by Lynn Meskell, pp. 166–183. Duke University Press, Durham, North Carolina.

2010   Colonialism, Conflict and Connectivity: Public Archaeology's Message in a Bottle. In *Handbook of Postcolonial Archaeology,* edited by Jane Lydon and Uzma Rizvi, pp. 459–470. Routledge, London.

2018   *Extremism, Ancient and Modern: Insurgency, Terror and Empire in the Middle East.* Routledge/Taylor and Francis, London.

Smith, Laurajane

2006   *The Uses of Heritage.* Routledge, New York.

Sofer, Sasson

2013   *The Courtiers of Civilization: A Study of Diplomacy.* SUNY Press, Albany, New York.

Spivak, Gayatri

1988   Can the Subaltern Speak? In *Marxism and the Interpretation of Culture,* edited by C. Nelson and L. Grossberg, pp. 271–313. University of Illinois Press, Urbana.

Steadman, Sharon, and Jennifer Ross

2010   *Agency and Identity in the Ancient Near East: New Paths Forward.* Equinox Press, London.

van Exel, Job, and Gjalt de Graaf

2005   *Q Methodology: A Sneak Preview.* Available from www.jobvanexel.nl.

USAID (United States Agency for International Development)

2013   *Evaluation of USAID's Afro-Colombian and Indigenous Program.* Washington, D.C.

Zimmerman, Larry J.

2019   Help Needed! Reflections on a Critical Pedagogy of Heritage. In *History and Approaches to Heritage Studies,* edited by Phyllis Mauch Messenger and Susan J. Bender, pp. 215–236. University Press of Florida, Gainesville.

7

Do the Homeless Have Heritage?

Archaeology and the Pedagogy of Discomfort

ELIZABETH KRYDER-REID

In the fall of 2011, eleven students enrolled in "Issues in Cultural Heritage," a combined undergraduate and graduate class cross-listed in anthropology and museum studies, and team-taught by the author and Dr. Larry J. Zimmerman. While developing the class for this first-time offering at IUPUI,[1] an urban university in central Indiana, we recognized that the challenge was less how to present the information about cultural heritage management, and more how to engage students in meaningful ways. Specifically, how could we help students move from the idea that heritage is a discrete set of objects and buildings to an understanding of heritage as a political act inextricable from the power dynamics of "nationalism, imperialism, colonialism, cultural elitism, Western triumphalism, social exclusion based on class and ethnicity, and the fetishising of expert knowledge" (ACHS 2012)? How could we help them grapple with complex ideas such as the value and stewardship of heritage resources, the uses of the past, and the inequalities of access and representation so often implicated in heritage management (Baird 2013; Byrne 2014; González-Ruibal and Hall 2015; Herwitz 2012; Little and Shackel 2014; Soderland 2010). And, equally significantly, what experiences could we design so that students who come from a range of majors and diverse backgrounds could both apply these ideas to real world settings and be provoked to challenge their own assumptions, stereotypes, and worldviews? How might they make connections between heritage and social justice issues (Baird 2014; Ševčenko 2011)? In short, how could we design a pedagogy of heritage that taught not only skills and knowledge, but had the potential to change attitudes and behaviors as well?

Our teaching philosophy is embedded in critical pedagogy (Freire 1970) and, more particularly, in critical literacy. The goals of the pedagogical approaches to critical literacy are to investigate and raise students' consciousness about the inequalities that exist across society (Mulcahy 2008: 18). Our teaching practice is also predicated on experiential, problem-based, collaborative learning, so we knew there had to be an applied project. Ideally it would be one that gave students opportunities to work with community partners and engage with issues relevant to those communities. The solution we came up with was to involve the students in Zimmerman's long-standing research project on the archaeology of homelessness and to pose the basic question, "Do the homeless have heritage?"

Context

The curricular and research context of the course is significant for understanding how the course's goals are part of a broader project to train self-reflective practitioners committed to community engagement. Our anthropology department is an applied anthropology program, and our museum studies program is similarly committed to civically engaged teaching and public scholarship (Holzman et al. 2014; Labode et al. 2013). Not coincidentally, our urban university includes civic engagement as one of the three main platforms of our mission, and the culture of teaching and learning on campus embraces community engagement. Specifically, we are in the IU School of Liberal Arts in Indianapolis, part of the partnership known as IUPUI, and our leadership values community collaboration, applied or "translational" research, and public scholarship as faculty practices across both teaching and research (Wood et al. 2016). Our faculty regularly incorporate community-based projects in their courses, and they employ critical pedagogy in various ways to help students, as Henry Giroux (2010) has put it, "develop consciousness of freedom, recognize authoritarian tendencies, and connect knowledge to power and the ability to take constructive action." For example, our colleague Susan Hyatt has developed a number of projects within her urban anthropology and ethnographic methods courses including the "Neighborhood of Saturdays." This project, which has been documented through a digital humanities collection and a community-published book, was a collaboration of the Department of Anthropology at IUPUI along with a number of community-based organizations to reconstruct a diverse neighborhood on Indianapolis' Southside (Hyatt et al. 2013;

Neighborhood of Saturdays 2010). Using archival research and oral histories, students documented the experiences of African Americans and Sephardic communities from the 1920s up to the 1960s when many of the Jewish residents migrated north and the remaining residents were subsequently dislocated by highway construction. Another colleague, Paul Mullins, has a long-standing community archaeology project investigating the intersections of race, racism, and consumer culture in Indianapolis' near Westside, the neighborhood largely displaced by the construction of the campus in the late 1960s and early 1970s (Mullins, 2003, 2006, 2008; Mullins and Jones 2011; Mullins et al. 2011). The faculty have also been involved in national projects with similar critical literacy and community engagement goals. For example, Modupe Labode, Laura Holzman, and I have been part of both the Guantanamo Public Memory and the States of Incarceration projects, wherein students in universities across the United States worked collaboratively to develop digital humanities projects and a traveling exhibit to engage diverse communities in dialogue about these topics (Guantanamo Public Memory Project 2009; Humanities Action Lab's Global Dialogues on Incarceration 2016). Significantly, many of these projects invest heavily in public-facing products, both digital (blogs such as Mullins and Hyatt's [2016] "Invisible Indianapolis" project), and "tangible" (such as exhibits, walking tours, community forums, and public presentations).

Within this context of critical, engaged research and teaching, we recognized that Zimmerman's archaeology of homelessness project offered both a robust body of scholarship and an opportunity for students to connect with the issues of heritage intellectually and emotionally. Zimmerman's investigation of the archaeology of homelessness started with his work in Minneapolis (Zimmerman 2004). Beginning in 2005, he developed a collaborative research project focused on downtown Indianapolis, a city of 853,173 and the fourteenth-largest metropolitan area in the United States. Using a mixed-methods research design of site mapping, material culture inventories and surface mapping, and ethnography, the project has produced cogent results (compare Pluckhahn, this volume). Zimmerman and his students Jessica Welch and Courtney Singleton have identified and inventoried different types of sites, including routes, short-term sites, and camp sites. They have similarly classified and inventoried types of shelters. Finally, their analysis has produced interpretations of material patterns including site formation, subsistence, and caching, as well as evidence of gender and ethnicity (Zimmerman and Welch 2011; Zimmerman et al. 2010).

The archaeology of homelessness project had the potential, we hoped, to challenge students to think critically about what heritage means and explore its connections with identity, politics, and structural inequalities. It also allowed students to compare public memory practices familiar in dominant culture heritage with the marginalized, displaced, and often invisible heritage of those living homeless. It provided a chance as well "to understand the . . . root causes, social context, ideology, and personal consequences" (Shor 1992: 129) of homelessness and the myriad issues it raises, including civil and human rights and ideas about public space and personal property in the United States. As Paul Shackel argues, "An educator's responsibility is about critical education, engaged citizenship, and social responsibility" (Shackel 2019). The project's activist goals seemed well suited for realizing higher education's goals to instill in students the notion that they are not only a part of their community, but that they could play a role in creating a more just society (Giroux 2007: 5; Little and Shackel 2014: 102). Finally, the archaeology of homelessness project presented an opportunity for students to confront, on a personal and emotional level, their own attitudes, stereotypes, and beliefs about people living homeless. In education theory, this kind of "pedagogy of discomfort" places a central focus on "how emotions define how and what one chooses to see, and conversely, not to see" (Boler 1999: 2). Specifically, if educators seek to disrupt oppression, students must step outside their comfort zones to acknowledge and question how one's privilege implicates one in the oppression of others (Ivits 2009: ii). The potential of the project was, therefore, the possibility of expanding students' perspectives on the uses of cultural heritage, on a marginalized population, and on their own positions of privilege.

Issues in Cultural Heritage Seminar

In the "Issues in Cultural Heritage" seminar students learned about the structures, laws, ethics, and current issues of cultural heritage through readings, discussions, and lectures. They simultaneously worked in three small teams throughout the semester on the archaeology of homelessness project. Each student team was tasked with producing a public humanities project. One team wrote a self-published book (Figure 7.1) and created a

Figure 7.1. Students and members of the homeless community examining the student-curated exhibit, "What does homelessness look like? It depends on who is looking," at the Indianapolis Central Library, December 6, 2011. Photograph used with permission of Museum Studies Program, Indiana University–Purdue University–Indianapolis.

Facebook group page. A second team curated an exhibit at the Indianapolis Central Library (Figure 7.2), and a third team curated an exhibit in the IU School of Liberal Arts building, Cavanaugh Hall, on the IUPUI campus. All of the students helped organize and promote a public forum held at the downtown library branch in conjunction with the exhibit (Zimmerman 2011). After the public forum the whole class, along with the presenters and faculty, went out to dinner with guests from the homeless community. In addition to readings and lectures on homelessness by the instructors and by guest speakers, the students had the opportunity to visit the project site and talk with the members of the homeless community. They participated in a portion of the research project in which the homeless were given disposable cameras to record their routes and activities throughout a day. Furthermore, the students were required to complete several assignments designed to provoke self-reflection. It should also be noted that students had a great deal more support than is typical for a class this size. In addition to two full-time faculty teaching the class, the eleven students were supported by a graduate service learning assistant funded by a grant from the university's

Figure 7.2. Cover of *Urban Heritage? Archaeology & Homelessness in Indianapolis*. Used with permission of Museum Studies Program, Indiana University–Purdue University–Indianapolis.

Center for Service and Learning, and the Library Exhibit team was assisted by a museum studies student with graphic design skills. The students were also able to communicate with Courtney Singleton, a Columbia PhD candidate doing her dissertation with the project, who shared her research files. And, finally, the museum studies program paid for the exhibit printing and fabrication costs while Dr. Zimmerman allocated research funds to support the forum, including Rachael Kiddey's keynote presentation.

Student Learning Outcomes

IUPUI requires that all undergraduate courses fulfill one or more of the Principles of Undergraduate Learning, and this class was identified as fulfilling the outcome of "Understanding society and culture" demonstrated by the student's ability to:

1. Compare and contrast the range of diversity and universality in human history, societies, and ways of life;
2. Analyze and understand the interconnectedness of global and local communities; and
3. Operate with civility in a complex world.

On a more particular level, explicit learning objectives listed on the assignment guidelines emphasized skills development and the application of concepts and theories. For example, the objective of a discussion of 9/11 memorial sites and commemorative practices after watching portions of the film "Objects and Memory" was "to recognize master narratives, and the significance of counter-narratives, telling different stories" (Fein and Danitz 2008). The explicit learning objectives for the team projects were that students would increase research, exhibit development and collaboration skills, demonstrate the application of theories of cultural heritage, and demonstrate critical self-reflection on the roles of heritage professionals in the stewardship and interpretation of cultural heritage. Implicitly our goals were more ambitious. We wanted students to challenge their own assumptions and think critically about their worldview. We wanted them to investigate their own participation in systems of privilege and power and to develop empathy with marginalized populations.

Student learning was assessed in a number of ways. The skills development and application of theory and knowledge was most evident in the final presentations and projects that were graded by the instructors in the course. Their work in collaborative teams was assessed through self- and peer evaluations. For the subtler outcomes of changing paradigms, we had more indirect measures. We had the students map the stakeholders of the heritage of the homeless community at three points during the project. In addition to identifying the stakeholders, we asked them to articulate each constituency's particular interests or concerns. During the course of the semester, the students' lists became longer and they were more detailed in identifying the concerns, suggesting an increasing awareness of the complexity and range of stakeholders with interests in the city's homeless. We also asked students to reflect on their experiences in the class in assigned essays and on the end-of-semester course evaluations. While the small sample size relegates our findings to anecdotal evidence, the students' essays suggest that our more rudimentary learning objectives were met to at least some degree, and that some students did indeed engage with the critical pedagogy goals. These final projects and reflective essays indicate that the course's learning objectives were met in a number of ways.

First, all of the students demonstrated an increase in their knowledge of the vocabulary and concepts of cultural heritage. Several commented on their increased confidence and took pride in their growing knowledge. Reflecting on her time with Rachael Kiddey (Kiddey 2014, 2017a, 2017b; Kiddey and Schofield 2011; Kiddey et al. 2015), who was then a doctoral student at the University of York and a keynote presenter at the public forum, one undergraduate student wrote,

> I drew upon experiences going to the homeless site, classroom lectures, reading assignments, and curating the Cavanaugh exhibit to answer her questions. I introduced her to members of the homeless community who I personally knew from my site visits. I was able to lead discussions which would provide important understandings for her research. . . . Before taking this course and preparing for this project, I could not have held a conversation which had the potential to help her focus her research.

Another indication of the students' learning was that they came to see the homeless as individuals, not a "social caste." They came to know their names, learn their roles within the encampment, and understand some of their needs and concerns. The book project authors, in particular, came to know and like the men they talked with. As a result, their goal for the publication shifted from documenting the encampment to seeking to change attitudes about people living homeless by sharing their personal stories (Figure 7.3). Students found the possessions that the men had carefully saved, such as photographs and books, powerful symbols to convey the enduring importance of relationships and personal narratives. In their essays the students reflected on the unexpected experience of coming to see the individuals in the encampment as friends.

Students also came to appreciate the resourcefulness and skills required to "live rough." They recognized the ingenuity and careful planning it took to survive in the conditions, the complex self-governance of the encampment residents, and the careful negotiations of rules and public policy enforced in

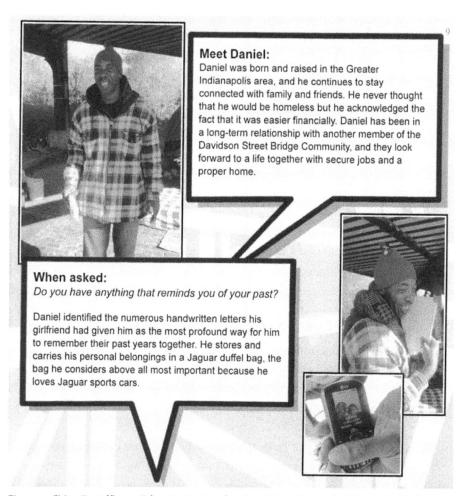

Figure 7.3. "Meet Daniel," p. 9, *Urban Heritage? Archaeology & Homelessness in Indianapolis*. Used with permission of Museum Studies Program, Indiana University–Purdue University–Indianapolis.

sometimes idiosyncratic ways. The students came away with respect for the strategies of those living homeless in curating their cultural heritage, given their transient lifestyle and lack of secure storage spaces. One student observed, "Each person created their own spatial identity and carried a collection of 'stuff' that had been deemed valuable or useful by their community." The students also recognized how those living homeless created meaningful landscapes, whether in downtown public plazas or what otherwise might have been seen as peripheral wasteland. One student observed,

While there are certainly "tangible" aspects of this project, there is also a transient element which would be hard to interpret without input from the community itself. . . . The camera project gave invaluable insight to the daily travel sights [*sic*] routes and meeting areas. Especially notable was that each camera came back with a picture of the Legion Mall. What is the function of this space? What does it mean to the community? Is it safe? Are their [*sic*] resources available there? These questions all relate to the Heritage of the homeless population—tangible and intangible, fluid and stable.

Students also connected this increased awareness of the range and complexity of tangible and intangible heritage within the homeless community to the global patterns of the marginalization, displacement, and removal.

Some of the students made connections between the project and broader agendas of activist or translational archaeology (Atalay 2014; Stottman 2010; Zimmerman at al. 2010). A few articulated a relationship between their research findings and larger issues and practices of the homelessness industry and governmental policy. Several identified the desire to find ways to continue to help and to encourage others to take action. For example, the Central Library exhibit curators included a section that offered suggestions for people who wanted to offer assistance to those living homeless, and one student began to explore a vocation in activist archaeology.

Lastly, students' self-reflective essays demonstrated an awareness of the role of heritage professionals in shaping the narratives and constructs of heritage sites. Some saw themselves as stakeholders in cultural heritage for the first time. They read Smith and Waterton (2009), and we discussed the notions of "authorized heritage discourse" in class, but a telling moment was when the Central Library exhibit curatorial team announced their title: "What does homelessness look like?: It depends on who is looking." The exhibit text expanded on this notion of perspectival knowledge by identifying divergent perspectives including the homeless services industry, those who proudly claim living "home free," and archaeologists themselves.

This is not to say that the students' experiences in the course were all transformative or even equally valuable. At least one student continued to assert that time is the central paradigm for the value of heritage, meaning the older something was, the more significant it was; and this same student continued to challenge the relevance of translational archaeology. Other students' self-assessments focused on the practical skills gained, and demonstrated neither self-reflective growth nor changed perspectives on issues of homelessness or the politics of cultural heritage. Some of the students, including those who were otherwise deeply invested in the readings and in the curatorial projects, never took advantage of the opportunities to go into the encampment and talk with people there.

As instructors in the class, Zimmerman and I questioned what we could have done to better support students in going into unfamiliar settings and potentially challenging encounters. The premise of the pedagogy of discomfort is that students are willing to engage with the material and to connect emotionally as well as intellectually. It was clear from the range of responses in the essays that, however curious and sympathetic, some students remained safely in their academic roles as observers. They documented, analyzed, and interpreted, but they did not necessarily connect with the homeless community through personal relationships or convey any sense that their comfortable worldviews were disrupted. We recognized that despite considerable experience in teaching, doing applied research, and working with community partners (Zimmerman and Branam 2014), our training as archaeologists has not necessarily equipped us with the sophisticated tools needed for effective critical pedagogy, and that deeper training and reading in the field would be beneficial (for example, Boler and Zembylas 2003; Carmona and Luschen 2014; Darder et al. 2009; Freire 1970; Trifonas 2003). We agreed that providing more explicit training in ethnographic methods or coordinating with the courses offered by colleagues in urban anthropology or ethnographic methods would better prepare the students for the fieldwork portion of the class, as well as orient them toward the growing use of ethnography in heritage studies (Brumann and Berliner 2016).

But there were some for whom this course was a formative experience. Two students continued to be active in the project and maintained the Facebook pages for several years. For others, the longer term impact may be less visible. In an essay she titled "Admitting the Truth," a student wrote,

> Homelessness is a topic I did not necessarily think about. I have seen homeless areas off the interstate and even saw homeless people while driving in the neighborhoods. Even though I saw them, I never re-

ally noticed them. It would not faze me to see a woman sitting near an abandoned building wrapped in a blanket. . . . I knew they were there, just truly never thought about them. "Displaced and Invisible" is a perfect name for homeless people. Having to see them and admit they are there would mean we have to admit there is a problem.

Later in the essay, she reflected, "Homelessness is a community, societal issue. I understand now that there is something [in which] everyone can participate. We can offer resolutions to the issues that surround homelessness. . . . [This class] is the beginning of a very long road in doing my part to help make the problem better."

Conclusion

The "Issues in Cultural Heritage" course offers examples of strategies to engage students in issues such as civic engagement and social justice. We share this experiment in the pedagogy of discomfort as an example of experiences designed not only to challenge students to think deeply and critically about the structures and systems of power implicated in cultural heritage management, but to feel empathy and even distress at the injustice they observe and the privileged positions they enjoy. As faculty we, like others that seek to deconstruct privilege in ways that transform it into "usable knowledge" (McIntosh 2013), wanted students to translate their learning into action. The class gave students the chance to experience community-based archaeology and to observe the potential for translational and activist archaeology to affect policy and address contemporary social issues. Finally, the critical pedagogy of heritage, which included grappling with the emotionally fraught and even painful experiences of living on society's fringes, changed their perspectives on the stakeholders of heritage and spurred some to question the nature of heritage itself.

We learned a number of things from the class that we applied to subsequent courses that similarly incorporated critical pedagogy strategies and addressed social justice issues. For example, we spent two and a half years working as part of a national collaborative project, States of Incarceration (SOI), spearheaded by Liz Ševčenko and the Humanities Action Lab. The project brought together more than 500 students and faculty from twenty universities to "explore the roots of mass incarceration in our own communities [and] to open national dialogue on what should happen next" (Humanities Action Lab 2016). We taught a series of classes in which students developed exhibit components, digital humanities projects, and public programming. As part of that series, in the fall of 2016 I designed a course titled "Interpreting Incarceration." Students developed public programs to accompany the SOI exhibit's run at the Indianapolis Central Library in the spring of 2017, and I drew on our experiences from the homeless heritage project. First, recognizing how difficult it had been for students to visit the homeless encampment, I invited people affected by incarceration to come to the classroom instead. Students spoke for two hours with a man who had been released after serving twenty-six years for murder. They met a woman who, as part of her response to her son's incarceration, had established a not-for-profit to give rides to families of those in prison. We also brought the students, who were mainly museum studies graduate students, to Recycle Force, a work release setting where they toured the job-training site and then had an extended conversation with a group of people going through the program. I also addressed directly the emotional work of the project. In addition to readings about mass incarceration, students read about the challenges of justice work and the need for self-care (Rockquemore 2015). We did in-class exercises to reflect on our backgrounds and to acknowledge some of our experiences and feelings in confronting painful and contentious issues, and students wrote self-reflective essays about their experience in the class. Despite these preparatory experiences, only two (out of eleven) students went on an optional tour of a prison facility, an experience that, like the visit to the homeless encampment, is both intense and potentially intimidating. But all of the students reported that the most significant learning experiences were talking with people who were formerly incarcerated, hearing their personal stories, and putting a human face on the larger social issue. They also said that the experiences in the class changed how they perceived the work they envisioned for themselves as they went on to pursue their museum careers. The class demonstrated that changing attitudes is possible, and students can tackle challenging, even uncomfortable, situations, but it requires a great deal of preparation and support.

A second lesson learned is somewhat counterintuitive. As noted, the Issues in Cultural Heritage class was resource-intensive. It yielded some impressive student-generated products that reached a public audience, particularly the exhibit and forum in the Central Library, but even those were ephemeral. One takeaway was to tackle larger projects, such as States of Incarceration. While the investment of effort and money was larger, the payoff was substantially greater as well. We were able to secure grants for the more ambitious SOI project from both university and external funders, as well as sponsorship for the exhibit opening and some programming from a community group, the Circle City Chapter of Links, Inc. The higher profile project helped us make connections with key community partners, such as the Central Library, and secure far more marketing and media coverage than a typical class-based project engenders. We involved students in three courses over two academic years, which expanded the number of students who benefited, and it shared the work of fund raising, organizing, and implementing the project among multiple faculty. Participating in the SOI project also gave us access to the resources that the Humanities Action Lab developed, including a sophisticated website through which the students' digital projects reached an international audience, a symposium held in conjunction with the exhibit opening in New York that fifteen of our students attended and at which a small group presented, and a National Endowment for the Humanities "Humanities in the Public Square" grant that helped support our public programming. While we still do more modest course-based projects, an indication of the benefits we see from working at this sort of "economy of scale" is that we have signed on for the next Humanities Action Lab project—a four-course sequence focusing on the history of environmental justice and migration within the context of climate change, culminating in hosting an exhibit in the winter of 2020.

As the fields of critical pedagogy and critical heritage studies develop, there is an increasing body of research on issues, such as the student resistance to deconstructing privilege (Case and Cole 2013), that we observed in the Issues in Cultural Heritage class. As Elizabeth Chilton argues, the field of heritage studies has developed over time and is rapidly changing (Chilton 2019). Even in the few years since we taught the course, the literature, particularly in the area of critical heritage studies, has grown significantly in publications and with the creation of the Association of Critical Heritage Studies (for example, Baird 2017; Harrison 2013, 2015; Smith 2012; Waterton and Watson 2011; ACHS 2012). The preparation of scholars and practitioners for this important work will require a similarly sophisticated pedagogy of critical heritage studies that embeds these approaches to social inequalities and the politics of heritage in classroom learning experiences.

Note

1. IUPUI is the partnership between two statewide universities, Indiana University and Purdue University, on the Indianapolis campus.

References Cited

Association for Critical Heritage Studies (ACHS)
2012   Manifesto. http://www.criticalheritagestudies.org/history/, accessed 9/26/16.
Atalay, Sonya (editor)
2014   *Transforming Archaeology: Activist Practices and Prospects.* Left Coast Press, Walnut Creek, California.
Baird, Melissa F.
2013   "The Breath of the Mountain is my Heart": Indigenous Cultural Landscapes and the Politics of Heritage. *International Journal of Heritage Studies* 19(4): 327–340.
2014   Heritage, Human Rights, and Social Justice. *Heritage & Society* 7(2): 139–155.
2017   *Critical Theory and the Anthropology of Heritage Landscapes.* University Press of Florida, Gainesville.
Boler, Megan
1999   *Feeling Power: Emotion and Education.* Routledge, New York.
Boler, Megan, and M. Zembylas
2003   Discomforting Truths: The Emotional Terrain of Understanding Difference. In *Pedagogies of Difference: Rethinking Education for Social Change,* edited by Peter Pericles Trifonas, pp. 110–136. RoutledgeFalmer, New York.
Brumann, Christoph, and David Berliner (editors)
2016   *World Heritage on the Ground: Ethnographic Perspectives.* Berghahn Books, New York.
Byrne, Denis
2014   *Counterheritage: Critical Perspectives on Heritage Conservation in Asia.* Routledge, New York.
Carmona, Judith Flores, and Kristen V. Luschen (editors)
2014   *Crafting Critical Stories: Toward Pedagogies and Methodologies of Collaboration, Inclusion, and Voice.* Peter Lang, New York.
Case, Kim A., and Elizabeth R. Cole
2013   Deconstructing Privilege When Students Resist: The Journey Back into the Community of Engaged Learners. In *Deconstructing Privilege: Teaching and Learning as Allies in the Classroom,* edited by Kim A. Case, pp. 34–48. Routledge, New York.
Chilton, Elizabeth
2019   The Heritage of Heritage: Defining the Past in Contemporary Societies. In *History and Approaches to Heritage Studies,* edited by Phyllis Mauch Messenger and Susan J. Bender, pp. 24–31. University Press of Florida, Gainesville.
Darder, Antonia, Marta P. Baltodano, and Rodolfo D. Torres (editors)
2009   *The Critical Pedagogy Reader.* 2nd ed. Routledge, New York.

Fein, Jonathan, and Brian Danitz

200   *Objects and Memory: A Documentary Film.* An EVER production.

Freire, Paulo

1970   *Pedagogy of the Oppressed.* Herder and Herder, New York.

Giroux, Henry

2007   *The University in Chains: Confronting the Military-Industrial-Academic Complex.* Paradigm, Boulder, Colorado.

2010   Lessons from Paulo Freire. *Chronicle of Higher Education,* October 27, 57(09). (serial on the Internet).

González-Ruibal, Alfredo, and Martin Hall

2015   Heritage and Violence. In *Global Heritage: A Reader,* edited by Lynn Meskell, pp. 150–170. Wiley-Blackwell, Oxford, UK.

Guantanamo Public Memory Project, Liz Ševčenko, Director.

2009   http://gitmomemory.org/about, accessed June 3, 2015.

Harrison, Rodney

2013   *Heritage: Critical Approaches.* Routledge, New York.

2015   Beyond "Natural" and "Cultural" Heritage: Toward an Ontological Politics of Heritage in the Age of Anthropocene. *Heritage & Society* 8(1): 24–42.

Herwitz, Daniel Alan

2012   *Heritage, Culture, and Politics in the Postcolony.* Columbia University Press, New York,

Holzman, Laura, Elizabeth Wood, Holly Cusack-McVeigh, Elizabeth Kryder-Reid, Modupe Labode, and Larry J. Zimmerman

2014   A Random Walk to Public Scholarship? Exploring Our Convergent Paths. *Public: A Journal of Imagining America* 2(2), Online: http://public.imaginingamerica.org/ blog/article/a-random-walk-to-public-scholarship-exploring-our-convergent-paths, accessed June 3, 2018

Humanities Action Lab, States of Incarceration. Liz Ševčenko, Director.

2016   http://statesofincarceration.org, accessed January 16, 2018.

Hyatt, Susan (Project Director), Benjamin J. Linder, and Margaret Baurley (Editorial and Research Assistants)

2013   *The Neighborhood of Saturdays: Memories of a Multi-Ethnic Neighborhood on Indianapolis' Southside.* Dog Ear Press, Indianapolis.

Ivits, Shantel

2009   Disturbing the Comfortable: An Ethical Inquiry into Pedagogies of Discomfort and Crisis. M.A. thesis, Society, Culture and Politics in Education, University of British Columbia, Vancouver.

Kiddey, Rachael

2014   Punks and Drunks: Counter-mapping Homelessness in Bristol and York. In *Who Needs Experts? Counter Mapping Cultural Heritage,* edited by John Schofield, pp. 165–179. Routledge, London.

2017a   From the Ground Up: Cultural Heritage Practices as Tools for Empowerment in the Homeless Heritage Project. *International Journal of Heritage Studies.* Online: http://www.tandfonline.com/action/showCitFormats?doi=10.1080/13527258 .2016.1274669, accessed June 3, 2018.

2017b   *Homeless Heritage: Collaborative Social Archaeology as Therapeutic Practice.* Oxford University Press, Oxford.

Kiddey, Rachael, Andrew Dafnis, Jane Hallam, and art by Mats Brate

2015   Journeys in the City: Homeless Archaeologists, or Archaeologies of Homelessness. *Journal of Contemporary Archaeology* 2(2): 217–259.

Kiddey, Rachael, and John Schofield

2011   Embrace the Margins: Adventures in Archaeology and Homelessness. *Public Archaeology* 10(1): 4–22.

Labode, Modupe, Elizabeth Kryder-Reid, and Laura Holzman

2013   Hybrid Discourse: Exploring Art, Race, and Space in Indianapolis. *Public: A Journal of Imagining America* 1(1–2). Online http://public.imaginingamerica.org/blog/article/hybrid-discourse-exploring-art-race-and-space-in-indianapolis, accessed September 26, 2016.

Little, Barbara J., and Paul A. Shackel

2014   *Archaeology, Heritage, and Civic Engagement: Working toward the Public Good.* Left Coast Press, Walnut Creek, California.

McIntosh, Peggy

2013   Foreword: Teaching about Privilege: Transforming Learned Ignorance into Usable Knowledge. In *Deconstructing Privilege: Teaching and Learning as Allies in the Classroom,* edited by Kim A. Case, pp. xi–xvi. Routledge, New York.

Mulcahy, Cara M.

2008   The Tangled Web We Weave: Critical Literacy and Critical Thinking. In *Critical Literacy as Resistance: Teaching for Social Justice across the Secondary Curriculum,* edited by Laraine Wallowitz, pp. 15–27. Peter Lang, New York.

Mullins, Paul

2003   Engagement and the Color Line: Race, Renewal, and Public Archaeology in the Urban Midwest. *Urban Anthropology* 32(2): 205–230.

2006   Racializing the Commonplace Landscape: An Archaeology of Urban Renewal along the Color Line. *World Archaeology* 38(1): 60–71.

2008   Marketing in a Multicultural Neighborhood: An Archaeology of Corner Stores in the Urban Midwest. *Historical Archaeology* 42(1): 88–96.

Mullins, Paul, and Susan Hyatt

2016   Invisible Indianapolis: Race, Heritage and Community Memory in the Circle City. https://invisibleindianapolis.wordpress.com/, accessed September 26, 2016.

Mullins, Paul, and Lewis C. Jones

2011   Race, Displacement, and 20th Century University Landscapes: An Archaeology of Renewal and Urban Universities. In *The Archaeology of the Recent African American Past,* edited by Jodi A. Barnes, pp. 250–262. University of South Carolina Press, Charleston.

Mullins, Paul, Modupe Labode, Lewis C. Jones, Michael E. Essex, Alex Kruse, and Brandon Muncy

2011   Consuming Lines of Difference: The Politics of Wealth and Poverty along the Color Line. In *Archaeologies of Poverty,* edited by Christopher Matthews, special issue of *Historical Archaeology* 45(3): 140–150.

Museum Studies Program, IUPUI

2011   *Urban Heritage: Archaeology and Homelessness in Indianapolis*. OnDemand Print book, Bookemon, http://www.bookemon.com/read-book/165231, accessed September 26, 2016.

Neighborhood of Saturdays. Digital Humanities site.

2010   http://www.ulib.iupui.edu/digitalscholarship/collections/NoS, accessed April 28, 2018.

Rockquemore, Kerry Ann

2015   Radical Self Care, *Inside Higher Education*, May 5: https://www.insidehighered. com/advice/2015/05/06/essay-how-faculty-members-can-keep-focused-amid-so-much-disturbing-news, accessed August 8, 2016.

Ševčenko, Liz

2011   Sites of Conscience: Heritage of and for Human Rights. In *Heritage, Memory & Identity. The Cultures and Globalization* Series 4, edited by Helmut Anheier and Yudhishthir Raj Isar, pp. 114–124. SAGE, London.

Shackel, Paul A.

2019   Civic Engagement, Representation, and Social Justice: Moving from CRM to Heritage Studies. In *History and Approaches to Heritage Studies*, edited by Phyllis Mauch Messenger and Susan J. Bender, pp. 9–23. University Press of Florida: Gainesville.

Shor, Ira

1992   *Empowering Education: Critical Teaching for Social Change*. University of Chicago Press, Chicago, Illinois.

Smith, Laurajane

2012   Editorial: A Critical Heritage Studies? *International Journal of Heritage Studies*. 18(6): 533–540.

Smith, Laurajane, and Emma Waterton

2009   *Heritage, Communities and Archaeology*. Duckworth, London.

Soderland, Hilary A.

2010   Values and the Evolving Critique of Heritage: The First Century of Archaeology and Law in the United States (1906–2006). In *Heritage Values in Contemporary Society*, edited by George S. Smith, Phyllis Mauch Messenger, and Hilary A. Soderland, pp. 129–143. Left Coast Press, Walnut Creek, California.

Stottman, M. Jay (editor)

2010   *Archaeologists as Activists: Can Archaeologists Change the World?* University of Alabama Press, Tuscaloosa.

Trifonas, Peter Pericles (editor)

2003   *Pedagogies of Difference: Rethinking Education for Social Change*. Routledge-Farlmer, New York.

Waterton, Emma, and Steve Watson, (editors)

2011   *Heritage and Community Engagement: Collaboration or Contestation?* Routledge, London.

Wood, Elizabeth, Youngbok Hong, Mary F. Price, Kathleen Stanton-Nichols, Julie A. Hatcher, David M. Craig, Jason M. Kelly, Ross D. Silverman, and Kristi L. Palmer

2016   Public Scholarship at Indiana University–Purdue University. White paper published online: http://hdl.handle.net/1805/9713, accessed January 16, 2018.

Zimmerman, Larry J.

2004   Archaeological Evaluation of the Hillside Garden Areas at the James J. Hill House (21RA21), St. Paul, Minnesota. *Minnesota Archaeologist* 63: 118–136.

2011   Interview, Indianapolis Marion County Public Library (IMCPL). http://www.youtube.com/watch?v=1y5Cf_zRJIc&list=UUmmPGTJTRuJ5HM5Gqzz4k5A&index=88, accessed September 26, 2016.

Zimmerman, Larry J., and Kelly M. Branam

2014   Collaborating with Stakeholders. In *Archaeology in Practice: A Student Guide to Archaeological Analysis*, 2nd ed., edited by Jane Balme and Alistair Paterson, pp. 1–25. Blackwell, Malden, Massachusetts.

Zimmerman, Larry J., Courtney Singleton, and Jessica Welch

2010   Activism and Creating a Translational Archaeology of Homelessness. *World Archaeology* 42(3): 443–454.

Zimmerman, Larry J., and Jessica Welch

2011   Displaced and Barely Visible: Archaeology and the Material Culture of Homelessness. *Historical Archaeology* 45(1): 67–85.

8

Learning to Listen

A. GWYNN HENDERSON AND NICOLAS R. LARACUENTE

Over the past two decades, the expectation of what archaeology should be has expanded, bringing more archaeologists out of the field and lab and into the public sphere (Nassaney 2009: 4–5). Archaeologists who began their careers not explicitly intending to engage the public are acknowledging the need to explain their work to interested citizens or descendants or the media. Twenty-first-century archaeologists highlight the disenfranchised in politicized situations (Little 2007; Shackel 2019), and they use their archaeology to take on causes (Stottman 2010). These diverse approaches and various contexts require that archaeologists work with multiple publics in meaningful and informed ways.

Twenty-first-century archaeologists are not alone. They are part of a larger conversation taking place among heritage studies practitioners, and many developments in archaeology education and public archaeology mirror those taking place within heritage pedagogy and heritage studies. We, like others, include public archaeology as one of the many disciplines sheltered under the broad umbrella of heritage studies. Thus, despite the fact that the disciplinary context from which we draw our inspiration is public archaeology, we think heritage practitioners of all persuasions may discover from our experiences and find in our suggestions relevance for their own practice.

This chapter offers insights, identifies challenges, and offers suggestions gained from our experience in a University of Kentucky Department of Anthropology graduate seminar in public archaeology, developed and taught by Henderson and taken by Laracuente; and from our reflection, separately and together, on that experience. Our insights also draw upon conversations we have had with instructors who teach and with students who have taken public archaeology courses in somewhat similar contexts as ours.[1]

A New Skill Set

Working at public archaeology is not like collaborating with colleagues on a common research problem whose tangible products are intended primarily for the eyes of the professional. Working at public archaeology involves translating, interpreting, and communicating (often technical) specialized knowledge and information using a different, more inclusive vocabulary, for different purposes, to the nonprofessional, in often unpredictable and unfamiliar social contexts.

This "de-siloing" of archaeology—making it more accessible and inclusive—is a healthy and important development, but it requires that archaeologists with established careers and especially students embarking on new careers receive training in this new skill set. Today's archaeology majors need to understand the importance of communicating archaeology's findings outside of our discipline's comfort zone. Their graduate school years, especially, must give them opportunities to gain experience in practicing their new skills (that is to say, apprentice themselves). Indeed, a public archaeology course may be as critical, or perhaps even more critical, to students' career success as traditional methods courses (for example, lithic or faunal analysis) or skill-building courses (for example, statistics or archaeological geophysics). Understanding public archaeology issues and getting experience doing public archaeology diversify and broaden students' employment options and prepare graduates for social and intellectual work (as also discussed in Shackel and Mortensen 2006; Smith 2006; and Weisman 2006).

Unfortunately, many graduates are entering the archaeological workforce without basic experiences in sharing what they do and what they have learned with people who are not archaeologists; without an understanding of audiences' learning types; and without practice in the skills needed to explain archaeology's big ideas. This is because many colleges and universities today are not providing training to graduate students in the skills they will need to effectively move within the public sphere upon receipt of their degrees (see Henderson and Laracuente 2012). Smith and Krass' 2000 survey of how the subject of public archaeology (often considered synonymous with cultural resource management [CRM]) was taught at the collegiate level revealed that forty departments (only about one-third of the respondents) offered one or more courses primarily dedicated to this subject (Smith and Krass 2000: 21). Most of these courses focused on national historic preservation laws. In 2012, we had difficulty finding public archaeology courses listed as formal course offerings with elements that reflected our broader conceptualization of "public archaeology," which encompasses knowledge of laws and the skills for CRM, certainly, but also oral and written communication, people's learning styles, interpretation, and the like (but see Pluckhahn, this volume).

Our Course

Out of a concern for its lack of graduate course offerings in public archaeology, in 2009–2010, the University of Kentucky's Department of Anthropology developed a pair of complementary public anthropology courses that it planned to offer occasionally and as a series in the special topics track. The target audience was cultural anthropology and archaeology graduate students with a strong interest in conveying academic information to the general public. One course focused on cultural identity politics and cultural property issues on a worldwide scale. The other was predominantly experiential, providing students opportunities to engage in diverse hands-on activities. It was envisioned that, at the end of the series, students who had taken both courses would have gained not only a solid introduction to issues in public anthropology/archaeology, but also a structured personal experience working in the public sphere.

Our course, "Seminar in Public Anthropology" (Henderson 2010), was the predominantly experiential course and was the first one offered in the series.[2] It focused almost exclusively on public archaeology. Its outward appearance—a traditional, graduate-level seminar held once a week for 2.5 hours during the fifteen-week semester—belied its experiential nature.

The course began and ended by asking students to consider, through readings, case studies, and discussion, the definition of "public archaeology," its purpose, its important issues, and its relevance for today. The course introduced students to public archaeology's fundamental concepts (for example, how people learn; how teaching, learning, and assessment are structured) and to the tools public archaeologists use (writing and speaking) when working with diverse publics in multiple venues (both formal and informal learning settings, like public school classrooms, museums, or outdoor classrooms). The course gave students opportunities to observe

A. Gwynn Henderson and Nicolas R. Laracuente

"the public" (in this case, upper elementary public school children and their instructors) in both formal classroom contexts (by viewing a half-hour video of a master teacher on Annenberg Learner (www.learner.org) and informal outdoor classroom contexts (their own hands-on experience). Since much of public archaeology is in the doing, the course provided opportunities for students to explore and experience some of the diverse methods and techniques used in oral (following best interpretation practice) and written communication with the public.

The course was built around a guided, structured, hands-on outdoor classroom experience with upper elementary school children at a historic archaeological site on the grounds of a nearby city-owned nature sanctuary. All aspects of the course were linked in one way or another to preparing the students for that hands-on experience and for reflecting on it afterward. This experiential learning[3] component was a response to Bender's (2000: 37) call for universities and colleges in the twenty-first century to include real-world problem solving in today's archaeology courses.

Grades for the course were based on class participation (20 percent); three experience observations prepared after (1) viewing the video of a master teacher in the classroom, (2) working with students during the hands-on outdoor classroom experience, and (3) observing an interpretive walk by the nature sanctuary's staff (20 percent); and a ten-minute interpretive presentation and critique of their classmates' presentations (20 percent).

Like traditional seminar courses, a student project was part of the course. In this case, students prepared a *Learning Object:* a focused lesson for upper elementary school teachers, which counted for 40 percent of their grade. A Learning Object was selected as the course project because it combined almost all of the methodological and practical aspects the students would experience during the course.[4] Topics targeted the archaeological resources of the nature sanctuary—for example, the historic cemetery, the dry-laid stone walls, the Indigenous sites. It was hoped that, at the conclusion of the semester, the nature sanctuary staff would be able to use the Learning Objects with visiting school groups during on-site programming.

Afterward

Our "Seminar in Public Anthropology," conceived of in earnest to fill a desperate need in graduate education, and inspired by countless discussions with colleagues in public archaeology and by consideration of numerous treatises on the issues (for example, Bender and Smith 2000), was not, in practice, wildly successful (Henderson and Laracuente 2012). Sharply mixed course evaluations from the students (half gave it high marks; half considered it a dismal failure) compelled critical examination of the course and a search for answers to this question: "What elements are part of an effective public archaeology course?" Corollary questions included:

- What learning goals do public archaeology courses share?
- *Are* there other public archaeology courses like this?
- What pedagogical elements make for successful instruction? Are there standard best practice techniques? Overarching pitfalls?
- What issues have other instructors grappled with while teaching public archaeology courses?

In our search for answers to these questions, we considered information from a variety of sources:

- the six returned graduate student course evaluations;
- our own wide-ranging conversations and personal reflections on the course;
- syllabi from established public archaeology courses;
- informal telephone interviews with six public archaeology course instructors; and
- anonymous responses from eight students who had taken a public archaeology course in the United States and the United Kingdom.[5]

After reviewing the data, we identified four main problem areas: course structure and content; lack of fit to the student audience; students' perception of the course's applicability and relevance to their chosen career path; and role reversal and threats to student egos. We will consider each of these problems in turn, below.

Problem Areas

Course Structure and Content

The students who took this course were unsettled by its unconventional structure. They were used to lecture classes or traditional seminars. The last

A. Gwynn Henderson and Nicolas R. Laracuente

active learning experience that most of them had had was likely in upper elementary school.

Although titled "Seminar in Public Anthropology," the course was not conducted as a seminar, and only occasionally were students required to come to class prepared to discuss assigned readings with minimal instructor moderation. In the traditional seminar room, discussion mainly considers the conceptual and theoretical, and the focus is on ideas and on critiquing others' research. Students rarely are asked to consider the practical application of theories in seminars.

This course was mainly about practical methods and techniques. Discussion focused more on critiquing concrete hands-on experiences than ideas and theories. This experiential learning format also required the students to apply archaeological facts and ideas outside an archaeological context and audience, which took them out of their learning comfort zone. In addition, the course introduced students to subject matter that was, in many cases, more likely to be covered in an education course (for example, exploring the topic of how humans learn) or in an English Department writing course than in an anthropology graduate seminar.

Lack of Fit to the Audience

The course's goals and objectives were unrealistic for the targeted audience. It is our hypothesis that the students who gave it high marks were those who had had previous experiences in public archaeology. Reference to Levstik and Barton's (2001: 37) categories for assessing student performance (from lowest to highest, they are: novice, apprentice, proficient, and distinguished) helps illustrate this point.

The seven graduate students in this course were second-year students (or more), and they all had field and lab experience (some in significant amounts). However, they brought to the course a wide range of previous public archaeology experience: from none ("novice") to some ("apprentice"). The former expressed interest in finding out about public archaeology, but the course structure and format did not provide enough scaffolding for their learning. It assumed too much prior knowledge. These students struggled and became frustrated.

The "apprentices" came to the course looking for ways to fit a conceptual and methodological framework to experiences they had already had. They hoped to learn new techniques and tools, and to receive training in how to do public archaeology more effectively than they had done it in the past, for their previous public archaeology work (like that of many professional archaeologists) had been purely seat-of-the-pants. They also hoped the course would introduce them to the burgeoning theoretical literature of public archaeology. They got what they wanted.

But even the apprentice-level students had trouble transferring to different situations and different audiences the pedagogical skills they were learning. They did not realize how the course activities had broad applicability to many "publics," and how the tools and techniques considered successful for working with the course's targeted audience, public school students, could apply to adults as well. For example, research shows that people of all ages learn in different ways (Bransford et al. 2000). Thus, incorporating into a course or lesson or public presentation as many different ways of learning as is feasible for the subject helps to ensure that all participants are engaged and learning. Effective interpretation requires public archaeologists to find ways to make an emotional link between the subject they are talking about and the audience they are addressing, irrespective of age or venue or subject (Brochu and Merriman 2008). Writing for children or the general public is difficult and it requires a whole different set of skills from those needed in writing for archaeologists (Allen 2002; Kane and Keeton 2003).

Students' Perception of Course Relevance

It is possible that some of the students, once involved in the course, did not or could not maintain a serious interest in the subject matter because they did not see its value, its relevance. Students with a more academic career path may have been of this mindset.

If correct, this perception reveals a deeper issue. Gaining the skills required to successfully communicate archaeology's significance and its findings to nonarchaeologists is relevant for all graduate students, irrespective of personal career path (whether applied or academic). Relegating public archaeology's relevance to only those who expect to interact routinely with the lay public is shortsighted. We would contend that teaching archaeology in a university or college setting is public archaeology, too, and thus public archaeology's concepts, methods, and techniques are applicable and relevant (indeed, necessary) skills for even the most academic of career paths.

Not until challenged to explain an archaeological idea, method, or fact to a nonarchaeologist (in whatever venue and in whatever form, written or oral), can students truly understand exactly how difficult—and how challenging and rewarding—it is to communicate with diverse "publics" and do it well, honestly, respectfully, responsibly, and accurately. This kind of communication is every bit as hard to do as writing and speaking in an academic context. In addition, the former takes humility. There is an art to this communication, yes, but there is also a *science* to it. Learning to use those skills takes practice.

Role Reversal and Threatened Egos

In graduate school, students are becoming experts in their chosen field. They feel the need to project an aura of "the expert" in a seminar setting as they evaluate scholarly books and journal articles, argue over the meaning of archaeological interpretations, and decide where particular concepts and ideas are applicable. Critiquing strengthens the student's role as expert.

Public archaeology flips this model on its head, and, thus, so will a course in public archaeology. A public archaeologist often does not get to maintain the role of expert. Coming into a community to work with residents without listening to them smacks of elitism and could be counterproductive to developing any type of collaborative relationship. Meaningful engagement requires listening. It requires working outside one's comfort zone. It requires compromising and taking some blows to one's ego. These are experiences best had within the context of a course before confronting them in a real-world context.

This sharp contrast can be unsettling to the fragile graduate student ego. According to Zellner (2011), graduate students suffer from the "imposter syndrome" and lack the confidence of seasoned professionals. They fear that other students, as well as faculty, can see through the farce: that they really are the dumbest person in the room, unworthy to be there, and undeserving of financial and faculty support.

The challenge in a public archaeology course is to show students how to apply their knowledge of the subject matter, while at the same time modeling for them the many hats a public archaeologist wears: the hats of listener, collaborator, facilitator, leader, *and* expert.

Decision Points for Structuring an Effective Course

Our course experiences as teacher and student, our subsequent personal reflections, and our research provide insights into structuring a public archaeology course that, we believe, are relevant for heritage practitioners. In this section, we highlight three important decision points that instructors should consider when developing a course in public archaeology. In our view, public archaeology, by its very nature, is in the doing, in the application, and it is not synonymous with CRM. Thus, from our perspective, a course in public archaeology must include an element of experiential, active, and hands-on learning.

These decision points address three continua: course purpose (from introduction through immersion), course format (from discussion/critique through action/creation), and the character of the hands-on learning experience (from simulation through authentic). The amount of prospective students' prior public archaeology experience—their location on the experience spectrum (novice, apprentice, proficient, and distinguished)—is another consideration that must be folded into the mix.

Course Purpose: From Introduction through Immersion

If students are novices (and our research indicates that most students, both graduate and undergraduate, are novices), then the purpose of a public archaeology course should be to introduce students to the breadth of the subject. The course serves as a "tasting room." For apprentice students who have some public archaeology experience, the course should cover methods and techniques, and provide structured learning opportunities, including hands-on learning experiences. Proficient and distinguished students require more. These learners want to know about the details and nuances of learning theory and interpretation. They may be ready to experiment with new techniques and to critique time-honored approaches. With guidance, they are seeking the challenges of creating and implementing their own public archaeology projects.

Course Format: From Discussion/Critique through Action/Creation

Unlike the task of developing a traditional lecture course or a seminar, instructors developing a public archaeology course must decide not only on course content (for example, Touch on the laws? Require writing for the

A. Gwynn Henderson and Nicolas R. Laracuente

public? Include a component on site protection and stewardship instead of considering learning theory?), but also on course format. That is because, as we mentioned previously, a course in public archaeology should include hands-on learning experiences. So the issue becomes: How much course time should be devoted to introducing concepts and ideas, and how much to hands-on learning?

Our research found that there are many good structures, and all contribute to successful student learning. Depending on the instructor's interests and the students' experience, the course format can range from primarily discussion, to discussion and in-class, hands-on exercises, to primarily involvement in a real-world project.

For novices, critiquing provides the better learning context. For apprentice students with more practical experience, asking them to prepare a course project is a better assignment. The instructors we spoke to mentioned a host of tangible student projects: brochures or signs; classroom lessons; booklets, comics; a website/trail study for a city park (see also Pluckhahn, this volume). Advanced students' class projects could be prepared with the understanding that the best will live on as gifts to the collaborating school, park, or organization. These projects also could take the form of written assessments critiquing the educational effectiveness of (1) a particular type of public archaeology technique, (2) a certain learning model, or (3) selected media. For example, students could research the importance of understanding children's psychological development for successful instruction and then recommend how to change the content of a particular public archaeology project to better match the intended audience.

Laracuente's online survey (albeit a very small sample, see Henderson and Laracuente 2012) suggests that course format choice could have unintended consequences for student learning, however. A comparison of the responses from those who had taken a formal course with those who had learned public archaeology by the seat of their pants identified a difference in how students spoke about the public. Those who had taken a formal public archaeology class (it is unclear if hands-on activities were course components) discussed the need to be careful when communicating; the need for engagement to keep the public interested; and the need to keep in mind the politics of these situations. The respondents who had never taken a class discussed topics like being approachable; forming communities; building confidence; gaining the trust and respect of the public; the importance of relevance; and the value of archaeological projects. This suggests that *doing* (versus *reading about doing*) public archaeology impacts the positionality of students in a way that promotes a role of "partner" with a community rather than "us versus them."

Character of Hands-on Learning (From Simulation through Authentic)

To insure effective learning, where on the continuum of active and passive learning should the hands-on learning component of a course in public archaeology fall? Are in-class exercises or simulations effective experiential learning tools, or should actual archaeological experiences be course elements? This depends on the students. Some will be ready for actual experiences; others will not.

Two instructors we spoke to definitely do NOT insert students taking a semester-long course into the relationships they have built up over years of professional involvement with an organization or site. They cited two reasons: (1) they do not want students turned loose without experience; and (2) they consider it unethical to use the public as a guinea pig for a college course. These informants said that, once trained, students can be involved in real-world public archaeology experiences. For these instructors, reading and considering case studies was the better approach.

But how will students know how to *do* public archaeology if they are not given the opportunity to do it and get feedback in a safe environment? An experience Laracuente had can provide an answer. At a public venue, as part of a research assistantship, he watched a seasoned public archaeologist present to the public a few times. Then he did the presentation himself while the veteran watched. Afterward, the veteran provided a critique and answered Laracuente's questions about methods and techniques. In other words, the veteran served as a coach. Perhaps public archaeology coaching could work in the same way as medical students who shadow surgeons: the students don't cut; they watch, critique, watch. Then, they cut in the presence of their mentor.

Concluding Thoughts

We do not advocate that all archaeologists embrace public archaeology as their specialty (after all, there is no expectation that every archaeologist should be skilled at ceramic analysis or comfortable interpreting geophysical data). However, we do expect all archaeologists to know that the interpretation of the past is no longer the exclusive purview of our discipline. The archaeology of today is more inclusive, with respect not only to the members of the academic disciplines with whom we work, but to the constituencies with whom we converse and to whom we must listen.

We also expect all archaeologists to always consider both their audience and the story they want to share before engaging *any* situation where interaction with nonarchaeologists will take place. All archaeologists should ask: "Can I convey this to my audience accurately, responsibly, and respectfully in a way that *they* can understand?" If their answer is "Yes," they will be successful.

But if their answer is "No," we expect them to seek out the advice or the services of a public archaeologist. Archaeologists routinely work with experts. They ask experts for aid in everything from understanding the history of soil formation at a site to the age of an artifact. If you are not an expert in lithic analysis, you leave to experts the detailed lithic analysis your project requires. A growing literature in public archaeology theories, issues, methods, and techniques reflects its subdisciplinary status (King 2016; McDavid 2009; Merriman 2004; Richardson and Almansa-Sánchez 2015). A cadre of public archaeology experts now exists. Work with or hire such experts when you do public archaeology.

The statement we made at the beginning of this chapter bears repeating. *We believe that, for today's students, a public archaeology course may be as critical, or perhaps even more critical, to students' career success as traditional methods courses.* We believe that every archaeology/anthropology department should offer a public archaeology course and that it should be a routinely offered, permanent course in the curriculum (see Pluckhahn, this volume). In the twenty-first century, students must have the opportunity to be introduced to and gain experience in doing public archaeology. American anthropology departments must implement the curricular reform Bender and Smith proposed (Bender and Smith 2000).

The routine inclusion of a public archaeology course will require a paradigm shift in two venues. First, university and college curriculum committees will need to value public archaeology and consider working with and communicating to the public as valuable and worthwhile skills for twenty-first-century students. We think they are as important to these students as archaeology's stand-by skills of ceramic or lithic artifact analysis were to early twentieth-century students, or geophysical or GIS data collection and manipulation methods were to late twentieth-century students. Although we concede that this is easier said than done, anthropology departments *must* make room in the twenty-first-century curriculum for public archaeology.

Second, a shift in perspective within public archaeology itself must take place. Public archaeologists in the twenty-first century need to move beyond discussions of what public archaeology is, to what it does: facilitate the flow of information about the past and past peoples to the public (King 2016; Richardson and Almansa-Sánchez 2015). The information and understanding gained through archaeology is one of the many ways to understand heritage.

This change in perspective will challenge public archaeologists to focus their energies on engaging publics beyond laypeople, museum patrons, or school children and their teachers—groups commonly considered our "publics." Repositioning other professions (architecture, city planning and design, finance) and other academic disciplines (chemistry, music, physics, geography, zoology) as "publics" beneath the "heritage studies" umbrella will promote interdisciplinary communication (see Chilton 2019).

Shifting the roles archaeologists play in these interactions will require as much listening as teaching. In this way, archaeologists will be more successful in sharing our fascinating findings on our listeners' terms. This will help facilitate academic collaboration, resulting in a more holistic archaeology that operationalizes a true anthropological archaeology.

Public archaeology takes place in the rarified, challenging, rewarding place where the discipline of anthropology intersects with the real world and with the many disciplines that heritage studies embrace. It is interaction between practitioners and various stakeholders. It is interpretation. It is communication-being heard, but also listening.

Acknowledgments

We would like to thank the symposium organizers, now our editors, Phyllis Mauch Messenger and Susan J. Bender, for organizing "Lessons from the Trenches: The Pedagogy of Archaeology and Heritage," an electronic symposium held in 2012 at the 77th Annual Meeting of the Society for American Archaeology in Memphis, Tennessee. Heartfelt thanks go to the many individuals who, in 2009–2010, provided Henderson with insights, feedback, and critiques as she was developing her public archaeology course. We would like to thank Bev Chiarulli, Pam Cressey, John Jameson, Patti Jeppson, Tom Pluckhahn, and Carol McDavid for sharing during our informal telephone interviews their thoughts about public archaeology and how to teach it, and we thank the eight anonymous students who replied to our online query of the same questions on March 7, 2012. Henderson also would like to thank all the students who took her "Seminar in Public Anthropology (ANT770)" course in 2010.

Much has happened since 2010, when we were teaching/taking the "Seminar in Public Anthropology (ANT770)" at the University of Kentucky." Still, we remain as committed as ever to the relevance and importance of formal training in public archaeology. Successfully translating our discipline's jargon is critical to ensuring the protection of heritage resources. Training will provide the next generation of heritage professionals the tools they need to ensure that everyone sees the shared value in what we do.

Notes

1. We identified public archaeology course instructors in three ways: (1) by following the thread of available online course syllabi at the time of our work on our 2012 paper, such as the ones on the Society for American Archaeology's Archaeology for the Public webpages, (http://www.saa.org/publicftp/public/home/home.html) and the MATRIX Project (Pyburn and Smith 2015); (2) by contacting individuals who responded in 2009–2010 with information and suggestions as Henderson was developing her "Seminar in Public Anthropology-ANT770"; and (3) by searching the World Wide Web for universities with public archaeology courses listed as part of their curriculum. We queried the six instructors using a set of informal questions.

2. For a variety of reasons, the first offering of the companion course, "Seminar in Public Anthropology: Cultural Identity Politics and Cultural Property," did not take place in the fall of 2010. At the time of our 2012 research, the University of Kentucky's Department of Anthropology did not offer a course that focused mainly on CRM/historic preservation laws/Section 106 and the like. There was an underused independent study format course on the books, "CRM Clerkship," in which the student spends time working in the department's different archaeology units (museum, contract program, public outreach program, and State Archaeologist office).

3. Various terms, such as "learning by doing" (Dewey and Dewey 1915) or "experienced-based learning" (Wolfe and Byrne 1975) have been used to label the process of learning from experience or learning from the "real-world." We use the term "experien-

tial learning" (Kolb 2015) or "hands-on learning" (Levstik and Barton 2001) throughout this chapter. While "most pedagogies allow students to learn experientially to some extent, the resultant learning can be in error unless care is taken to assure that the right learning conditions are met. Certain approaches are more likely to facilitate experiential learning than others" (Gentry 1990: 9).

4. The major elements of the Learning Objects prepared by the students were the same as those developed for Kentucky archaeological sites featured on the PBS Learning Media website (e.g., http://ket.pbslearningmedia.org/resource/hisarch. ss.archeology/historic-archaeology-at-ashland-artifacts-in-a-privy/): 1. Background Content Essay (one to two pages written for the instructor to provide factual background information on the topic); 2. Fieldtrip/Outdoor Learning Experience (including previsit discussion questions and a suggested discovery activity at the case study site); 3. Fieldtrip/Outdoor Learning Experience Follow-up (postvisit discussion questions and at least one suggested follow-up activity); 4. List of curriculum alignments to the relevant subjects for fourth and/or fifth grade (based on the Program of Studies for those grades/subjects as required by Kentucky's Department of Education); 5. List of links and resources for further reference.

5. We adapted the informal set of questions into a Google survey form that allowed open-ended, essay-style responses to each question. We then created a link to the survey, distributed through Laracuente's Twitter, Google+, and Facebook accounts, which permitted archaeologists and archaeology students to respond anonymously.

References Cited

Allen, Mitch
2002   Reaching the Hidden Audience: Ten Rules for the Archaeological Writer. In *Public Benefits of Archaeology*, edited by Barbara J. Little, pp. 244–251. University Press of Florida, Gainesville.
Bender, Susan J. (editor)
2000   A Proposal to Guide Curricular Reform for the Twenty-first Century. In *Teaching Archaeology in the Twenty-first Century*, edited by Susan J. Bender and George S. Smith, pp. 31–48. Society for American Archaeology, Washington, D.C.
Bender, Susan J., and George S. Smith
2000   *Teaching Archaeology in the Twenty-first Century*. Society for American Archaeology, Washington, D.C.
Bransford, John D., Ann L. Brown, Rodney R. Cocking, M. Suzanne Donovan, and James W. Pellegrino (editors)
2000   *How People Learn: Brain, Mind, Experience, and School* (expanded edition). National Academy Press, Washington, D.C.
Brochu, Lisa, and Tim Merriman
2008   *Personal Interpretation: Connecting Your Audience to Heritage Resources*. Interpress, National Association for Interpretation.
Chilton, Elizabeth
2019   The Heritage of Heritage: Defining the Role of the Past in Contemporary Societ-

ies. In *History and Approaches to Heritage Studies*, edited by Phyllis Mauch Messenger and Susan J. Bender, pp. 24–31. University Press of Florida, Gainesville.

Dewey, John, and Evelyn Dewey
1915   *Schools of Tomorrow.* E. P. Dutton, New York.

Gentry, James W.
1990   What Is Experiential Learning? In *Guide to Business Gaming and Experiential Learning*, 9: 20.

Henderson, A. Gwynn
2010   Syllabus for "Seminar in Public Anthropology (ANT770)." Spring Semester 2010. Accessible through Henderson's page on www.Academia.edu.

Henderson, A. Gwynn, and Nicolas R. Laracuente
2012   Teachable Moments: Pedagogical Considerations in Teaching Public Archaeology at the Graduate Level. Paper prepared for Lessons from the Trenches: The Pedagogy of Archaeology and Heritage, an electronic symposium presented at the 77th Annual Meeting of the Society for American Archaeology, Memphis, Tennessee. Accessible through Henderson's page on www. Academia.edu.

Kane, Sharyn, and Richard Keeton
2003   Archaeology as a Compelling Story: The Art of Writing Popular Histories. In *Ancient Muses: Archaeology and the Arts,* edited by John H. Jameson Jr., John E. Ehrenhard, and Christine A. Finn, pp. 65–71. University of Alabama Press, Tuscaloosa.

King, Eleanor (issue editor)
2016   *Advances in Archaeological Practice* 4(4).

Kolb, David A.
2015   *Experiential Learning: Experience as the Source of Learning and Development.* 2nd ed. Pearson Education, Upper Saddle River, New Jersey.

Levstik, Linda S., and Keith C. Barton
2001   *Doing History: Investigating with Children in Elementary and Middle Schools.* 2nd ed. Lawrence Erlbaum, Mahwah, New Jersey.

Little, Barbara J.
2007   *Historical Archaeology: Why the Past Matters.* Left Coast Press, Walnut Creek, California.

McDavid, Carol
2009   Back to the Futurist: Response to Dawdy. *Archaeological Dialogues* 16(2): 163–169.

Merriman, Nick (editor)
2004   *Public Archaeology.* Routledge, London.

Nassaney, Michael S.
2009   The Reform of Archaeological Pedagogy and Practice through Community Service Learning. In *Archaeology and Community Service Learning*, edited by Michael S. Nassaney and Mary Ann Levine, pp. 3–35. University Press of Florida, Gainesville.

Pyburn, Anne K., and George S. Smith
2015   The MATRIX Project (Making Archaeology Relevant in the XXIst Century). In

Sharing Archaeology: Academe, Practice and the Public, edited by Peter G. Stone and Zhao Hui, pp. 132–140. Routledge, New York.

Richardson, Lorna-Jane, and Jaime Almansa-Sánchez

2015   Do You Even Know What Public Archaeology Is? Trends, Theory, Practice, Ethics. *World Archaeology* 47(2): 194–211.

Shackel, Paul A.

2019   Civic Engagement, Representation, and Social Justice: Moving from CRM to Heritage Studies. In *History and Approaches to Heritage Studies*, edited by Phyllis Mauch Messenger and Susan J. Bender, pp. 9–23. University Press of Florida: Gainsville.

Shackel, Paul A., and Lena Mortensen

2006   Some Thoughts about the Graduate Curriculum. *SAA Archaeological Record* 6(5): 23–24.

Smith, George S.

2006   Skills, Knowledge, and Abilities: Archaeology in the 21st Century. *SAA Archaeological Record* 6(5):30–31.

Smith, George S., and Dorothy Schlotthauer Krass

2000   SAA Surveys regarding Public Archaeology/Cultural Resource Management and Teaching. In *Teaching Archaeology in the Twenty-first Century*, edited by Susan J. Bender and George S. Smith, pp. 21–27. Society for American Archaeology, Washington, D.C.

Stottman, M. Jay (editor)

2010   *Archaeologists as Activists: Can Archaeologists Change the World?* University of Alabama Press, Tuscaloosa.

Weisman, Brent R.

2006   The New Curriculum is More Than Courses. *SAA Archaeological Record* 6(5):27–28.

Wolfe, Douglas E., and Eugene T. Byrne

1975   Research on Experiential Learning: Enhancing the Process. *Business Games and Experiential Learning in Action* 2: 325–336.

Zellner, Andrea

2011   Banishing Imposter Syndrome. Posted September 2, 2011, on www.gradhacker. org, accessed March 20, 2012. http://www.gradhacker.org/2011/09/02/banishing-impostor-syndrome/.

9

Experiencing Antiquity in the First Person through Archaeological Fiction

The Pedagogical Opportunities of BACAB CAAS

LEWIS C. MESSENGER JR.

As an anthropological archaeologist and a teacher of undergraduates, I am interested in the nature of students' engagement with ancient material culture and their understanding of it. I am also interested in students' attitudes and understandings of the ancient peoples who created the material culture, as well as their descendant communities. This chapter discusses a pedagogical strategy I have developed that helps students achieve greater understanding and empathy for peoples of the past (a writing assignment named BACAB CAAS).

The nature of work for people majoring in anthropology (and cultural studies in general) is changing, and it is becoming increasingly clear that the important stakeholders and their relationships are changing as well (compare Smith 2006, Smith et al. 2010). Archaeology is now done in the context of development, environmental assessment, and other public activities—all contributing to a need for our students to develop new perspectives vis-à-vis archaeological knowledge, empathy, and understanding, and all things that increasingly have significant parts to play in agenda setting in research and structuring the way we study cultures (compare Messenger and Smith 2010).

Our way of knowing about the past lifeways of peoples is through the lens of archaeology, applying certain scientific principles and formally presenting and publishing our findings. On a personal level, I think what many of us really want to do is use the tools available to us to vicariously go back in time. We want to know what it would have been like to live in places like Pueblo Bonito, Tikal, or Angkor. We want to be able to empathize with those *persons* in such places; we wish we could think and speak *in the first person* as one who lived in those ancient places. Is it possible to do that in a way that is respectful of the history and heritage of a culture that is not our own?

Such considerations have strongly motivated me in my own archaeological practice and in the ways in which I try to teach such subjects to my students. I was influenced by my professor, Janet Spector, and with regard to using archaeological fiction in my teaching, by her use of narrative in *What This Awl Means* (Spector 1993). Other models for the use of fiction as a portal to understanding archaeology include Sabloff (1989), von Hagen and Morris (1998), Fagan (2005), and Nelson (2015). These scholars all model what I want my students to do in their research and writing for archaeology classes. I want them to confront the nature of archaeological epistemology—how we know what we know about cultures in the past—in a way that transcends just the learning of archaeological facts. I want them to take ownership of the process, to have them feel the need to constantly critique the epistemology of what they learn. I want them to be mindful that they are ultimately dealing with ancient *persons*.

BACAB CAAS

Since 1986, I taught North American Archaeology with a pretty standard research assignment. Students focused on an area of their choice, writing a term paper reflecting their archaeological knowledge of a site or region, and demonstrating their ability to apply the hypothetico-deductive approach in archaeology. This was geared toward getting them to think like processual archaeologists. It fit with the current paradigm and students wrote fairly good papers. At the same time, I always felt that such writing exercises were viewed mostly as something they had to do for the grade. Generally speaking, for students it was just an assignment.

I developed my first creative writing assignment in 1992. In addition to what I had learned from Janet Spector, I drew inspiration from several examples of archaeological fiction (for example, Anthony 1991, King 1983, Shuler 1988, Gear and Gear 1992), as well as some well-grounded speculative fiction (for example, Silverberg 1980), which brought civilizations to life through detailed descriptions of environments and cultures, even to the creation of fictional "First Nations." At the same time, I was frustrated by authors who used endnotes and bibliographies to make their more fanciful takes on prehistory seem solidly rooted in archaeological evidence (for example, Auel 1980).

When I first introduced the new assignment, it was "Option B," described as an assignment involving the creation of fiction based on archaeological findings. Initially, students opted for this assignment over the original hypothetico-deductive one I had been using (Option A). After the class was over, a number of students confessed that they had chosen Option B because they thought writing creative fiction would be fun and easy! I was gratified that virtually every student told me that the easier choice would have been Option A, because the other assignment forced them to confront directly how they knew what they knew about events and people in prehistory. They found that they wanted to find ways of knowing things like: what sleeping conditions were like, what kinds of food people ate, whether things people used were prone to breaking, how they kept warm at night, and so on. Finding out these things became students' personal agendas. They ended up researching information and writing their papers more for themselves than for me. This resulted in some of the most impressive and archaeologically rich papers than I have ever received in my classes—and with a heightened concern for style and communication, as well.

What I wanted this assignment to do for my students was to make them think about their understandings of the epistemology of archaeology as well as empathize with ancient people through the writing of well-grounded archaeological fiction. Their stories were to document their grounding using endnotes, where they would indicate the sources for all of the details of daily life that emerged in their fictional accounts, as well as noting where they were taking liberties in the absence of archaeologically derived facts about past lifeways.

After a couple of years, I decided to give this assignment a name and a central place in my syllabus. I created the acronym BACAB CAAS ("Bringing Ancient Cultures Alive by Creating Archaeologically Accountable Stories"). Not only does it describe what the assignment is meant to do, but ironically (for this Mayanist), it seems to point to another meaning. For the Yucatec Maya, there are four Bacabs, or supernatural beings, whose responsibility it is to hold up the four corners of our heavens.

Since 1992, I have incorporated the BACAB CAAS approach in all my North American Archaeology courses at Hamline, later adding it into my Ancient Civilizations of Middle America and my Ancient Civilizations of Southeast Asia survey courses (Messenger 2004, 2006, 2007). Since I began having students do this creative writing project, I have received some 400 papers. Several anthropology majors have received Hamline's prestigious Stedman Award for writing on the strength of their BACAB CAAS papers, and another student used the assignment as the basis for a successful senior honors project. This methodology was employed as a contribution to the Society for American Archaeology MATRIX project (Pyburn and Smith 2015). Later, one of my MATRIX colleagues at another university, who adopted the BACAB CAAS methodology, reported that one of her students won the National Collegiate Honors Society for Anthropology award for the assignment (Troutman 2010).

Adapting the BACAB CAAS Methodology to the Classroom

I set up my course assignments in a sequential manner, and students work on two tracks throughout the semester. One track is primarily content-oriented toward acquiring knowledge and expertise in a particular world region and/ or analytic approach. The other track is the student research project. BACAB CAAS involves student research done throughout the semester, in tandem with their content-focused track. It involves eight assignments, with each of them designed to provide a base for the next assignment. Students work individually, although they may share books and other resources. This individual work is necessary because their ultimate goal is to focus on the experience of an individual in antiquity: they are asked to imagine themselves living in a past time and place.

One adjustment that I have made in recent iterations of this project is to insist that students focus on a day in the life of their subject. I found that when students had the liberty of creating a plot line and a set of characters, they often forgot about the context of daily life. I want to know what they are learning about the details of life in their specific time and place, not how creative they can be in their story telling. This change has resulted in consistently better results for all students. The following is a description of the writing assignments from a fall 2015 North American Archaeology class (see Table 9.1 for a schedule of the assignments).

Table 9.1. BACAB CAAS schedule of writing assignments

Assignments	Status	Dates
Assignment 1—Autoethnoarchaeological survey	Hand-out:	September 9: Wednesday
	Due:	September 11: Friday
Assignment 2—Proposed culture	Due:	September 18: Friday
Assignment 3—First Reference (first of four)	Due:	September 25: Friday
Assignment 4—Second Reference	Due:	October 9: Friday
Assignment 5—Third Reference	Due:	October 26: Monday
Assignment 6—Fourth Reference	Due:	November 6: Friday
Assignment 7—First Draft	Due:	November 13: Friday
Assignment 8—Final Draft	Due:	December 4: Friday

Source: From page 13 of Topics in Archaeology: North American Archaeology syllabus (Anthropology 3040) by Lewis C. Messenger Jr. (Messenger 2015: 35).

- Assignment 1: Autoethnoarchaeological survey. On the first day of class, students receive the "Ethnoarchaeological Self-perspective Questionnaire," eight pages of questions beginning with number 1: "When you first open your eyes, what do you see within about 6 inches of your face?" and ending with number 46: "Would the answers to these questions be different for different times of the year? If so, why? and how?" There are questions about how you keep warm, what you eat and wear, how you feel about going out at night, even whether people are sleeping next to you and how they are related to you. Some questions may seem intimate, but they are designed to get students to think about their immediate surroundings and how they interact with them, with the goal of sensitizing them to what it must have been like for a person in the past to wake up and notice what was immediately around them. Throughout the semester I refer back to that form and what it taught them.
- Assignment 2: Proposed culture. Within the geographical parameters of the particular class (North American, Southeast Asian, or Mesoamerican archaeology), students are to look for a location, culture, and time period they could get interested in, reflecting on what they put down on their first-day questionnaire about what they would like to research in the class.

- Assignments 3–6: Four references. In the next four weeks students must turn in at least one page per week reporting on a reference (properly formatted) and its relevance to their chosen culture. They must discuss how this reference will provide information to allow reconstructions of ancient environmental and cultural scenarios that their persona, or avatar, will inhabit. I offer assistance throughout this process and am demanding about the kinds of references students submit.

By around the seventh week of the semester, students begin to have a general idea of at least the physical scenario, the "stage," or the environment and general material culture that would have been normal for the person who lived there. This is the point at which they confront the epistemological quandary of archaeology—what can we know about the past through the process of archaeology? Often at this point, students are saying, "I really don't know a lot of things and really want, and need, to know more!" This is when those worked stones, pieces of pottery, mounds, and other evidence they have researched become important, interesting, and worthy of future consideration.

- Assignment 7: First draft. At this stage, I check for chronological, locational, and cultural inconsistencies (twelfth-dynasty Egyptians encountering Classic Maya, or a person in ancient Monte Verde keeping a journal, for instance). This is when I find that, in spite of my warnings, some students have focused on plot anyway, and they learn they have a lot of additional research to do. I remind them that you don't need scientific information or research reports to do plot, and that I prefer a boring day-in-the-life account that is rich in detail over a fantastic plot that is creative fiction.

In the last weeks of the semester there are optional assignments in the form of one or two more drafts, but at this point, students are writing something they care about. They have crossed a threshold from the work being just an assignment, to it being an opportunity to learn and feel personally enriched. Those readers who are educators know what it means to see the light go on in students. I have been fortunate to see this happen often as part of this assignment, and I also feel that students have in some measure internalized an ethic whereby their stewardship of the past will become more natural (compare Messenger 2007).

- Assignment 8: Final draft. By this point, students have gone through the entire sequence and taken advantage of the feedback provided in each section. They also are familiar with the standard form that will be used to evaluate their final draft. If they have followed all the steps, they should be able to hand in something they have a stake in, are proud of, and that will help them achieve their hoped-for grade in the class.

As often as I have taught this writing assignment, I have continued to fine-tune it and have enjoyed the many ways my students have responded to it. The following examples indicate the kinds of writing my students have produced.

BACAB CAAS Student Stories

In "The Raven" (Wold 1992), a delirious Huron man is being taken by his two friends in a canoe to see if the Jesuit priest at the mission can help. Lying in the bottom of the canoe, he falls asleep. When he awakens, he finds that, instead of his two friends, at the bow and stern are two of his animal totems. They stop at a village, which seems familiar to him, yet things are different now. There are no metal pots hanging over the fire, no brightly colored trade beads or woven trade cloth. He tries to ask someone what village it is, but all ignore him as if he is not there. He finally realizes that he has died and gone back to a time before the coming of the whites. Sending the main character's ghost back in time allowed the author to chronicle cultural changes in a Huron village.

"The Rain Bowl" (Lehman 1998) begins and ends with contemporary life at San Ildefonso Pueblo; in between, the author helps us imaginatively enter the life of an Anasazi cliff dweller during the later half of the thirteenth century. She places the process of pottery making within the larger context of daily life during a time of increasing environmental and social stress. The main character, "Yellow Corn," watches the changes that are taking place in her world while she carries on with the routines of daily life.

"The Maya Stone-Carver of *K'umarcaaj*" offers a day in the life of a jade carver from Utatlán, a late–Postclassic Period Quiché Maya city in the Guatemala highlands (Schousboe 2008). The story is filled with subtle cultural and linguistic observations, with recognized chronological, archaeological, and locational specifics. Schousboe's story takes place "in the month *Tequexepual*, the time when lords collected tribute." Her persona is a jade worker, of the *ah c'ajol*, or commoner, rank. Written in an engaging manner, this story was also well documented with extensive endnotes, and the author was careful to inform the reader about the linguistic liberties she was taking, using both Quiché and Cakchiquel, recognizing that they are two separate languages. She received Hamline's Stedman Award for excellence in writing.

A small number of students accepted a new challenge I introduced a decade ago—to direct their BACAB CAAS writings toward younger audiences by producing children's books. These also had to be rigorously researched, but were evaluated by the way they presented both visual and textual information to children (see also Bender, this volume), as well as for development of detailed information for parents to help them make the book meaningful for their children. The parent guide was critically evaluated like other BACAB CAAS assignments. Within that framework, students produced several beautifully illustrated and contextually narrated children's books.

One story, "Suchin and the Prince in Angkor Thom," uses a small family dog that runs away and is roaming around the central area of ancient Angkor Thom. As the children give chase through the site, this ancient Khmer community comes alive (Wetherby 2006).

Another student, Emma Swank, wrote a beautifully illustrated children's story, "Rainforest Adventure . . . Involving Silvery Gibbons and Jamu Fruit Doves," set on the island of Java. The goal of the story was to teach children what it would have been like to live there during the Saelendra dynasty (eighth century), when the great Buddhist temple mountain, Borobudur, was new and in active use (Figure 9.1). The author created a visual narrative from the perspective of a group of gibbons traveling through the ancient Javanese forests as they looked for different kinds of food. Her images and accompanying texts gave the reader a sense of both the natural and anthropogenic landscapes of the times. She included a concise detailed discussion for parents (see Figure 9.2), complete with a well-formatted bibliography (Swank 2006).

The funny hairless apes in the field were humans.
The loose colorful skins that hung from their bodies were clothes.
They wore woven reed hats to protect their
furless faces from the hot sun.

The flat lands were rice paddies.
The human beings stomped in the soft muddy ground
to prepare it for the cultivation of rice. It took many feet
to soften the ground for the rice seedlings.

They worked and worked as the rain tumbled down. These humans,
like the animals of the forest, were used to the heavy rains on the
island. They needed the rainwater to grow their rice and to quench
their thirst during hot sunny days.

15

Figure 9.1. Description and illustration of people and landscape around Borobudur on Java
(Swank 2009, original in color). Used with permission of Emma Swank.

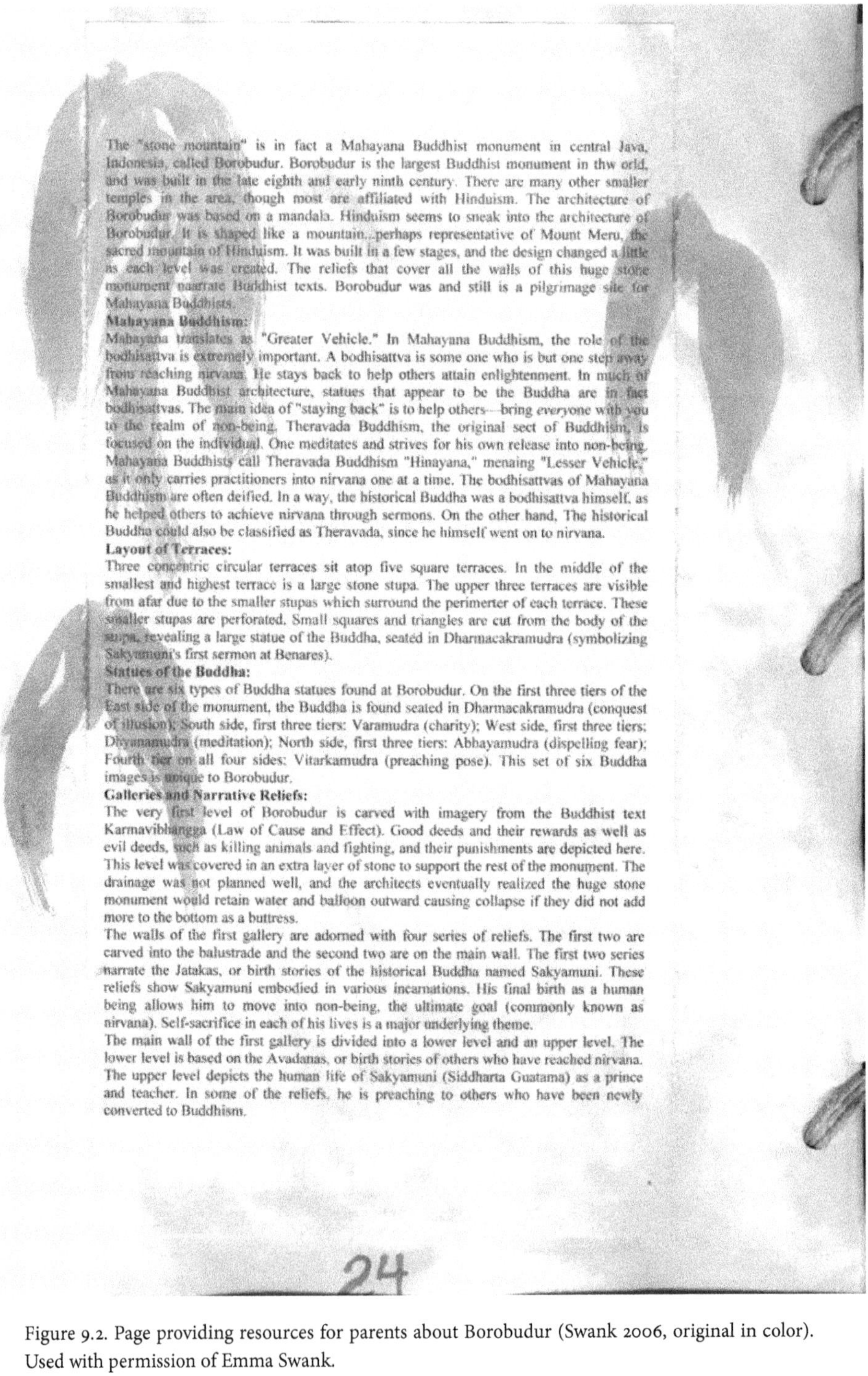

The "stone mountain" is in fact a Mahayana Buddhist monument in central Java, Indonesia, called Borobudur. Borobudur is the largest Buddhist monument in thw orld, and was built in the late eighth and early ninth century. There are many other smaller temples in the area, though most are affiliated with Hinduism. The architecture of Borobudur was based on a mandala. Hinduism seems to sneak into the architecture of Borobudur. It is shaped like a mountain...perhaps representative of Mount Meru, the sacred mountain of Hinduism. It was built in a few stages, and the design changed a little as each level was created. The reliefs that cover all the walls of this huge stone monument naarrate Buddhist texts. Borobudur was and still is a pilgrimage site for Mahayana Buddhists.

Mahayana Buddhism:
Mahayana translates as "Greater Vehicle." In Mahayana Buddhism, the role of the bodhisattva is extremely important. A bodhisattva is some one who is but one step away from reaching nirvana. He stays back to help others attain enlightenment. In much of Mahayana Buddhist architecture, statues that appear to be the Buddha are in fact bodhisattvas. The main idea of "staying back" is to help others—bring everyone with you to the realm of non-being. Theravada Buddhism, the original sect of Buddhism, is focused on the individual. One meditates and strives for his own release into non-being. Mahayana Buddhists call Theravada Buddhism "Hinayana," menaing "Lesser Vehicle," as it only carries practitioners into nirvana one at a time. The bodhisattvas of Mahayana Buddhism are often deified. In a way, the historical Buddha was a bodhisattva himself, as he helped others to achieve nirvana through sermons. On the other hand, The historical Buddha could also be classified as Theravada, since he himself went on to nirvana.

Layout of Terraces:
Three concentric circular terraces sit atop five square terraces. In the middle of the smallest and highest terrace is a large stone stupa. The upper three terraces are visible from afar due to the smaller stupas which surround the perimeter of each terrace. These smaller stupas are perforated. Small squares and triangles are cut from the body of the stupa, revealing a large statue of the Buddha, seated in Dharmacakramudra (symbolizing Sakyamuni's first sermon at Benares).

Statues of the Buddha:
There are six types of Buddha statues found at Borobudur. On the first three tiers of the East side of the monument, the Buddha is found seated in Dharmacakramudra (conquest of illusion); South side, first three tiers: Varamudra (charity); West side, first three tiers: Dhyanamudra (meditation); North side, first three tiers: Abhayamudra (dispelling fear); Fourth tier on all four sides: Vitarkamudra (preaching pose). This set of six Buddha images is unique to Borobudur.

Galleries and Narrative Reliefs:
The very first level of Borobudur is carved with imagery from the Buddhist text Karmavibhangga (Law of Cause and Effect). Good deeds and their rewards as well as evil deeds, such as killing animals and fighting, and their punishments are depicted here. This level was covered in an extra layer of stone to support the rest of the monument. The drainage was not planned well, and the architects eventually realized the huge stone monument would retain water and balloon outward causing collapse if they did not add more to the bottom as a buttress.

The walls of the first gallery are adorned with four series of reliefs. The first two are carved into the balustrade and the second two are on the main wall. The first two series narrate the Jatakas, or birth stories of the historical Buddha named Sakyamuni. These reliefs show Sakyamuni embodied in various incarnations. His final birth as a human being allows him to move into non-being, the ultimate goal (commonly known as nirvana). Self-sacrifice in each of his lives is a major underlying theme.

The main wall of the first gallery is divided into a lower level and an upper level. The lower level is based on the Avadanas, or birth stories of others who have reached nirvana. The upper level depicts the human life of Sakyamuni (Siddharta Guatama) as a prince and teacher. In some of the reliefs, he is preaching to others who have been newly converted to Buddhism.

24

Figure 9.2. Page providing resources for parents about Borobudur (Swank 2006, original in color). Used with permission of Emma Swank.

BACAB CAAS Assessment

How can we know what students are learning? Can the BACAB CAAS assignment be assessed as a pedagogical methodology, and if so, do my assumptions about its impact upon students hold up under scrutiny? Since 2007, I have utilized three assessment instruments in addition to anecdotal evidence: (1) questionnaires sent to participants in past BACAB CAAS creative writing projects, (2) surveys on fiction writing in archaeology administered at the beginning and end of the semester, and (3) anthropology final exam essays.

My goal was to learn the impact this BACAB CAAS writing project had upon students' perspectives and lives—their studies, work, and life experiences. Did it affect how they perceive archaeological sites, archaeological materials, and any descendant communities they have interacted with? Has this project impacted their archaeological epistemology, the kinds of questions they ask of the archaeological record, or their vocation? Has it produced an enhanced ethic toward the stewardship of archaeological heritage?

The following examples give a flavor of responses from both students and recent graduates.

- "The creative writing assignment I did at Hamline allowed me to look at the archeological sites and artifacts I have seen as not just 'cold faceless objects,' but instead as products of living cultures and peoples."
- "Storytelling is key to archaeology because it allows people to imagine the past instead of just seeing artifacts."
- "Working on these various projects was the most useful exercise I encountered at Hamline. I do not think that I would have pursued archaeology as a vocation without them."
- "It allows the archaeology to 'speak' and reminds us that there once were living, breathing humans who occupied the ancient archaeological sites."
- "By putting data into such a personal, human context it is easier to think about the importance of the data you gather and the things you plan to do with it. Rather than just writing or learning for the sake of doing it, this style of output really requires you to think about the human implications of your research."

The following student essay response summarizes much of what I hope students learn from the BACAB CAAS assignments.

In my field, people often make generalizations about Native American beliefs—saying things like "Native Americans are much more connected with the earth than we are" or "Native Americans have such and such opinion." This is not the case now, and has never been. I think in this class I learned how important thinking about groups of people as real people is: individuals who are a part of a culture that influences their beliefs, but individuals nonetheless.

I was also greatly impacted by the difficulty of drawing conclusions from objects left behind by ancient peoples. After writing the BACAB CAAS paper, I learned firsthand the difficulty archaeologists have deciding whether they are justified in drawing conclusions about a past civilization. This is just as true today, in more fields than just archaeology. When looking through information, it is important to understand where it is coming from, and if the person relaying the information is justified in drawing the conclusions that they do.

Conclusion

We are influenced by stories, especially those that we find compelling, and we may find that they have influenced our thoughts, our perception of the world—our ontology—and hence what motivates us to interact with it, in particular ways. Stories reify our perceptual paradigms; Thomas Kuhn's (1962) work is still relevant today. We are blind to seeing beyond those paradigms, unless someone narrates the world differently in a way that engages us. Even as professional archaeologists, we may wish we could go back to places or times we are studying just to sit in the shadows and watch and listen. How wonderful it would be if we could somehow enter a time machine and learn directly what the ontological frameworks were that people took for granted in Cahokia, or Tiwanaku, or, better yet, in some small village in their hinterlands.

BACAB CAAS as a pedagogical approach guides students to gather information so that they can imagine what life was like for a person at a particular place and time in antiquity, and to do so in the first person. This has proven to be a powerful way for students to cross-culturally empathize with those in the past and reconstruct a lifeway—recognizing that it is someone else's heritage, but treating and valuing it as if it were their own.

References Cited

Anthony, Piers
1991   *Tatham Mound*. Avon Books, New York.
Auel, Jean
1980   *Clan of the Cave Bear*. Crown, New York.
Fagan, Brian
2005   *Writing Archaeology: Telling Stories about the Past*. Left Coast Press, Walnut Creek, California.
Gear, W. Michael, and Kathleen O'Neal Gear
1992   *People of the River*. Tom Doherty, New York.
King, Kathleen
1983   *Cricket Sings: A Novel of Pre-Columbian Cahokia*. Ohio University Press, Athens, Ohio.
Kuhn, Thomas S.
1962   *The Structure of Scientific Revolutions*. University of Chicago Press, Chicago.
Lehman, Caroline
1998   The Rain Bowl: A Short Story about the Pottery-Making Tradition of the Mesa Verde Anasazi and Its Significance in Contemporary Pueblo Culture. Student paper submitted for North American Archaeology, Department of Anthropology, Hamline University, St. Paul, Minnesota.
Messenger, Lewis C., Jr.
2004   North American Archaeology. Anthropology 3040: Topics in Archaeology Course Syllabus. (Course manual containing BACAB CAAS instructions). Fall 2004. Department of Anthropology, Hamline University, St. Paul, Minnesota.
2006   Ancient Civilizations of Middle America: Fall 2006 Course Syllabus. (containing BACAB CAAS instructions). Department of Anthropology, Hamline University, St. Paul, Minnesota.
2007   BACAB CAAS: Seeking the "First Person" in Antiquity and Taking Personal Ownership of the Preservation of Heritage Resources. Paper presented at the 3rd Annual Ename International Colloquium, The Future of Heritage: Changing Visions, Attitudes, and Contexts in the 21st Century, Ghent, Belgium.
2015   North American Archaeology. Anthropology 3040: Topics in Archaeology Course Syllabus. (Course manual containing BACAB CAAS instructions). Fall 2015. Department of Anthropology, Hamline University, St. Paul, Minnesota.
Messenger, Phyllis Mauch, and George S. Smith (editors)
2010   *Cultural Heritage Management: A Global Perspective*. University Press of Florida, Gainesville.
Nelson, Sarah Milledge
2015   *Shamans, Queens, and Figurines: The Development of Gender Archaeology*. Left Coast Press, Walnut Creek, California.
Pyburn, K. Anne, and George S. Smith
2015   The MATRIX Project (Making Archaeology Teaching Relevant in the XXIst Century: An Approach to the Efficient Sharing of Professional Knowledge

and Skills with a Large Audience). In *Sharing Archaeology: Academe, Practice, and the Public*, edited by Peter G. Stone and Zhao Hui, pp. 132–140. Routledge Press, New York.

Sabloff, Jeremy A.

1989 *The Cities of Ancient Mexico: Reconstructing a Lost World.* Thames and Hudson, New York.

Schousboe, Ellen

2008 The Maya Stone-Carver of K'umarcaaj. Student paper submitted for Ancient Civilizations of Middle America, Department of Anthropology, Hamline University, St. Paul, Minnesota.

Shuler, Linda Lay

1988 *She Who Remembers.* Signet, New American Library, New York.

Silverberg, Robert

1980 *Lord Valentine's Castle.* Bantam Books, New York.

Smith, George S.

2006 Heritage Resource Management Work Group: Preserving the World's Heritage Resources Workshop, November 2–6, 2005. Paper presented at the 71st Annual Meeting of the Society for American Archaeology, San Juan, Puerto Rico.

Smith, George S., Phyllis Mauch Messenger, and Hilary A. Soderland (editors)

2010 *Heritage Values in Contemporary Society.* Left Coast Press, Walnut Creek, California.

Spector, Janet

1993 *What This Awl Means: Feminist Archaeology at a Wahpeton Dakota Village.* Minnesota Historical Society Press, St. Paul, Minnesota.

Swank, Emma J.

2006 Rainforest Adventure . . . Involving Silvery Gibbons and Jamu Fruit Doves. Student paper submitted for Ancient Civilizations of Southeast Asia, Department of Anthropology, Hamline University, St. Paul, Minnesota.

von Hagen, Adriana, and Craig Morris

1998 *The Cities of the Ancient Andes.* Thames and Hudson, London.

Troutman, Michele

2010 A Tale of Two Scribes: Scribes in the Aftermath of 18 Rabbit's Sacrifice. Mesoamerican Archaeology (Anthropology 323) Spring 2010. Dr. Beverly Chiarulli. Department of Anthropology, Indiana University of Pennsylvania.

Wetherby, Bonnie S.

2006 Suchin and the Prince in Angkor Thom. Student paper submitted for Ancient Civilizations of Southeast Asia, Department of Anthropology, Hamline University, St. Paul, Minnesota.

Wold, Bob

1992 The Raven's Gift. Student paper submitted for North American Archaeology, Department of Anthropology, Hamline University, St. Paul, Minnesota.

IDENTITY AND HERITAGE

A Faculty Interview on the Use of Image in the Classroom

SUSAN J. BENDER

Like Messenger's use of the construction of narrative (this volume), pedagogical approaches more commonly associated with the humanities may provide students alternative ways to connect to past cultures. While Messenger asks his students to construct verbal narratives that can be supported with imagery, the following summarizes an assignment created by Heather Hurst, Skidmore College, in which she plunges her students into the task of reading and constructing visual narrative. While neither assignment was initially designed to engage students in the study of heritage, they arguably accomplish this end by encouraging students to grasp the many ways that the identities, and ultimately heritages, of people (both past and present) can be expressed in material remains.

Archaeological instruction often demands that students gain command of numerous facts (geographic, historic, and socioeconomic), in addition to conceptualizing less tangible elements of cultural belief systems, such as aspects of practice and worldview, which are often distant from their own. When addressing the latter, the typical pedagogical format of reading, synthesis, and writing has limitations because a certain degree of familiarity and experience needs to be cultivated in order to successfully "see" an unfamiliar worldview (compare Moe, this volume). To bridge this gap, we populate our classes with images of ancient tools, pottery, figurines, artwork, and site plans with the intent to help students improve their literacy. Using these visual media in the classroom can be particularly successful when systematic, close observation is employed. In contrast to memorization of an image's attributes, when students are instructed to identify pattern and meaning, they come to know a cultural framework living within the object itself.

Hurst uses the iconography of Chavín de Huántar in highland Peru as the basis of this exercise in visual learning. The people of ancient Chavín de Huántar (1000–500 B.C.) created visually dense sculpture that was a central focus in the site's role as a pilgrimage center, where complex art and architecture are highly organized around principles that express the worldview of this formative Andean monumental center. Students can find these works impenetrable and express their poor understanding by simplifications such as "ritualistic" or "animistic." However, replicating anthropological practice (observation, description, and analysis) used to discern underlying principles of structure and meaning within Chavín visual culture, and then asking students to apply this framework to their own visual culture, can help them make connections to the active nature by which identity, authority, and belief systems manifest in material remains.

The assignment progresses through several incremental steps: (1) students identify sets of similar and contrasting elements in a relatively simple Chavín iconographic example; (2) they are introduced to basic principles that structure Chavín iconography and then work to identify these within various artworks (see Burger 1992, Kembel and Rick 2004); (3) working with a complex sculpture (for example, Figure A), students diagram the image using the vocabulary gained in step 1 and guiding principles realized in step 2; and then (4) students apply the principles of repeated patterns to generate their own monument using a personalized symbol set they create themselves. Within this structured approach, students are asked to craft an understanding of the meanings embedded in the construction of Chavín monuments through their own powers of observation, and they are coached through this process in manageable increments that become increasingly sophisticated (compare Messenger, this volume).

As they move through more complex images and identify repeated patterns of elimination and substitution, students begin to discern that these images convey messages to the onlooker about the foundations of power and its acquisition by leaders at Chavin de Huántar. By increasing their own proficiency to "read" Chavín symbolism, they learn about the relationship between power, transformation, and religion-based authority in the ancient society. Other understandings emerge as well—for example, when students begin to build a picture of Chavín de Huántar's natural landscape as

Figure A. Raimondi Stone, Chavín de Huántar. Used with permission of Richard Burger.

they identify the range of animals depicted in its imagery. Once they have worked their way through this step of the assignment, students have grasped that a set of symbols and structures dominated how pilgrims to Chavín de Huántar understood the world to be organized and their role in it (Burger 1992; Druc 2004; Kembel 2008).

The students are then asked to apply these insights in the creation of their own monument, one that expresses their identity and worldview. Hurst asks students to develop their own symbol bank and articulate this vocabulary into a monument by applying the rules that structure Chavín iconography. While they are given free rein in the choice and definition of symbols (for example, brand logos, sports' mascots), they must provide a rationale for them. Why does "X" represent "Y"? What is the power relationship between facets of personal choice and things they "like," versus aspects of their identity that are inherited or assigned (Figure B)? At this point, the assignment becomes quite complex and challenging. Students are asked to operate on a metalevel that is unfamiliar to them. They must consider what structures their lives in terms of economy, movement, landscape, and so on. In actually making a monument about themselves, students internalize concepts of symbolic structure and worldview in ways that would not happen in writing an essay about the cultural sphere of Chavín de Huántar.

Several sources—the monuments that students create, final reflection papers, and their informal commentary—reveal what students learn from such an assignment. These outcomes reflect the deep questioning that students engage in when choosing a symbol set, asking themselves probing questions about who they are. Hurst's students researched the history and changing meanings associated with the symbols they chose, and came to understand that they are deeply enmeshed in a consumer culture, and that their identity is socially (rather than professionally) constructed at this point in their lives. Similar to the efforts by site leaders at Chavín de Huántar to both attract followers and establish their authority, students identified frameworks that compete to shape their cultural participation.

The assignment gives students tools to reflect critically on visual materials and identity construction. In coming to their conclusions, many students engage in deep, serious self-reflection about who they are and what they consume, until now, often without thought to wider

Figure B. Student monument. Used with permission of Samantha Primiano.

impacts. In this process of self-discovery and expression, students are willing to spend more hours on research than they might in a more straightforward writing assignment (compare Messenger, this volume). Ultimately, asking students to access understanding through an unconventional mode, and then to apply it in a form of self-expression, helps them to embed the knowledge more securely in their knowledge structures (see Moe, this volume), such that they are unlikely to forget the power of worldview to propel behavior.

In raising critical issues about identity and worldview, this type of assignment can serve as a bridge into several dimensions of heritage study. At a very basic level, Hurst's assignment makes something, at first impenetrable, legible to students. In this, the assignment encourages students to observe closely and look for patterns to grasp meaning instead of simply rejecting or ignoring what seem to be incomprehensible cultural differences. It asks students to be open to and develop empathy with diverse worldviews. On a more sophisticated level, the assignment requires students to bring the lens of self-reflection to their own identity, to grasp that their identity and ultimately heritage are constructs. From this stems the realization that heritages are fluid, constructed for a purpose, and can be challenged. Here they are fully engaged in a critical thinking exercise (see Shackel 2019; Zimmerman 2019). From this perspective, students are then in a position to engage in multivocal dialogue about the American past and present, and they have gotten to this place by studying the past to learn about principles that also apply to the present.

References Cited

Burger, Richard L.
1992   *Chavín and the Origins of Andean Civilization.* Thames and Hudson, London.

Druc, Isabelle C.
2004   Ceramic Diversity in Chavín de Huántar, Peru. *Latin American Antiquity* 15(3): 344–363.

Kembel, Silva R.
2008   Architecture at the Monumental Center of Chavín de Huántar: Sequence, Transformations, and Chronology. In *Chavín: Art, Architecture and Culture*, edited by J. Quilter and W. Conklin, pp. 35–84. Cotsen Institute of Archaeology, Los Angeles, California.

Kembel, Silva R., and John W. Rick
2004   Building Authority at Chavín de Huántar: Models of Social Organization and Development in the Initial Period and Early Horizon. In *Andean Archaeology*, edited by Helaine Silverman, pp. 51–76. Blackwell Studies in Global Archaeology, Victoria, Australia.

Shackel, Paul A.
2019   Civic Engagement, Representation, and Social Justice: Moving from CRM to Heritage Studies. In *History and Approaches to Heritage Studies*, edited by Phyllis Mauch Messenger and Susan J. Bender, pp. 9–23. University Press of Florida, Gainesville.

Zimmerman, Larry J.
2019   Help Needed! Reflections on Archaeology's Role in Theorizing a Critical Pedagogy of Heritage. In *History and Approaches to Heritage Studies*, edited by Phyllis Mauch Messenger and Susan J. Bender, pp. 215–236. University Press of Florida, Gainesville.

10

Connecting the Dots

Teaching Archaeology and Social Relevance

SHEREEN LERNER AND RICHARD EFFLAND

From an archaeological perspective, heritage education provides us with the opportunity to learn about the common threads connecting ancient civilizations, guides us to a better understanding of the nature of society and humanity in the past, and connects the past to our world today. The elements that we share across time and space provide us with a story of humanity and its successes and failures. We rely on this perspective when we teach world archaeology and focus our pedagogical strategy on creative uses of technology blended with a thematic approach, connecting regions to themes such as trade, use of water, urbanization, and political power. This integrated approach, using active learning techniques, helps students to understand the importance and value of our past and its connection to the present. In the process, students gain a greater understanding of a world heritage that is tied to issues they are confronting today. Of course there remains a question of whether or not students truly understand these connections; our best understanding of this has been through their final reflections, which include:

- "This course has also hammered in the fact that culture is 'What makes you, you.' This culture comes from your traditions, beliefs, and way of life and customs. Learning about the past has helped me better understand the present."
- "If I have learned anything from this class, it's that I have very little knowledge about other cultures, and there is always more to learn and to be able to better understand others."

- "I never really liked history, which at first I thought the class was going to be all about history, but after seeing the assignments it wasn't like our regular history class. It was so much more than that."

Freshman- and sophomore-level archaeology classes are often filled with students who have little knowledge of the past, but who enroll because it "sounds interesting." In teaching these students, we long ago determined that our focus was not to encourage students to major in anthropology as much as to teach them the value and importance of their heritage by gaining an understanding of the past and its connection to the present. We are fortunate that our class sizes are no larger than thirty-five, so active student engagement and participation is not only possible, but encouraged. Our emphasis has been to teach about how culture helped humans adapt to their world and how contemporary human cultures are contingent upon the past; in other words, we are conditioned by our past experiences. One of the many questions we consider in this course is how and whether we learn from the past and why we often ignore it.

Structuring Principles

Little and Shackel discuss the concept of heritage as a way to begin to think about the uses of the past and its connection to the public good. They point out the importance of "raising consciousness about the past and connecting it to the present." It is this notion that a "socially useful heritage can stimulate and empower" (2014: 21) that is a foundation of our course.

We teach our introductory archaeology classes in such a way that we take this concept of heritage and apply it through the use of themes, current events, activities, and reflections. We have learned that it is critical to engage students and involve them in the learning process and that the delivery of information is an important component of this engagement. As part of our overall course design, we have redirected its organization from a traditional culture–historical approach to one that combines regions with themes and connects ancient cultures and concepts from the past to the present. We use a variety of "seed questions" to spark student thinking about the big picture, while they are learning the details of a culture.

Thematic Approach

Examples of some of the themes and seed questions that we pose include:

Power and Leadership: What are the qualities that make for good leadership? How does one become a leader and how are leaders selected by society? What is divine kingship and why do civilizations turn to this form repeatedly? What characteristics can be defined that distinguish a "god-king" across civilizations? Is a leader always a political figure? Can there be people who shape a society without having political power?

Trade and Economics: Why is trade important? What are the positive and negative impacts of trade? What are the implications of having access (or not having access) to resources? How is conflict related to trade, economics, and resources?

Religion and Ideology: How does religion help shape a society and affect power and leadership in a society? What do religions say about wealth and power and its connection to politics?

Social Organization and Social Stress: What do we mean by social organization? How are the different forms of social organization reflected in various societies and how do they affect power and leadership and the functioning of society? Why do social organizations change and what tends to drive that change?

Art, Architecture, Literacy, and Control of Information: What does information mean for societies (how do we define it)? What are the different forms of information? How does the control and exchange of information affect a society and the development of cultures and civilizations? Who has access to information, and do access and control impact power? Can art and architecture be considered information and, if they are, how are they used to transmit messages and express the beliefs of people?

Impact of People on the Environment: What factors tend to put societies at risk in terms of how they relate to the environment? What was the impact of the agricultural revolution on the environment and societies? How does a society's subsistence system affect the environment?

Connection to the Present

Of course one cannot teach a class on world prehistory without understanding how archaeology provides insight into our cultural heritage. Our purpose here is to explore the nature of archaeology and how archaeologists contribute to understandings of the past. We want to dispel the images of "Indiana Jones" archaeology with a more accurate depiction of what archaeologists hope to learn not only about the past but also about the present. As part of this consideration, we emphasize that while excavation does occur, it is just one method to retrieve insights about how a culture operated. Most importantly, students learn that archaeologists pursue their investigations systematically as they move through a series of questions aimed at yielding new insights. We engage students with Renfrew and Bahn's (2016) view of archaeology as the examination of the history of humanity, which is seen through the process by which humans use material things to interact with their world. In this emphasis lies the understanding that archaeology strives to explain human behavior by looking at things in the past for the purpose of understanding humanity at large and at the same time craft an understanding of the present.

Social Relevance

Another of our goals is to have students connect the past to important contemporary social issues, something we term "social relevance." We agree with Brian Fagan who notes that "archaeology is unique among all the sciences, as it is the only reliable way of studying and explaining how human societies have changed—or remained the same—over very long periods of time. Quite apart from studying our origins among the nonhuman primates, the long time frame of archaeology allows us to trace the origins of modern humanity" (2005: 32). We use Fagan's concept to engage students in how archaeological research allows us to identify the commonalities and/or differences in why and how cultures change and how this relates to our cultural heritage in today's world.

Pedagogical Methods

Current Events Reporting

How do we use current events in an archaeology class? Each student is required to present a current event related to archaeology. The presentations often spark discussion about how archaeological research is conducted, what the ethical considerations are, or how the current discovery relates to past information. These discussions in turn open the door for students to learn more about a topic that would not otherwise be covered in the class. For example, when a student brought in information on a recent television program on National Geographic ("Diggers"), it sparked an extensive discussion pertaining to laws that protect heritage resources and burials, as well as how those laws differ among countries around the world. It also allowed a historical digression that focused on how archaeology was conducted in the past versus today. A more recent article on the destruction of the ancient archaeological site of Nimrud by ISIS (National Geographic 2015) prompted a discussion pertaining to religion, war, and conflict, and how these have been interrelated for thousands of years. We also discussed what it means to lose a place such as Nimrud with regard to our heritage and understanding of the history of humanity. Typically, as the semester progresses, many students actively seek out articles that are directly related to a topic or region under discussion. In the presentation of their article, students must connect the information to the course content and to current issues in today's world.

Case Studies

Throughout the class, we use case studies to address specific concepts and issues that arise during the course. We want students to understand that every element of discovery through archaeology can yield information and provide insight into the past and, potentially, the present. Ultimately, archaeology is anthropology and as such shares in the goal of understanding humanity at large. For example, we can tell the story of how we understand Stonehenge as one that unfolds over time. It also reveals how archaeologists build an understanding of time and space in an effort to see how human cultures operate. From this perspective, we tie Stonehenge, and many other examples, to our discussions of social change processes or transformations.

As in many world prehistory courses, Easter Island provides a good case study of human impact on the environment, which can then be connected to current issues of climate change. Paul Bahn and John Flenly (1992) propose a model for the decline of the forest and its impact on the society. They raise the question of collapse and use a model of continued exploitation and overuse of the environment to examine it. The central issue is that the environment could not sustain a growing population over the long term. Bahn and Flenly posit: "Yes, there was war and famine, and yes, there was a population crash, but ultimately the Easter Islanders were reconciled with nature and achieved, for a time, a sustainable stability. Will we Earth Islanders have the sense to do the same thing before our skyscrapers come tumbling about our ears? Or is the human personality always the same as that of the person who felled the last tree?" (1992: 63). These are questions we discuss with students to help them develop a sense of how what happened in the past relates to the present. Students are quick to see the connection to their future. In response, they bring in current event articles about climate change and how the governments of the world cannot agree on approaches to slowing environmental degradation. While they are aware that our lifeway is not sustainable at the current rate of environmental impacts, connecting these concepts to what happened to ancient societies gives them a greater sense of urgency.

Another good example that emphasizes social and environmental issues comes from Jared Diamond's book, *Collapse: How Societies Choose to Fail or Succeed* (2011), where he examines the Norse expansion into Greenland and ultimately North America. Diamond believes that the Norse came to Greenland within a time frame of mild climatic conditions, allowing them to settle and adapt to a harsh environment. The Norse were hierarchically structured, and their leaders tended to enhance their social positions through trade. Ultimately, short-term enhancement of social position was more important than attending to long-term survival needs, leading to the eventual cultural collapse of their North American settlements. Diamond, at the end of *Collapse*, asks a very fundamental question based on all that we know about the past civilizations he discusses: do we "have the courage to make the most fundamental reappraisal now facing us: how much of our traditional consumer values and First World living standard can we afford to retain?" (2011: 524). That is the fundamental question Diamond is asking. In the face of what we are doing today, can we really learn from the past?

We also use current news as a means to connect to our archaeological case studies. Based on the writing of Zou Hanru, a columnist for the *China Daily*, Thomas Friedman reports on developments that reiterate environmental issues documented for ancient societies, "We no longer have abundant forest cover, our land is no longer that green, our water tables are depleting and our numbers are expanding faster than ever. . . . China itself uses 45 billion pairs of disposable chopsticks a year, or 1.66 million cubic meters of timber, or 25 million full-grown trees." The more affluent the Chinese become, he added, "the more the demand for bigger homes and a wide range of furniture" (October 26, 2005).

As part of our thematic structure, we ask the students to connect what they read about the Chinese, with their growing appetite for material wealth, to what they have learned about Easter Island or Greenland. The students consider the issues and raise questions regarding short-term desire versus long-term needs. Ultimately, students conclude that, as with ancient societies, while there may be concern about environmental impacts, the Chinese people are placing greater emphasis on the continued growth and prosperity of their economy.

Students also tend to believe that these problems can be solved because we have superior knowledge and technology to handle them today than in the past. This is an aspect of ethnocentrism, as it has been traditionally defined, that goes largely unchallenged. We feel we are more capable of handling problems than people in the past. However, the archaeological record tells us of great human accomplishments in the past. One look at the ancient temple of Angkor Wat tells us that the ancient Khmer people were ingenious in their building and use of symbolism. We have the students conduct independent research on the connections among the culture, religion, and architecture of Angkor Wat and they come away in awe of what ancient people can accomplish. They learn that the issues that confronted the ancient people of Angkor Wat are not that different from those of today. For example, studies have shown that the collapse of Angkor was a complex process brought about by social, political, and environmental factors that included war, land overexploitation, and drought, and that technology is not always sufficient to prevent major collapse during times of severe instability (Choi 2012). Unfortunately, this is all too easy for students to connect to issues in today's world.

As a result of projects such as Angkor Wat, students gain a greater understanding that there are many lessons to be learned from the ancient world and many things that the ancient people of the world can teach us about our own cultural heritage. The issue is whether we care to learn and make these relevant to ourselves. This is why social relevance is an important part of what we discuss in our course. Questions that relate to sustainability, conflict, resource acquisition, trade, economics, and communication are crucial as part of our connecting the past to the present. The past can tell us some things about how other people faced these same questions, yet we have to listen with an open mind to learn from it.

Using the Web to Enhance Learning

With the growth in online learning and the use of various learning management systems, we have seen technology play a greater role in student learning. We have learned that we must not only make course content more meaningful, but also offer it to the students in a format that helps them "want to learn." We have approached this challenge in two ways: (1) as discussed, we have created our introductory archaeology course to focus on themes that are relevant to the past and present, and (2) we have enhanced our use of technology to offer students a variety of avenues for learning. Most importantly, we have moved away from test taking and memorization toward increased writing and critical thinking. We have used this approach for both our online and face-to-face classes. In both arenas we have found that students are thinking about what they are learning and relating the content to the modern world more effectively.

The Web pages we have developed are highly visual, interactive, and engaging, and are constructed around a definitive problem set related to a course theme. Students are encouraged to engage in interactive activities in order to explore problems. The problems are formulated in a way that encourages the student (learner) to ponder the implications of what they are discovering in the process. We have added video clips and TED talks to enhance the reading materials. Over the years, we have converted many of the Web pages into e-books or open educational resources to provide students with much of the same content but in a manner that is easier to access.

As mentioned earlier, one of the activities in the course is to study Angkor Wat. We have created a Web area that requires students to interact with material that includes a primer furnishing important facts, visuals, and video clips. We then provide the students with a data section that contains a variety of resources, including architectural maps, descriptions, and background on religion, ancient mathematics, astronomy, and the history of the Khmer civilization. Angkor Wat is filled with symbolism designed to convey meaning to those who entered into it. We ask the students to examine Angkor Wat and, using scientific inquiry, attempt to reconstruct the meaning of one part of the temple. By the time they conduct their study of Angkor Wat, they have already studied other ancient cultures and are prepared to consider how the powerful exert their influence on society and how Angkor compares or contrasts with other civilizations. As a final component, we ask the students to find a modern corollary and compare what they have learned about Angkor Wat to a current culture (see also Bender, this volume).

We have created a similar Web area that probes the consequences of agriculture on human societies. A central question guides students as they think about these consequences. The problem is set up by an overview of the agricultural revolution; it is highly visual and includes concise text. Students then can select three of seven different articles that focus on the impacts of agriculture on ancient societies. Each article raises specific issues pertaining to the impact of agriculture on health, diet, population demography, social organization, and more. Perhaps most interesting about this Web area is that one has choices of readings to answer the central question. There is no right or wrong response. However, a specific problem is defined and students have choices as to how to approach it. There is a combination of visual dressing, multimedia power, and problem orientation. We have found that students become more engaged when they are interacting with the material in a variety of forms. As a final component of this activity, students connect the impacts of agriculture on ancient societies to issues of sustainability in today's world (see also Hayashida, this volume).

A more recent activity that we have incorporated takes advantage of the Chaco Digital Archive (http://www.chacoarchive.org/cra/about/), which was developed by Steve Plog at the University of Virginia. As noted on the website, "The Chaco Research Archive is a collaborative effort to create an online archive and analytical database that integrates much of the widely dispersed archaeological data collected from Chaco Canyon from the late 1890s through the first half of the 20th century." From a teaching perspective, it allows our students the opportunity to use an online database and address specific research objectives (for example, mapping the construction periods of Pueblo Bonito or identifying the distribution of artifacts and structures at various sites in Chaco Canyon) that help them understand relationships between behavior and the landscape.

Think Pieces

In addition to these Web-based exercises, we have students read a number of articles throughout the semester and respond with what we call "think pieces," which address a number of questions that pertain to the articles and are directly related to the themes and seed questions. The purpose of the responses is to help the student think about the readings and activities and relate them to the ideas presented in the course. The goal of the think piece is to explore what the student is learning and relate that to the themes that are being discussed.

Project-Based Learning

With regard to the themes, our goal is to have students think critically about the content they are learning. For their final projects, students are divided into groups at the beginning of term with an emphasis on a particular topic that they have selected as an area of interest (for example, trade networks, mortuary practices, social stratification, exploration/nautical, beliefs/religion, abandonment/collapse). They must connect these topics to the overarching themes of the course. Throughout the semester, students meet and develop the information within their topics as it pertains to course content. At the end of term, the students present the results of their findings using archaeological data and sites. It is common for students to conduct additional research to enhance their final presentation. Over the course of the semester, students explore the overarching thematic questions and learn that, with more information, their perspectives change. A goal is to have students seek new questions and try to relate what they are learning in class to the world around them today. We think of this process as: Define . . . Revisit . . . and Add.

The purpose of this assignment is to have students conduct research related to an overarching course theme through a specific topic and identify ideas they have generated as the semester progresses. As part of the process, students report back to the instructor every two weeks with information, including what team members have researched, new information that has been obtained, insights that have formed with respect to the questions being pursued, and identification of any new questions that have arisen in their exploration of the theme topic. This approach requires students to not only learn the content discussed in class, but be independent thinkers.

We have also been working on avenues to reach out to the growing area of students in the online environment. It is easy to have online students focus on sites and artifacts without making connections to the present or our cultural heritage. It is more challenging to provide project-based learning to online students, but, as growth in this area continues, it is more important than ever to learn how to integrate elements of the past with the present in an interactive and engaging manner. Are such courses teaching heritage preservation and the value of our past, or are they focused on the details of archaeological sites and past cultures? While details can be interesting to archaeologists, those who are nonmajors are often more captivated by the big picture and understanding how it relates to our world today. Our challenge is to teach these students from a thematic perspective so they can gain insight into how learning about the past helps them understand the present, and how they can take that knowledge and apply it to the issues of today.

We also know that traditional lecture formats present challenges to teaching and learning. Studies have shown that active, problem-based learning, and student-centered pedagogies are more effective pedagogical strategies which is why our emphasis has been to create learning environments that are tied to problem-based learning and connect the course content of ancient societies to cultural heritage and present-day issues. Joe Cuseo states: "When students think critically, they think deeply; they not only know the facts, but they take the additional step of going beyond the facts to do something with them. Critical thinking involves reflecting on the information received, moving away from 'surface' memorization and toward deeper levels of learning. It also involves a shift away from viewing learning as the reception of information from teacher or text (in pre-packaged and final form) to viewing learning as an elaboration and transformation of received information into a different form by the learner" (2005).

Thousands of students enroll in archaeology courses each year to fulfill general education requirements or simply out of interest—but have no intention of majoring in archaeology. At the college level, we need to teach these students broad principles that pertain to heritage and culture and the value of understanding the past and how it connects to the present. The model we use in our anthropology courses is that our content should be socially relevant to our students—that they can walk away with a better understanding of humanity, who we are today, and how we got here.

The Significance of Heritage

The thematic approach provides students the opportunity to examine global concepts such as: sustainability, world population, hunger, housing, conflict, health, literacy, community building, cultural differences in a global world, preservation of culture, spiritual and inner peace, and technology transformation. These themes enable students to focus on things that will be relevant to their future. Michael Wesch wrote: "The most significant problem with education today is the problem of significance itself. Students—our most important critics—are struggling to find meaning and significance in their education" (2008: 5). This means that students tend to see education as less than a true learning experience and largely irrelevant to their lives. They memorize for tests or learn strategies for passing tests so they can graduate. Our effort, and in keeping with ideas set forth by Little and Shackel, is to have students consider the "tangible parts of our heritage" and how it can become a "powerful force in social, cultural, and political life" (2014: 21). We also recognize, as Bender and Messenger note in the Introduction to this volume, that the majority of undergraduates taking our classes do not easily connect the past to the present; it is our job to help them identify those linkages.

Toward the end of the semester, we provide our students with final think pieces that ask them to consider how we can use the past to help us think productively about cultural heritage by examining the present and the future. They respond to questions such as what role water supplies, drought, and environmental change play in regulating human life; what role status and wealth play in the organization and success of societies; and/or what role warfare, trade, and economics play. In each case, they also address how human choices play a deciding role in outcomes and how this applies to the modern world. They must use examples from the past and tie them to the present.

Overall, our approach has recognized that, as educators, we are often bound by structural limitations that inhibit our ability to unlock our own imagination and creativity. New concepts such as hybrid or flipped classrooms are providing opportunities for instructors to offer students the opportunity to participate in more hands-on learning in the manner we have discussed in this chapter. It is what we term a "frame-breaking" mindset, which provides the potential for exploration of what is possible with the encouragement of creative thinking. Innovators provide vision of what can be done because they see beyond the "boxes" that so confine our thinking. This approach is what will drive the evolutionary process by which instructors use problem-based learning, creative projects, and the Web as a platform for learning, and it is how we can teach our students to learn by considering concepts pertaining to cultural heritage on a broad scale. Given the opportunity, students become more engaged in their own learning and often discover interdisciplinary connections among the various classes they are taking.

References Cited

Bahn, Paul, and John Flenley
1992   *Easter Island, Earth Island*. Thames and Hudson, New York.
Choi, Charles Q.
2012   *Drought Led to Demise of Ancient City of Angkor*. Electronic document, http://www.livescience.com/17702-drought-collapse-ancient-city-angkor.html, accessed October 24, 2016.
Cuseo, Joe
2005   *Questions That Promote Deeper Thinking*. Electronic document, http://on-courseworkshop.com/life-long-learning/questions-promote-deeper-thinking/, accessed October 24, 2016.
Diamond, Jared
2011   *Collapse: How Societies Choose to Fail or Succeed*. Rev. ed. Penguin Books, New York.
Fagan, Brian
2005   *Archaeology: A Brief Introduction*. Prentice Hall, New York.
Friedman, Thomas
2005   Living Hand to Mouth. *N.Y. Times*, October 26. New York.
Little, Barbara J., and Paul A. Shackel
2014   *Archaeology, Heritage, and Civic Engagement: Working toward the Public Good*. Left Coast Press, Walnut Creek, California.
National Geographic
2015   Why ISIS Hates Archaeology and Blew Up Ancient Iraqi Palace. Electronic document, http://news.nationalgeographic.com/2015/04/150414-why-islamic-state-destroyed-assyrian-palace-nimrud-iraq-video-isis-isil-archaeology/, accessed February 13, 2017.
Renfrew, Colin, and Paul Bahn
2016   *Archaeology: Theories, Methods, and Practice*. 7th ed. Thames and Hudson, London.
Wesch, Michael
2008   *Anti-Teaching: Confronting the Crisis of Significance*, Canadian Education Association, Education Canada. 48(2): 4–7.

11

Making Connections in *Food, Foraging, and Farming*

FRANCES M. HAYASHIDA

Food, Foraging, and Farming takes a historical and comparative look at food acquisition, production, and distribution and how we are tied to the land, plants and animals, and people that sustain us. By learning about food production in very different times and places, students learn to critically examine our current system with its deep but often hidden or obscured social, health, and environmental costs. The course was originally designed as a capstone for undergraduates in the Department of Anthropology at the University of New Mexico (UNM)–Albuquerque, and encompasses the different subfields of anthropology.

Throughout the course, ideas about heritage (defined as "shared values that people have about their culture and their past" (Shackel 2019: 10) are considered at different scales and perspectives. It is relatively easy for students to map onto the idea of shared values in terms of what and how we eat. We can all think of "heritage foods" and of cooking and eating practices that are linked to culture and identity. This is particularly true in New Mexico, with its strong regional food traditions. What is more difficult to grasp is the concept that, for most of human history and until quite recently, food acquisition and production were equally laden with meaning. In the course, we discuss the ways in which people have been (and in many places still are) tied to the land, resources, and people that feed them; how these connections can be and have been broken; and the possibilities for creating new, or strengthening existing, ties and shared values through collective action today.

Setting and Students

Before discussing the course itself, I'd like to briefly introduce the setting and the students at UNM, both of which informed decisions about course structure, readings, and other material, assignments, and assessment.

As stated in a 2014 *Washington Post* commentary "on good indicators, the Land of Enchantment [New Mexico] often ranks near the bottom; on bad indicators, it's often near the top" (Chokshi 2014). Of the fifty states, New Mexico currently ranks near the bottom in per capita income, the number of bachelor's degrees, and in freshman graduation rates at public high schools (Chokshi 2014; National Center for Education Statistics 2012). It ranks at the very top in income inequality and child food insecurity (Center on Budget and Policy Priorities 2012; Feeding America 2014). Income, education, and food gaps are significant.

As the flagship campus in the state's university system, UNM–Albuquerque draws a student body that crosscuts New Mexico's population and encompasses a range of cultural, educational, and economic backgrounds. New Mexico (like California, Texas, and Hawaii) is a "minority majority" state, and UNM–Albuquerque is a minority majority campus. In spring 2016, the undergraduate population was 35.7 percent white; the remainder of the student body is predominantly Hispanic (46.05 percent), with smaller percentages of Native American (5.66 percent), African American (2.51 percent), and Asian American (3.48 percent) students (University of New Mexico Office of Institutional Analysis University of New Mexico 2016a).[1] Over 80 percent of undergraduates receive financial aid, and roughly half of all awards are based on economic need (University of New Mexico Office of Institutional Analysis 2011).[2] In addition to their studies, students must often meet work, family, or other outside obligations. Linked to these challenges, student retention is low (only 80 percent of freshmen return in the second year), and only half of our students graduate within six years (Anderson 2015).

Anthropology at UNM has roughly 150 undergraduate majors divided across three subfields (ethnology and linguistics, archaeology, and evolutionary anthropology). As at many public universities, departments at UNM are under pressure to have high student credit hours per faculty instructor. Introductory courses in our department have large enrollments and many are also taught online. Many of the upper division courses are lecture format. Opportunities for our majors to take smaller, discussion-based, writing-intensive courses are rare. *Food, Foraging, and Farming* has been offered three times as an elective (the capstone requirement never materialized) between 2010 and 2012, and drew about twenty students each time, making it possible to teach it as a seminar with discussions, brief regular writing assignments, essays, and research papers and presentations. I rarely lecture in this class, but instead use student responses and questions to guide the discussions. There are no exams.

What does all this mean for the course? First, students who are near graduation at UNM and who choose to take a relatively challenging elective value their education and have worked hard (both in and out of the classroom) to get as far as they have. Second, the diversity of their backgrounds and experiences informs their interactions with each other and with the course material. Class discussions are invariably rich and lively. Third, as New Mexicans, students are familiar (at times through personal experience) with some of the food justice issues that are addressed in the course. Fourth, the small format allows for a lot of interaction (with the instructor and each other) that strengthens skills in critical thinking and writing, public presentations, research, and thoughtful listening and speaking.

Course Content

Table 11.1 outlines the structure and content of the course. I begin with a simple exercise. Students are asked to keep a "food chain diary," where they record everything they consume in a 24-hour period, identify the ingredients, and find out (as best they can) where the ingredients came from; how they were raised, grown, and processed; how far they traveled and where they stopped as they went from field to plate (and to put those locations on a world map with lines back to Albuquerque); and who was involved in raising, harvesting, processing, transporting, and preparing their food and the conditions under which these people worked. I encourage students to use different means to gather this information, from checking labels, to combing through websites, to calling customer information lines, and to (very politely) asking servers or managers. In class, we then discuss their efforts and what they were able to find out.

In trying to complete what first appears to be an easy task, students quickly learn that the requested information can be extremely difficult to track down, unless you grow or raise your own food or get it directly from farmers (which most students do not). Labels may list ingredients, but not origins or how a crop or animal was raised. Websites provide information that is vague or incomplete. Company representatives are evasive in their responses. And even if you can get information about how something was

Table 11.1. Schedule for *Food, Foraging, and Farming*

Week	Module Topics	Assignment[a]	Presentation Topics
1	• Introduction • The biology and culture of food	• Readings, response, and discussion questions	
2	• Research skills • Personal food chain	• Readings, response, and discussion questions • Literature search workshop with research librarian • Food chain diary	
3	• Modern American food chains	• Readings, response, and discussion questions	
4	• Modern American food chains, continued • Diet and early human ancestors	• Readings, response, and discussion questions	• Paleolithic and wild primate diets: implications for modern diet
5	• Hunting and food sharing in evolutionary history • Hunter-gatherer resource management	• Readings, response, and discussion questions	• Hunting by chimpanzees • Indigenous knowledge and conservation
6	• The origins of agriculture, ecological and social factors	• Paper 1 on Paleolithic diet • Readings, response, and discussion questions	• Perspectives on the origin of agriculture from human behavioral ecology • Domestication as a status quest?
7	• Health and demographic effects of the transition to agriculture • Agriculture, status, and power: the role of storage	• Readings, response, and discussion questions	• Stature, health, and agriculture • Inka storage
8	• Agriculture, status, and power: the role of feasting	• Readings, response, and discussion questions	• Alcohol and the legitimation of power
9	Spring Break		
10	• Indigenous agroecologies • Indigenous knowledge and agrobiodiversity	• Readings, response, and discussion questions	• Mayan tropical forest farming • Indigenous soil management • Conservation of potato diversity in the Andes

continued

Table 11.1.—*continued*

Week	Module Topics	Assignment[a]	Presentation Topics
11	• Indigenous agriculture case study: Zapotec farming	• Readings, response, and discussion questions	• Indigenous knowledge and development • Cultigens, memory, and meaning
12	• Indigenous agriculture case study: Zapotec farming • Industrial agriculture and globalization: GMOs	• Readings, response, and discussion questions	• Mexican maize, globalization, and NAFTA • Transgenic maize in Mexico
13	• Industrial agriculture and food justice: growing and producing food • Industrial agriculture and food justice: access	• Paper 2 on Zapotec Science • Readings, response, and discussion questions	• CAFOS, race, and class • Farmworker welfare • Food deserts
14	• Industrial agriculture and food justice: consumption and food politics	• Readings, response, and discussion questions	• Stature, obesity, and poverty • Diabetes among the Pima
15	• Industrial agriculture and food justice: global systems and growing justice • Food justice: alternative food routes and place-based food culture	• Readings, response, and discussion questions	
16	• Food justice: politics and prospects	• Readings, response, and discussion questions	
17	Finals week	• Paper 3 on food justice	

Source: From Hayashida syllabus for *Food, Foraging and Farming*, 2012.
Note: a. Research papers are due one week after the presentation.

raised (for example, free range, grass-fed, organic, non-GMO), it's nearly impossible to find out if agricultural and food workers labored under safe conditions and were fairly compensated. It's easier to get information on farm animals than farm workers.

Students come to realize that they can't complete the exercise, no matter how hard they try. Even if they have never previously thought much about where their food comes from, they are surprised and disturbed. This is intentional, for the sense of unease provoked by the exercise helps to hook students into the course. I follow our discussion of the diary with a viewing of *Food, Inc.* (Kenner 2008), a film about American industrial food production. The reading that accompanies the exercise and film is *The Omnivore's Dilemma*, Michael Pollan's book (2007) on contemporary American food chains.

With this introduction to how disconnected we are from our food, we hurtle back in time to the Paleolithic, when food acquisition was tightly linked to our biological, cognitive, and cultural evolution. We then move forward rapidly, discussing our long history as foragers and the intimate ecological knowledge and cooperative practices required for survival;[3] the ecological and social components of the origins of agriculture; the health and demographic effects of a reliance on cultivated foods; intensification, surplus, inequality, and feasting; Indigenous knowledge, agroecology and agrobiodiversity in the past and present (accompanied by reading *Zapotec Science* [González 2001]); industrial agriculture and the loss of local farming knowledge and control over seeds; and other contemporary food justice issues (food security, worker welfare, local and global food justice movements, accompanied by reading *Food Justice* [Gottlieb and Joshi 2010]). In addition to the three assigned books, students are required to read a range of academic/scientific articles drawn from archaeology, cultural anthropology, and biological anthropology, and a report on food gaps in New Mexico (New Mexico Food Gap Task Force 2008).

To help students engage with the readings and the issues covered in the class, they are asked to submit a brief (200–250 word) response just before each class meeting, which can include what they found surprising in the readings, reflections on personal experiences tied to the day's topic, or links to other course material or items in the news. The responses are not shared with their classmates, but I may refer to the content during the class discussion (unless it is personal, in which case it is up to the student to share that information or not). They also prepare one or two questions that are meant to generate discussion among their classmates. They can (among other possibilities) survey the class on issues covered in the readings, or ask fellow students to compare competing perspectives, evaluate the evidence and arguments used in a paper, or tie the readings to current events. Students are expected to consider how they would respond to their own questions. I compile all of their questions (with their names) before class, group them by topic with a heading, then print and hand out the questions in class. The student-generated questions then drive the discussion. Occasionally, I will insert a question about an issue that I feel is important if no student has brought it up.

There are several advantages to organizing the discussion in this way. First, students come to realize that the success of the course depends on them: they have a shared responsibility to be prepared for class and to contribute to the "discussion commons." This may be less of an issue in a program that typically offers small enrollment seminars for their undergraduates. Second, students are engaged because we talk about issues that interest them. Third, the questions and the responses help me to understand what material or concepts might need further explanation. Finally, the format gives every student a voice. In the handout, all students can see the contributions of their classmates. The handout helps to equalize oral participation as well. We have all taken or taught courses where a few people dominate the class, and where students who are quieter or who take a little time to compose a thoughtful answer rarely participate (or try to participate, but become discouraged). This format helps to draw these students into the discussion (using their questions as a starting point) and reminds the more talkative ones that other people also have something to say.

Beginning in the fourth week (of a sixteen-week semester), readings and discussions of the core course topics outlined above are supplemented by student presentations and research papers on related topics. To provide some examples: during the surplus and feasting module, a student reports on archaeological research on alcohol and the legitimation of power; the module on the origins of agriculture includes a presentation on theories of domestication as status competition. Our section on Indigenous agroecologies features presentations on agrobiodiversity conservation, pre-Columbian agricultural systems (Maya forest farming, Andean raised fields), and local agricultural knowledge and development. The section that follows, on industrial agriculture and globalization, is complemented by talks on NAFTA and farming in Mexico, and the introduction of transgenic maize in Mexico. Presentations on CAFOs (concentrated animal feeding operations); race and class; farmworker welfare; poverty and obesity; and diabetes among Native American populations help to illustrate the issues raised while reading *Food Justice*.

The idea of the research presentation and paper is to broaden and deepen understanding of the core topics by study and analysis of complementary or contrasting issues and case studies. I provide a list of possible topics, but students are also free to propose something different. They submit their ranked choices at the beginning of the term, and I try to assign them to one of their top picks. I provide a couple of "seed articles" to get them started, but they are expected to do additional research. The research paper is due one week after the presentation. Three additional papers (essays linked to other course themes) are also required.

I provide detailed prompts for the presentation and the papers. One goal of these assignments is that students hone their ability to craft clear arguments that are well supported by evidence, which also helps them to discern robust from weaker positions in their readings as well as in the media. Students come to the course with uneven writing, public speaking, and research backgrounds, and the prompts (which we go over in detail in class) also include information on essay writing, constructing and supporting a thesis, and how to structure an effective presentation. Because many of the students have little experience with research papers using primary sources, we also visit the library during the first week, where the librarian assigned to our department provides a hands-on workshop on electronic bibliographic resources and how to access relevant articles and books.

The presentation exercise is also designed to help students improve their speaking and listening skills. In addition to my assessment, presenters receive feedback from the rest of the class. On a form that I provide, students identify themselves by name and make comments on the clarity and organization of the presentation, the strength of the argument (clear thesis that is well supported by the presented evidence), the presentation style, and the effective use of images and other visual aids. They are also asked to identify the most interesting thing that they learned. The feedback sheets are then provided to the presenter. Presenters benefit from the comments of their classmates (and my sense is that students step up their effort knowing that they are being evaluated by their peers), and reviewers increase their awareness of what makes a compelling presentation.

Heritage in *Food, Foraging, and Farming*

By the end of the course, students should have an understanding not only of what has been lost or eroded (in terms of food acquisition and production practices, crops, knowledge, and landscapes), but also of efforts to protect, maintain, or revive these tangible and intangible features because of their cultural and other values, such as food justice and security. For example, landscapes that have been successfully farmed (or foraged) over centuries encode information about long-term sustainability (Sandor and Eash 1991). Social identity and organization in irrigator communities is often closely tied to water distribution principles that have been maintained over generations, and that provide insight into the equitable management of common pool resources (Ostrom et al. 1999). Diverse cultigens that have been selected for by farmers for local conditions not only provide flexibility and food security, but form the basis for local cuisines and identity (Nabhan 2016).

In a class more explicitly focused on heritage issues, several themes could be explored in greater depth. For example, most of the food acquisition and production heritage discussed above and in the course is not "official," defined by Harrison (2013: 114) as "state led practices concerned with the preservation of historic objects, places and practices" (see also Chilton 2019). They are instead examples of "unofficial heritage," a "broad set of public attitudes towards the past" (2013: 114), or as defined by Shackel (2019: 10) as "shared values that people have about their culture and their past."

Why aren't more agricultural practices, knowledge, crops, and landscapes considered as part of official heritage? The answer is complex and highlights issues relating to the politics of heritage, persistent perceptions held by policymakers and the public (and to some extent academics) about what qualifies as "cultural," smallholder farmer rights, and contemporary conflicts over food security and sovereignty. All of these themes could be probed in a modified version of this course, or incorporated as a separate module in a general course on heritage, particularly one where the relatively recent official heritage categories of *cultural landscapes* and *intangible cultural heritage* are explored (UNESCO n.d.[a]; n.d.[b]).

A good place to start the discussion would be Erickson (2003), who argues for the protection and management of traditional agricultural landscapes, where "traditional" is defined as "local, shared, historically contingent cultural practices embedded in the land, cultural memory, and practice of everyday life." Erickson notes that while agricultural landscapes might fall under the UNESCO World Heritage category of *cultural landscapes,* the justification criteria can be difficult to apply. At the time that the article was written, only twenty-three cultural landscapes were on the list, and few were primarily agricultural landscapes (Erickson 2003: 201). While the number of registered cultural landscapes has increased (to ninety-two as of this writing), the number that include agricultural landscapes is still small (less than half), and in only a fraction of these are fields and other farming or herding features the focus, rather than just a backdrop for structures and settlements on the landscape (UNESCO n.d.[a]; see also Martínez Yáñez 2010). That said, an October 2013 issue of *World Heritage* featuring agricultural landscapes suggests an effort toward greater recognition.

In 2003, the UNESCO Convention for the Safeguarding of Intangible Cultural Heritage was created, where intangible cultural heritage is defined as:

> the practices, representations, expressions, knowledge, skills—as well as the instruments, objects, artefacts and cultural spaces associated therewith—that communities, groups and, in some cases, individuals recognize as part of their cultural heritage. This intangible cultural heritage, transmitted from generation to generation, is constantly recreated by communities and groups in response to their environment, their interaction with nature and their history, and provides them with a sense of identity and continuity, thus promoting respect for cultural diversity and human creativity. (UNESCO 2003)

While it would seem that many practices linked to foraging and farming would fall under this definition, in fact, intangible cultural heritage is described as "manifested *inter alia* in the following domains" (UNESCO 2003):

(a) oral traditions and expressions, including language as a vehicle of the intangible cultural heritage;
(b) performing arts;
(c) social practices, rituals, and festive events;
(d) knowledge and practices concerning nature and the universe;
(e) traditional craftsmanship.

Foraging and farming, although often deeply social and concerned with nature and the universe, are poorly represented. Of the 391 elements (the term used by UNESCO) currently on the list, only three are directly related to food acquisition or production (UNESCO n.d.[b]).[4] Many more are for festivals or ceremonies related to food production, with little or no mention of the food acquisition or production practices themselves and their safeguarding. In many of these cases, it is likely that the festival or ceremonies have persisted long after the foraging or farming activities that they were originally related to have disappeared, just as few Americans celebrate an actual harvest at Thanksgiving. Listings for traditional cuisines and culinary practices are somewhat more common,[5] reflecting perhaps again the propensity to consider consumption as cultural, while production is not, despite the fact that heritage cuisines depend on heritage wild resources and crops that have been managed, developed, and perpetuated over centuries by foragers and farmers.

In addition, current conflicts over water and land rights, crops and seeds, and access to wild resources that pit smallholder farmers and foragers against powerful business and political forces decrease the likelihood that nation-states will nominate food production landscapes and practices as culturally significant and worthy of safeguarding.[6] It is much more likely that heritage initiatives or initiatives that include a heritage component will be unofficial and collectively organized at local to global scales as a means to gain greater food sovereignty and justice (Holt-Giménez et al. 2009).

In short, a course focused on food, foragers, and farmers can be used to more formally address heritage issues, including an analysis of how, why, and when official and unofficial heritage actions may follow different paths, or be in conflict. Course activities might include a case-by-case analysis of food production landscapes and practices that make it onto the World Heritage lists, and additional research into the broader economic and political context of nominations. Results could be juxtaposed against unofficial heritage initiatives. When combined with what they have learned in their comparative and historical study of food acquisition and production from the Paleolithic to the present, students will be in a better position to critically assess other heritage conflicts and food justice issues.

Conclusion

In many parts of the United States, regional food traditions connect us to past generations and are a source of shared identity and local pride. Yet we seldom know, much less consider, how and where the crops and animals we consume were raised, who raised and processed them, and how they made their way from farm to plate. By taking a comparative and historical approach, *Food, Foraging, and Farming* is designed to help students see this disconnect as something recent and aberrant and to envision how we might work toward healthier, more just food systems. In the past, the course has focused on food production as unofficial heritage. The neglect of food production as part of official heritage is a topic that will be included in future offerings of the course. In this way, students will learn that unless foraging and farming knowledge, practices, and landscapes are recognized (both unofficially and officially) as deeply cultural and worthy of study, support, and protection, we will continue to lose this important part of our shared past.

Notes

1. Other categories listed in this report are Native Hawaiian (0.18 percent), foreign (1.64 percent), unknown (1.36 percent), and "Two or More" (3.42 percent)

2. Including Pell grants, need-based federal and state loans and other grants, and work-study. Note that the current reporting of student financial aid does not separately list all need-based awards (UNM Office of Institutional Analytics 2016b). The most recent report (UNM Office of Institutional Analytics 2011) including this information is cited here.

3. Here we do another "disconnect" exercise, where students are broken into groups and given class time to walk around outside and to list and name as many plants as possible and their uses. Their knowledge is then juxtaposed against that of people from groups who rely heavily on foraged plants for food and medicine (Peacock and Turner 2000). As I learned from experience, during the exercise it is important to warn enthusiastic students not to taste any of the plants (some may be toxic) that they are trying to identify.

4. These are shrimp fishing on horseback in Oostduinkerke (Belgium), irrigator tribunals of the Spanish Mediterranean coast, and the cultivation of the "vite ad alberello" (head-trained bush vines) of the community of Pantelleria (Italy).

5. These include the cuisines of Japan, France, and Mexico; the Mediterranean diet; kimchi making and sharing; and Turkish coffee culture.

6. For an additional perspective on how political events affect the nomination of agricultural landscapes, see discussions of the nomination by Palestine of the terraced fields of Battir as part of an effort to block the construction by Israel of a separation wall (BBC 2012; Lewis 2014). Battir was inscribed as a cultural landscape in 2014 (UNESCO 2014).

References Cited

Anderson, Diane
2015   Fall Enrollment Down Slightly; Retention, Graduation Rates Increase. Electronic document, http://news.unm.edu/news/fall-enrollment-down-slightly;-retention-graduation-rates-increase, accessed September 28, 2016.

BBC
2012   West Bank Barrier Threatens Villagers' Way of Life. Electronic document http://www.bbc.com/news/magazine-18012895, accessed September 18, 2014.

Center on Budget and Policy Priorities
2012   Pulling Apart: A State-by-State Analysis of Income Trends. Electronic document http://www.cbpp.org/files/11-15-12sfp.pdf, accessed September 3, 2014.

Chilton, Elizabeth S.
2019   The Heritage of Heritage: Defining the Role of the Past in Contemporary Societies. In *History and Approaches to Heritage Studies*, edited by Phyllis Mauch Messenger and Susan J. Bender, pp. 24–31. University Press of Florida, Gainesville.

Chokshi, Niraj
2014   Population Growth in New Mexico is Approaching Zero—and Other Bad Signs. *Washington Post,* January 17. Washington, D.C. Electronic document, http://www.washingtonpost.com/blogs/govbeat/wp/2014/01/17/population-growth-in-new-mexico-is-approaching-zero-and-other-bad-signs/, accessed August 23, 2014.

Erickson, Clark
2003   Agricultural Landscapes as World Heritage: Raised Field Agriculture in Bolivia and Peru. In *Managing Change: Sustainable Approaches to the Conservation of the Built Environment,* edited by J. M. Teutonico and F. Matero, pp. 181–204. Getty Conservation Institute, Los Angeles, California.

Feeding America
2014   Map the Meal Gap: Highlights of Findings for Overall and Child Food Insecurity. Electronic document, http://feedingamerica.org/hunger-in-america/hunger-studies/map-the-meal-gap/~/media/Files/research/map-meal-gap/2014-MMG-web-2014.ashx?.pdf, accessed August 23, 2014.

González, Roberto
2001   *Zapotec Science.* University of Texas Press, Austin.

Gottlieb, Robert, and Anupama Joshi
2010   *Food Justice.* MIT Press, Cambridge, Massachusetts.

Harrison, Rodney
2013   *Heritage: Critical Approaches.* Routledge, London.

Holt-Giménez, Eric, Raj Patel, and Annie Shattuck
2009   *Food Rebellions! Crisis and the Hunger for Justice.* Pambazuka Press, Cape Town; Food First Books, Oakland, California; Grassroots International, Boston, Massachusetts.

Kenner, Robert
2008   *Food, Inc.* Magnolia Pictures, DVD.

Lewis, Renee

2014   UNESCO Names West Bank's Battir a Protected World Heritage Site. Electronic
        document, http://america.aljazeera.com/articles/2014/6/23/unesco-palestine-
        battir.html, accessed September 18, 2014.

Martínez Yáñez, Celia

2010   The International Day for Monuments and Sites Theme for 2010—"The Heritage
        of Agriculture." Electronic document, http://www.icomos.org/18thapril/2010/18_
        April_2010_Agricultural %20Heritage_Eng_20100323.pdf, accessed September
        14, 2014.

Nabhan, Gary Paul

2016   *Ethnobiology for the Future: Linking Cultural and Ecological Diversity* (Southwest
        Center Series). University of Arizona Press, Tucson.

National Center for Education Statistics

2012   Trends in High School Dropout and Completion Rates in the United States:
        1972–2009. Electronic document, http://nces.ed.gov/pubs2012/2012006.pdf, ac-
        cessed August 24, 2014.

New Mexico Food Gap Task Force

2008   *Closing New Mexico's Food Gap: A Report on Food Access in New Mexico.* Sub-
        mitted to Governor Richardson and the New Mexico State Legislature by the
        NM Food Gap Task Force, November 30, 2008. Electronic document, http://
        www.farmtotablenm.org/wp-content/uploads/2013/01/NM_Food_Gap_Task_
        Force_Final_Report-December_20081.pdf, accessed January 2012.

Ostrom, Elinor, Joanna Burger, Christopher B. Field, Richard B, Norgaard, and David
        Policansky

1999   Revisiting the Commons: Local Lessons, Global Challenges. *Science* 284: 278–282.

Peacock, Sandra L., and Nancy J. Turner

2000   "Just Like a Garden": Traditional Resource Management and Biodiversity Con-
        servation on the Interior Plateau of British Columbia. In *Biodiversity and Native
        America*, edited by Paul E. Minnis and Wayne J. Elisens, pp. 133–179. University
        of Oklahoma Press, Norman.

Pollan, Michael

2007   *The Omnivore's Dilemma: A Natural History of Four Meals.* Penguin, New York.

Sandor, Jonathan A., and Neal S. Eash

1991   Significance of Ancient Agricultural Soils for Long-Term Agronomic Studies
        and Sustainable Agriculture Research. *Agronomy Journal* 83: 846–850.

Shackel, Paul A.

2019   Civic Engagement, Representation, and Social Justice: Moving from CRM to
        Heritage Studies. In *History and Approaches to Heritage Studies*, edited by Phyl-
        lis Mauch Messenger and Susan J. Bender, pp. 9–23. University Press of Florida,
        Gainesville.

UNESCO

2003   Convention for the Safeguarding of Intangible Cultural Heritage. Electronic
        document, http://www.unesco.org/culture/ich/index.php?lg=en&pg=00006,
        accessed September 18, 2014.

2014   Palestine: Land of Olives and Vines—Cultural Landscape of Southern Jerusa-
           lem, Battir. Electronic document, http://whc.unesco.org/en/list/1492, accessed
           September 14, 2014.
n.d.(a)   Cultural Landscape. Electronic document, http://whc.unesco.org/en/cultural-
           landscape/, accessed June 22, 2016.
n.d.(b)   Lists of Intangible Cultural Heritage and Register of Best Safeguarding Practices.
           Electronic document, http://www.unesco.org/culture/ich/index.php?lg=en&pg
           =00559, accessed June 22, 2016.
University of New Mexico Office of Institutional Analysis
2011   Five Year Academic Ledger—Albuquerque Campus (Fall 2006 to Fall 2010).
           Electronic document, http://oia.unm.edu/documents/ledger_docs/Five_Year_
           Academic_Ledger_2010_2011_v1.2.pdf, accessed August 24, 2014.
2016a   Official Enrollment Report, Spring 2016. Electronic document, http://oia.unm.
           edu/facts-and-figures/documents/Enrollment%20Reports/spring-2016-oer.pdf,
           accessed September 28, 2016.
2016b   Data Visualizations: Financial Aid. Electronic document, http://oia.unm.edu/
           facts-and-figures/data-visualizations/financial-aid.html, accessed September
           28, 2016.

Contributors

SUSAN J. BENDER is professor emerita at Skidmore College and served as research director of the South Park (Colorado) Archaeology Project. She has contributed to the Society for American Archaeology's initiative to reform the undergraduate curriculum for the twenty-first century and worked collaboratively with the South Park National Heritage Area as part of her research interests in hunter-gatherer settlement in mountainous regions of the American West.

RICHARD EFFLAND is faculty emeritus from Mesa Community College where he taught anthropology for more than twenty-five years. Effland was an award recipient for his innovative use of technology for teaching and learning and the pedagogy of teaching excellence. His interests are why societies fail, power in political systems, and differences in simple and complex societies. He was the China Study Abroad Coordinator for fifteen years.

RICARDO J. ELIA is associate professor in the Archaeology Department at Boston University. His research interests focus on international heritage management, especially the problems of archaeological looting and the preservation of cultural heritage during armed conflict. He has been co-director of the Menorca Field School since 2009.

FRANCES M. HAYASHIDA is associate professor of anthropology at the University of New Mexico. She works in Peru and Chile on late prehispanic political economy and political ecology. Her research centers on agriculture and water management, and she has also written about Inka craft production, the ethnoarchaeology of beer brewing, humans, and the environment, and how archaeological studies can inform current environmental conservation.

A. GWYNN HENDERSON is staff archaeologist and education coordinator at the Kentucky Archaeological Survey, and adjunct assistant professor in the University of Kentucky's Department of Anthropology. Her archaeological research targets the prehistoric farming cultures of the Ohio Valley, and her work as a public archaeologist includes researching and assessing how children learn about the past. Her book *Kentuckians before Boone* is used in elementary school classrooms, and she is an award-winning freelance writer of children's nonfiction.

ELIZABETH KRYDER-REID is professor of anthropology and museum studies in the Indiana University School of Liberal Arts at Indiana University–Purdue University Indianapolis (IUPUI), director of the Cultural Heritage Research Center, and the former director of the IUPUI Museum Studies Program. With a background in archaeology, art history, and public history, her research investigates cultural heritage with a particular focus on the intersections of landscape and power and the contestation of social inequalities across gender, race, class, ethnicity, and religion. She is the author of *California Mission Landscapes: Race, Memory, and the Politics of Heritage*, a contributing author to *Keywords in American Landscape Design*, and PI of Shaping Outcomes (www.shapingoutcomes.org).

MEREDITH ANDERSON LANGLITZ earned a master's in archaeological heritage management and a BA in archaeology and history from Boston University. She has worked in the Programs Department at the Archaeological Institute of America since 2009, and her research interests include the preservation of archaeological sites, site interpretation, and public engagement in archaeology. She first came to Menorca as a student in 2006 and returned as a staff member in 2010.

NICOLAS R. LARACUENTE is the site protection program manager at the Kentucky State Historic Preservation Office. He is also the director of the award-winning Jack Jouett Archaeology Project, a community archaeology project focused on investigations of early whiskey distilleries in Central Kentucky. His archaeological research focuses exclusively on the distilling industry, and all of his projects involve the public to the maximum extent possible. The public has returned the favor by giving Nick the title, "The Bourbon Archaeologist."

SHEREEN LERNER is professor of anthropology and director of honors at Mesa Community College. Her areas of interest are southwestern archaeology and broad concepts pertaining to cultural heritage. She has presented numerous papers on teaching archaeology and social relevance and has published articles on archaeology, historic preservation, and educating the public on the connections between the past and present.

ALICIA EBBITT MCGILL is assistant professor in the Department of History at North Carolina State University, where in addition to teaching undergraduate and graduate courses, she contributes to the graduate programs in public history. Her research in Belize focuses on how constructions of heritage are promoted through public venues (for example, tourism, education, and archaeological practice) and the ways cultural actors like teachers and youth negotiate heritage constructions and navigate colonial legacies and cultural politics. In her scholarship she brings a historical lens to examinations of heritage practices and an ethnographic approach to public history.

LEWIS C. MESSENGER JR. is professor emeritus at Hamline University, Saint Paul, Minnesota. He has done archaeological field work in the Maya area of southern Mexico, Belize, and Honduras, as well as in Minnesota. He has led study-abroad programs in Peru, Mexico, and Southeast Asia and has developed teaching methodologies that focus on student engagement in collaborative projects, both for understanding past human-ecological interaction and for developing archaeologically based fictional first-person accounts of the past.

PHYLLIS MAUCH MESSENGER, RPA, holds a master's in anthropology and a doctorate in education and has worked on archaeological projects in Mexico, Honduras, and the United States. She is grants consultant for the Institute for Advanced Study (IAS) at the University of Minnesota, an editor of the university's online journal, *Open Rivers*, and was founding director of the Center for Anthropology and Cultural Heritage Education at Hamline University. She has edited several volumes, including *The Ethics of Collecting Cultural Property* (2nd edition), *Cultural Heritage Management* (with George Smith) and *Heritage Values in Contemporary Society* (with George Smith and Hilary Soderland).

JEANNE M. MOE works for the Bureau of Land Management and is the director of Project Archaeology, a national archaeology education program housed at Montana State University in Bozeman. Her research interests include students' conceptual understanding of science through archaeological inquiry, archaeology as culturally relevant science content for underserved audiences, and changing attitudes about the protection of archaeological sites and artifacts.

AMALIA PÉREZ-JUEZ is adjunct associate professor in the Archaeology Department at Boston University and the director of BU programs in Spain. Her research interests are the archaeology of Spain and heritage management. She has participated or directed excavations ranging from prehistory to the twentieth century and has been a codirector for the Menorca Field School since it began in 2002.

THOMAS J. PLUCKHAHN is associate professor of anthropology at the University of South Florida. He is the author of several books and numerous articles on the archaeology of the American Southeast. He maintains a strong interest in cultural resource management and public archaeology, where he worked extensively before his current position.

SANDRA SCHAM has had a varied career in international development (evaluation, countering violent extremism), teaching and research (University of Maryland and Catholic University), and government labor and financial regulation. She is coeditor of two journals, *Journal of Eastern Mediterranean Archaeology* and *Heritage Studies,* and is the author of many publications, both academic and popular. Her most recent book is *Extremism: Ancient and Modern.*

CHARLES S. WHITE was associate professor of education at Boston University until 2016. He now continues his work in civic engagement and heritage education as an independent scholar. He authored (with Kathleen Hunter) *Teaching with Historic Places: A Curriculum Framework for Professional Training and Development of Teachers, Preservationists, and Museum and Site Interpreters.* He was also coauthor of Houghton Mifflin's *K-6 Social Studies* (2005) and McDougal Littell's *World Cultures and Geography* (2008).

Index

Page numbers followed by the letters *f* and *t* indicate figures and tables.

CULTURAL HERITAGE STUDIES
Edited by Paul A. Shackel, University of Maryland

Heritage of Value, Archaeology of Renown: Reshaping Archaeological Assessment and Significance, edited by Clay Mathers, Timothy Darvill, and Barbara J. Little (2005)

Archaeology, Cultural Heritage, and the Antiquities Trade, edited by Neil Brodie, Morag M. Kersel, Christina Luke, and Kathryn Walker Tubb (2006)

Archaeological Site Museums in Latin America, edited by Helaine Silverman (2006)

Crossroads and Cosmologies: Diasporas and Ethnogenesis in the New World, by Christopher C. Fennell (2007)

Ethnographies and Archaeologies: Iterations of the Past, by Lena Mortensen and Julie Hollowell (2009)

Cultural Heritage Management: A Global Perspective, by Phyllis Mauch Messenger and George S. Smith (2010; first paperback edition, 2014)

God's Fields: An Archaeology of Religion and Race in Moravian Wachovia, by Leland Ferguson (2011; first paperback edition, 2013)

Ancestors of Worthy Life: Plantation Slavery and Black Heritage at Mount Clare, by Teresa S. Moyer (2015)

Slavery behind the Wall: An Archaeology of a Cuban Coffee Plantation, by Theresa A. Singleton (2015; first paperback edition, 2016)

Excavating Memory: Sites of Remembering and Forgetting, edited by Maria Theresia Starzmann and John R. Roby (2016)

Mythic Frontiers: Remembering, Forgetting, and Profiting with Cultural Heritage Tourism, by Daniel R. Maher (2016; first paperback edition, 2019)

Critical Theory and the Anthropology of Heritage, by Melissa F. Baird (2018)

Heritage at the Interface: Interpretation and Identity, edited by Glenn Hooper (2018)

Cuban Cultural Heritage: A Rebel Past for a Revolutionary Nation, by Pablo Alonso González (2018)

The Rosewood Massacre: An Archaeology and History of Intersectional Violence, by Edward González-Tennant (2018)

Race, Place, and Memory: Deep Currents in Wilmington, North Carolina, by Margaret M. Mulrooney (2018)

An Archaeology of Structural Violence: Life in a Twentieth-Century Coal Town, by Michael Roller (2018)

Colonialism, Community, and Heritage in Native New England, by Siobhan M. Hart (2019)

Pedagogy and Practice in Heritage Studies, edited by Susan J. Bender and Phyllis Mauch Messenger (2019)

History and Approaches to Heritage Studies, edited by Phyllis Mauch Messenger and Susan J. Bender (2019)

Lightning Source UK Ltd.
Milton Keynes UK
UKHW011341240119
336130UK00001B/41/P